CITIES FOR PROFIT

CITIES FOR PROFIT

The Real Estate Turn in Asia's Urban Politics

GAVIN SHATKIN

CORNELL UNIVERSITY PRESS
ITHACA AND LONDON

First published 2017 by Cornell University Press

Printed in the United States of America

Library of Congress Cataloging-in-Publication Data

Names: Shatkin, Gavin, author.
Title: Cities for profit : the real estate turn in Asia's urban politics / Gavin Shatkin.
Description: Ithaca : Cornell University Press, 2017. | Includes bibliographical references and index.
Identifiers: LCCN 2017003163 (print) | LCCN 2017004737 (ebook) | ISBN 9781501709906 (cloth : alk. paper) | ISBN 978-1-5017-1113-8 (pbk. : alk. paper) | ISBN 9781501712357 (epub/mobi) | ISBN 9781501709715 (pdf)
Subjects: LCSH: Real estate development—Government policy— Asia. | Real estate investment—Government policy—Asia. | Land use, Urban—Government policy—Asia. | City planning—Asia. | Urban policy—Asia.
Classification: LCC HD843.2 .S53 2017 (print) | LCC HD843.2 (ebook) | DDC 333.3095/091732—dc23
LC record available at https://lccn.loc.gov/2017003163

Cornell University Press strives to use environmentally responsible suppliers and materials to the fullest extent possible in the publishing of its books. Such materials include vegetable-based, low-VOC inks and acid-free papers that are recycled, totally chlorine-free, or partly composed of nonwood fibers. For further information, visit our website at cornellpress.cornell.edu.

For Arjun, Arushi, and Sudha

CONTENTS

List of Figures ix

Preface xi

Acknowledgments xvii

Introduction: The Real Estate Turn in Asia's Urban Politics 1

1. Origins and Consequences of the Real Estate Turn 35

2. Comparing State Agendas of Land Monetization 82

3. Planned Grab: Capitalizing on Land Dualism in
   New Order Jakarta 102

4. Experiments in Power: Urban Politics in Postliberalization
   Kolkata 137

5. Chongqing: The State Capitalist Growth Machine 176

Conclusion: Interpreting the Theoretical and Practical
Implications of the Real Estate Turn 212

viii   *Contents*

Notes   239

Bibliography   243

Index   261

Figures

I.1. Pipes used to pump silt into Boeung Kak   3
I.2. Rendering of Bonifacio Global City in Metro Manila   4
I.3. DLF City in Gurgaon   6
1.1. Villa in Lippo Karawaci, Jakarta Metropolitan Region   42
1.2. Songjiang City in Songjiang Province near Shanghai   42
1.3. Xintiandi, Shanghai   43
1.4. Muang Thong Thani, Nonthaburi Province near Bangkok   43
1.5. Annual inward and outward foreign direct investment flows into Indonesia, the Philippines, and Thailand, 1985–1997 (millions of US dollars)   49
1.6. Foreign direct investment in India, five largest sectoral recipients between 2005 and 2011 (millions of US dollars)   57
1.7. Jiangbeizui central business district model   70
1.8. Calcutta Riverside   76
2.1. A comparative framework for analyzing land-management systems   95
3.1. Jakarta skyline, with *kampung* in the foreground   105
3.2. Map of Jakarta   110
3.3. Walled-in *kampung*, BSD City   127

3.4. Residential street, BSD City phase one   129
3.5. The Green, phase 2, BSD City   131
4.1. Map of Kolkata   161
4.2. Election wall painting in Kolkata, 2010   163
4.3. Rendering of Calcutta Riverside   169
5.1. Map of Chongqing   195
5.2. Min Xin Jia Yuan public rental housing complex   203

PREFACE

At some point in the mid-2000s, as I sat in presentations at major conferences in urban studies and planning, I began to notice a distinct trend. It was becoming commonplace for academics presenting papers on Asian cities to show PowerPoint images of glossy renderings of massive "new town" urban real estate projects. These images were strikingly similar, whether the city being discussed was Jakarta, Shanghai, or Phnom Penh. They presented shimmering landscapes of sleek towers that seemingly hovered, like spaceships, over their surroundings. These surroundings were inevitably depicted as a verdant blue and green landscape, or alternatively as a solid black void. This representation of these projects as separate from any urban context marked them as visions of something entirely new, a revolutionary departure from the city of the present. Yet the scholars presenting these images usually had little to say about what these renderings meant or about the significance of the projects they were intended to represent. Rather, it seemed that these images were used to make a more general point about the audacity (or foolishness?) of developers and government officials. The images, it seemed, spoke for themselves. The audience would laugh knowingly, leaving me puzzled as to what they had inferred. And then the presenter would move on.

This book represents my effort to understand the meaning of the projects depicted in these images for Asian cities. Such renderings emerged in a context in which cities in much of Asia were indeed experiencing wrenching change, rapidly expanding out into their hinterlands and increasingly exposed to surges of investment (as well as periods of disinvestment) and rapid infusions (and extractions) of speculative finance capital. The urban fabric was being transformed through massive development of malls, highways, high-rise condominiums, "Grade A" office complexes, and flyovers. To put it briefly, urban space was, and indeed in most places still is, being rescripted on a large scale to facilitate the circulation and accumulation of capital. The research for this book started from a sense that the images of massive urban real estate megaprojects expressed something about the desires of powerful people to move beyond incremental change and to seek instead to wipe the slate clean, to completely revolutionize the process of city building. But how did these projects come into being? Whose interest, exactly, did they serve? And what fate awaited them? Did they ever achieve the revolution they so clearly sought? If not, why not? If so, what were the consequences for the cities in which they took root?

My initial effort to answer these questions focused on the most obvious object of analysis, the developers of these proposed projects and the architects and urban designers they employed. When I started to conduct exploratory field research I was focused on assessing how the effort to shape urban space on such a grand scale for profit were changing cities and whether this was leading to new issues of exclusion and inequality. Yet early on my efforts to address this question ran up against a simple obstacle: so few of these projects had actually broken ground, and (at least outside of China) when they did they rarely grew to resemble the fantastic renderings that I and so many scholars had found so fascinating. I began to view the representations of these megaprojects as not necessarily portraying meaningful, coherent urban schemes. Rather, they were often (and sometimes explicitly) intended as evocative urban visions, meant to excite desire, to galvanize public interest and acceptance of plans that served the interests of a powerful few. I shifted focus from the design of the schemes themselves to the question of the interests that lay behind them. When I did so, one aspect of these projects came sharply into focus: the strong role of state actors in backing these projects and enabling the corporate actors who were the more visible movers in shaping the plans and designs. Again and again, state actors specifically emerged as important protagonists in machinations and struggles around land, its acquisition, the dispossession of existing users, and the process of land use and ecological change and infrastructure provision.

Ultimately I came to focus my investigation primarily on the question of what interests state actors are pursuing through real estate megaprojects, and the ways that emerging relationships between state and nonstate actors are shifting the terrain of urban politics. The central argument that will be developed in the pages that follow is that in an era when state actors face intense fiscal constraints, and in which they experience economic fluctuations related to vacillations of global investment and finance, they have increasingly sought to exploit opportunities to monetize a critical resource over which they hold sway—urban land—as a means to power and authority. They do so in numerous ways: by selling state land, by using powers of compulsory acquisition to acquire land and lease it to private developers, by reclaiming land, by forming various forms of public-private partnerships in land development, and many other tactics. This push to monetize land has accompanied what I refer to as a real estate turn in urban politics, which has come to encompass a range of reforms in governance, land management, and state-community relations that represent a fundamental shift in perspective on the part of at least some state actors about their role in society and economy. The book further argues that the machinations of state actors in their effort to monetize land have broad implications for the actual changes we see in the built environment. In other words, urban form is quite often shaped less by the elegant designs of planners and architects than by the success or failure of state efforts to acquire land and by the extent to which state land-management policy shapes the incentives of corporate developers (for example to develop property versus speculatively hoarding land). State land-management practices also shape the agency of communities in pushing to ensure that their own interests are heard in deliberations over these projects.

Of course there are other actors beyond those within state institutions who also play a powerful role in these projects. Developers, in most contexts, make the most immediate decisions about what gets built, and they exercise powerful political influence in decisions over land development. Financiers often write the checks that determine whether developers are able to pursue their ambitions. The role of both is worth considerable further research, and indeed exceptional research and theorization of their roles is under way (see for example Halbert and Rouanet 2014; Searle 2014). My choice to focus on the role of the state, however, is driven by two considerations. First, the role of state actors is important and often too easily dismissed. As the stories of urban megaprojects in this book will reveal, state actors often use their regulatory, legal, and administrative powers to shape the development of real estate markets and real estate industries in fundamental ways. In some cases, it might even be said that today's real estate industry is an invention of the state. In China, all land is owned by the state, and the real estate industry has emerged through a deliberate and systematic agenda of state action. In Jakarta, the oligopolistic nature of the current real estate industry is a direct outcome of state land policies on the issuance of development permits for unregistered land. This research has therefore been partially motivated by a desire to explain this important area of state action and partly to interrogate the meaning of the real estate turn in policy for our understanding of urban politics and state action more generally. The second consideration is that because the state's role in land management is critical to the fate of real estate megaprojects, it is an important lever of opposition to these projects, or of change to their political, social, economic, and ecological outcomes. While the pages that follow will reveal significant structural issues that have led to regressive and ecologically destructive action on the part of state actors, it can nonetheless be argued that external pressures for reforms in the areas of property rights, land use planning and law, and urban governance hold the greatest promise for stopping destructive projects, or at least mitigating some of their worst impacts.

The chapters that follow examine how the real estate turn has played out in a number of Asian cities. Three chapters are dedicated to case studies of Jakarta, Kolkata, and Chongqing, but I touch on cases from many other cities throughout the book. The sheer diversity of such a massive region as that conventionally named "Asia" leads naturally to the question of whether it is possible to compare across such different cases, but the search for a metatheory of urban political economy in Asia is not the intent of the analysis that follows. Rather, the intent is to build toward an understanding of the highly divergent trajectories cities take as they experience similar pressures imposed by national economic reform and global economic integration. The case study chapters attempt to do this by examining one set of factors that render the experiences of particular cities unique: the historically rooted institutional, legal, cultural, and political relationships around the use of land and property rights. It is also worth noting that I do not wish to claim that Asia is somehow unique in experiencing the pressures discussed in this book. Indeed, they may be common to all cities that experience sudden increases in land prices as a result of surges in investment and speculative finance.

Ultimately, this book aspires to build bridges of knowledge across cities and to begin a conversation about the challenges of disruptive pressures on ecologies and communities many cities are facing because of the commodification of land. Given the rapidity of change and the permanence of many of the transformations being wrought, this is an urgent task.

ACKNOWLEDGMENTS

A project that takes this long to complete, and that involves a number of field sites, inevitably requires a great deal of help from many individuals. Below are the names of some of the individuals whose help made this book possible.

The India portion of this research benefited from the generous help and important insights of several people. I am grateful to the Center for Studies of the Social Sciences of Calcutta for hosting me during my time in Kolkata, and to Keya Dasgupta and Sohel Firdos for helping me to get the research started. Jaydatt Vaishnav, Arjun Joshi, and Anal Vaishnav helped tremendously with the research on the Calcutta Riverside project. Arunita Mukherjee provided valuable research assistance. I also enjoyed many insightful and enjoyable conversations about India's urban politics with Neha Sami. Discussions with Solomon Benjamin in both Ann Arbor and Kolkata were rich sources of ideas.

In Jakarta, I am particularly thankful to Jo Santoso, who went far out of his way to be helpful to me. I learned much about Jakarta from my conversations with him, and I remain inspired by his passion for the city. Numerous other people helped immeasurably in my efforts to understand Jakarta, including Kemal Taruc, Dian Tri Irawaty, and Suryono Herlambang. Victoria Beard and Chris Silver were provided critical introductions when I first set out to conduct research in Jakarta.

My research in Chongqing might have been impossible without the help of Wang Lin. Nick Smith was a valuable source of ideas and contacts. Yu Xiao accompanied me on some of the research trips and was full of insight on the field sites we visited.

This project benefited from two visiting positions, one nearer the beginning of the research and the other near the end, that provided wonderful opportunities to think, write, and interact with brilliant and engaging colleagues. At the National University of Singapore's Asia Research Institute, where I spent the summer of 2010, I would particularly like to thank Tim Bunnell and Michelle Miller. I also thank the Laboratoire Technique Territoire et Societes (LATTS) for hosting me as a visiting researcher in the summer of 2016. LATTS provided a stimulating environment for me to undertake the final revisions and edits to the manuscript. Thanks to Ludovic Halbert and Sylvy Jaglin for making the visit possible, and especially to Morgan Mouton for helping me feel at home in Paris.

I benefited from the excellent work of several graduate research assistants at the University of Michigan, Northeastern University, and the National University of Singapore. These include Shohei Nakamura, Vijayeta Singh, Antonio Vazquez Brust, and Rupinder Brar.

Numerous people made comments on versions of material presented in this book and on presentations at conferences and workshops. Among those whose input was helpful in refining these ideas are Liza Weinstein, Domonique Lorrain, Charles Goldblum, Abidin Kusno, Michael Leaf, John Friedmann, Terry McGee, Martin Murray, Anne Pitcher, Aihwa Ong, Ananya Roy, Michael Douglass, and Richard Walker.

Jim Lance at Cornell University Press was extremely supportive and helpful throughout the process. I thank him for his diligence, his encouragement, and his good cheer. I would also like to thank the anonymous reviewers of the draft of this book for the very helpful comments.

HOK and Hiland Incorporated generously allowed me to reproduce their material in this book. I would also like to thank several organizations that provided financial support for this project: the Fulbright program, which provided me with a Fulbright Senior Research Fellowship to conduct the India portion of this research, the Center for International Business Education at the University of Michigan, and the College of Social Sciences and Humanities Research Development Fund and Center for Emerging Markets at Northeastern University.

CITIES FOR PROFIT

Introduction

The Real Estate Turn in Asia's Urban Politics

In August of 2008, contractors commenced pumping sand into Boeung Kak, a lake lying near the heart of Phnom Penh, Cambodia's capital. A year and a half earlier, the Municipality of Phnom Penh had leased the rights to fill and develop the lake for US$79 million to Shukaku Incorporated, owned by Lao Meng Khin, a senator of the ruling Cambodian People's Party. Shukaku's stated intention was to develop a master planned commercial, office, and residential megaproject on the land to be created on the site (ninety hectares of lake plus forty-three hectares of land along the lakeshore), a total investment of more than US$2 billion. The Boeung Kak plan was one of several large real estate projects conceived around Phnom Penh during the late 2000s, and its lure lay in its promise to transform the largest undeveloped space in the center of the city into some of the city's most valuable real estate, a cluster of high-end condominiums, shopping centers, and office complexes.

The plan was controversial from the start. International organizations and local nongovernmental organizations argued that the project violated

Cambodian law and that it threatened to compromise the lake's important social and ecological functions. At the time of the lease signing the lake was home to about 4,250 households, who had built homes at its fringe and on stilts that extended out into the lake. Many of these households made their living from the lake itself, fishing and farming morning glory, a popular local vegetable that thrived on the shallow water. Most residents had settled along the lake with government consent in the gradual re-population of Phnom Penh following the end of the Khmer Rouge regime, which had largely depopulated the city. Some along the shore had legal land tenure, while those on the lake had gained the tacit support of the local authorities, who had provided them with household numbers, had given witness to land sales contracts, and had improved infrastructure (Bugalski and Pred 2011). The municipality's approach to the evictions was heavy-handed and was in apparent violation of principles of due process in cases of eviction outlined in international law and detailed by the Cambodia Land Management and Administration Project (LMAP), a donor-supported project undertaken by the Cambodian government (Biddulph 2014). The state's right to lease the land was itself legally questionable, for it appeared to violate provisions of the 2001 land law that designated water bodies as "state public property" that could not be leased to private users (Mgbako et al. 2010). An investigation undertaken by the World Bank as the evictions and the filling of the lake proceeded found that the lake acted as an important natural reservoir for the city and that the area surrounding the lake had experienced a significant increase in flooding as the filling had progressed (World Bank 2010a).

Ultimately, the coercive approach of the Cambodian government back-fired, although too late to stop much of the displacement and ecological damage that the project caused. The failure of the Boeung Kak scheme was precipitated most directly by the arrest in 2012 of thirteen women for protesting the evictions; although they were sentenced to up to two and a half years in prison, they were soon released due to strong international condemnation from local and international NGOs and the World Bank (Economist 2012). In 2012 the World Bank suspended all new lending to the Cambodian government, citing the lack of due process in the eviction of the Boeung Kak residents. By 2012 the filling of the lake was complete, but plans for the development had apparently ground to a halt. Today, the land created by the clearing of the lake stands empty, its future uncertain.

Figure I.1. Pipes used to pump silt into Boeung Kak. Source: Author.

Over the past three decades, variations on the Boeung Kak story have played out throughout Asia. In cities as disparate as Phnom Penh, Bangalore, Shanghai, Hanoi, and Jakarta, governments and elites have embraced the idea that enabling corporate developers to acquire massive amounts of land for the development of self-contained urban enclaves is an effective way to meet elusive goals of infrastructure modernization and create new lifestyles for a growing consumer class. These projects, which I will refer to in this book as urban real estate megaprojects, are built on a for-profit basis and contain a full suite of urban functions, including housing, commercial districts, office and industrial parks, and schools. They sometimes also contain highly specialized urban functions such as hospitals, university campuses, golf courses, export processing zones, convention centers, and sports stadia. They are a departure from the historical mainstream of urban development; while for-profit developers are responsible for much of the built environment in all capitalist societies, the scale at which they plan is usually constrained to specific buildings or perhaps a block or a handful of blocks. In urban real estate megaprojects, for-profit

Figure I.2. Rendering of Bonifacio Global City in Metro Manila. Images such as this, which present dramatic representations of new forms of urbanism utterly detached from their surrounding environment, demonstrate the discursive tactics that developers and government officials use to gain public approval for their schemes. Source: HOK No Date.

corporations dominate planning at much larger scales, conceiving of new urban districts and entire self-contained towns and planning infrastructure systems at an urban and regional scale. Developers and their state backers argue that the creation of new urban spaces from whole cloth on such a massive scale is necessary to enhance economic competitiveness in globalizing economies competing for foreign investment. At the same time, however, such projects raise troubling concerns about their potential to exacerbate already fraught issues of displacement, exclusion, segregation, and the ecological destruction that occurs with rapid urbanization.

In many parts of Asia, urban real estate megaprojects have emerged as a fundamental force shaping visions for urban futures. In some cases, they have already fundamentally changed urban form. In the Jakarta

Metropolitan Region, researchers have documented twenty-seven such projects that range in size from fifty to more than ten thousand hectares (Winarso and Firman 2002). In the mid-1990s, more than eighty thousand hectares of land were under permit for such projects, an area greater than the city of Jakarta itself, although to date a much smaller portion of this area has actually been developed (Firman 1997). In China, where government agencies and state enterprises predominate in the commercial real estate market, a nonexhaustive review conducted in 2011 as part of this research identified ninety-nine plans for projects with a combined area of more than seven thousand square kilometers and a projected population of more than thirty-six million.[1] "New town" developments with projected populations of half a million or more have been planned in Bangkok, Jakarta, Hanoi, Kolkata, Mumbai, and more than a dozen cities in China, while hundreds of smaller projects have been planned in cities such as Vientiane, Pune, and Phnom Penh (Dick and Rimmer 1998, Mitra 2002; Marshall 2003; Gorvett 2011).

But while glossy architectural renderings of massive, developer-planned urban enclaves have become ubiquitous in large Asian cities, the reality is that they have not always resulted in the production of the envisioned neat, globalized consumer landscapes on the ground. In many instances, desired elements of such plans—iconic skyscrapers, planned subdivisions, meticulously manicured public spaces—have either remained completely unrealized or have undergone a fundamental transformation when transitioning from ink to concrete and glass. A simple way to highlight this variation is to note the contrast in outcomes between two widely cited comparison cases, India and China. In China, where the property market is dominated by powerful state-owned corporations and politically connected developers and where the Chinese state has tremendous powers over land and economy, new towns of hundreds of thousands have sprouted in periods of a few years, replacing communities that have existed for decades if not for hundreds of years with rows of high-rise condominiums and wholly formed industrial and commercial districts. Even the failed projects, such as the widely discussed case of Chenggong, a new town in the Chinese city of Kunming that contains some one hundred thousand housing units but almost no residents, illustrate that Chinese new towns get built even where the market is apparently too weak to support them. In India, by stark contrast, state ambitions to seize land and

Figure I.3. DLF City in Gurgaon. The juxtapositions of planned and unplanned spaces illustrate the limits of efforts to create master planned consumer enclaves in Indian cities. Source: Author.

push through large-scale development has foundered on obstacles rooted in populist politics and difficulties in acquiring land. Large urban projects have consequently largely remained in the realm of the imagination. While there has been a proliferation of plans for large real estate developments, and billboards pronouncing their imminent arrival can be seen on the urban fringe of many Indian cities, many more such projects have been proposed than have broken ground. And even in the country's premier example of a privately built urban enclave, Gurgaon, the actual development resembles more a hybrid form of urbanism than the desired wholesale transformation: lone concrete blocks and stalks of glass and steel besieged by clogged traffic arteries and derelict urban spaces. This relatively successful project serves only to highlight the limits of the global ideal of the urban real estate megaproject in the Indian context.

The objectives of this book are to understand why urban real estate megaprojects have seized the imaginations of urban planners and policy makers and to contribute to efforts to explain the impacts they are having on Asian cities. The Boeung Kak story provides one illustrative example of the critical issues these projects raise for cities, issues of displacement, political conflict, the dislocation of local economies, and ecological damage. Yet these projects also have the potential to generate wealth and economic and social opportunity, and thus they also raise the question of how these benefits should be distributed. In developing a framework for analyzing these projects across national and urban contexts, the book starts with two puzzles. First, why have so many Asian governments taken on politically fraught contests over land and urban space in the aggressive pursuit of urban real estate megaprojects, even as these projects inevitably lead to conflict and to a loosening of direct state control over urban spatial development? That these projects are inevitably controversial and politically charged raises the question of what states hope to gain though their realization. What gains are to be had in the political empowerment and legitimation of the state? What changes in the conceptualization of the role of the state in society lie behind these projects? The second puzzle concerns how we explain the different outcomes of these projects in different cities. What are the circumstances that embolden governments to forge alliances with capital and gain control of land to push projects to realization? When states and corporations are met with opposition, what factors limit their ability to coerce compliance and allow communities and local economies to defend their own claims to property and the use of urban space? How does the necessity to legitimize such projects, to square them with historical state tropes of developmentalism and social equity, shape the bargaining and political deal making that go on around urban real estate megaprojects? How, in the end, does this process of negotiation shape real-world outcomes for urban politics and spatial change?

This book seeks to answer these questions both through a broad review of urban real estate megaprojects across Asia and through in-depth looks at the cases of Jakarta, Kolkata, and Chongqing. These case studies are intended to capture some of the variation in political economies of urban development, with a particular interest in differences in political systems and in state roles in land management. Each case study chapter explores the historical roots of contemporary dynamics of urban development in the city in question and examines one urban real estate megaproject in depth, exploring how the political and spatial dynamics of the city played out in one specific urban development initiative. The case studies of focus are Bumi Serpong Damai (BSD City) in Jakarta, Calcutta Riverside in Kolkata, and Western New City in Chongqing. These case studies of cities and urban real estate megaprojects were developed through interviews, site visits to projects, and data from a number of sources, including governmental and nongovernmental organization reports and data, urban plans, architectural renderings, annual reports and promotional materials of developers, academic studies, and newspaper and other media accounts.

Through a comparative exploration of urban real estate megaprojects, this book also seeks to address larger questions about the changing politics of urban development in Asian cities facing pressures of growth, competition, and fiscal austerity. Urban real estate megaprojects belong to a family of experiments in governance and urban politics that have spread across Asia and much of the rest of the world. These projects are broadly characterized by the increasing centrality of corporate actors and corporate-driven finance in the development of urban space and urban infrastructure on a large scale. Governments in many parts of the world have privatized urban land use planning and infrastructure development and have partnered with corporate developers in efforts to transform commercial areas and derelict urban spaces such as ports, airports, and other public lands (Marshall 2003; Orueta and Fainstein 2008). They have sought new means to finance affordable housing and infrastructure through capital markets and incentives to developers rather than through conventional government funding (Kusno 2012a; Rolnik 2013).

The meaning of this proliferation of market-based mechanisms of urban governance has fostered one of the central contemporary debates in the social sciences: the question of neoliberalism and neoliberalization. The term neoliberalism has been used to describe the global political trend toward the introduction of "market-driven calculations . . . in the management of populations and the administration of special spaces" (Ong 2006, 3–4). This trend, scholars have argued, is based on the conceptual premise that "human well-being can be best advanced by liberating individual entrepreneurial freedoms and skills within an institutional framework characterized by strong private property rights, free markets, and free trade" (Harvey 2005, 2). Yet the questions of *how* and *why* neoliberal ideas infiltrate urban politics and policy, how they interact with non-neoliberal social and political forms, and just how useful they are to understanding urban change in any given setting have animated an important debate. This book has simultaneously been inspired by some of the analytical insights of recent writings on neoliberalism and neoliberalization, but also by a sense that there still remains much to be said on this topic.

One side of the debate on neoliberalism takes a bleak view, arguing that neoliberalization at its heart is the product of collective action on the part of a global capitalist elite, propagated through international rule regimes and key thought leaders, that serves largely to ensure continued capital accumulation by multinational corporations (Harvey 2005). According to this perspective, governments in poorer and debt-ridden countries adopt neoliberal reforms as a defense mechanism, an effort to maintain competitiveness in a globalizing economy by stripping away welfare states and re-engineering economies and societies to function as platforms for corporate investment. What results is a process of "accumulation by dispossession," as places and people who (like the morning glory farmers of Boeung Kak) do not directly contribute to corporate accumulation, and therefore to government goals of fiscal stability through globalization-driven economic growth, are gradually dispossessed of their access to space and resources through the state-facilitated incursion of market norms (Harvey 2009).

More recently, however, some have argued that state actors are not quite so passive in this process of change. Brenner, Peck, and Theodore (2010, 330) have argued instead for an understanding of *neoliberalization* as a *process* of change, driven by adaptation of market-oriented governance to local contexts. This combination of global and local interests, they argue, "produces geo-institutional differentiation across places, territories, and scales; but it does this systemically, as a pervasive, endemic feature of its basic operational logic" (Brenner, Peck, and Theodore 2010, 330). Such a perspective leads to an analytical focus on the ways the imperatives created by global economic competition and fiscal austerity play out in local political and institutional responses and how they result in the selective use of global models of urban governance and planning (Peck and Theodore 2012). The concept of a "variegated neoliberalization" that results from this framework has opened up the field of investigation for explorations, like the one presented in this book, that seek to understand the particular social, political, and institutional factors that shape change in a given setting.

One important set of interventions that contributes to such a contextualized understanding is Aihwa Ong's work, which has argued that many

Asian governments have exercised considerable agency in setting their own course within a neoliberalizing global order and in defining their own developmental goals. Ong has characterized neoliberalism as a "mobile technology of governing" that is "selectively taken up in diverse political contexts" to achieve particular state objectives (Ong 2007, 3). In this view, state actors use market norms, alongside other logics of governing, where it suits their interest in creating governable subjects who, in their pursuit of material advancement through participation in markets, adhere to state norms of modernity and economic growth. Here neoliberal policy and planning ideas emerge not only through the imposition of global rule regimes, but also through selective appropriation or rejection based on the canny calculations of the state. What emerges is a combined logic, marked by the deliberate formation of spaces of "neoliberalization as exception," which coexist with "exceptions to neoliberalism."

Ong's framework is particularly compelling when applied to cases where strong states exercise considerable power over politics, society, and economy. Singapore, for example, adheres to market logics in its fiscal and trade policy as a means to achieve export-oriented economic growth, yet it has also developed a public housing system that, in a complete departure from any supposed neoliberal playbook, accommodates more than 80 percent of the Singaporean population. In the Singapore case, where a one-party state dominates social and political life, the state uses market logics as one of a range of "technologies" of social engineering and political control. Ong's framework, however, is less compelling in other cases, such as that of India, where the state appears far less powerful and where the process of commodifying land and labor is much less effectual. In many instances in India and elsewhere in Asia, changes to land-management practice appear less as "technologies of governing" than as what I will refer to as "strategies of accumulation." While the former refers to efforts to create entrepreneurial subjects through a coordinated set of governance initiatives, the latter refers to more limited efforts to monetize land and foster local economic development through improvised reforms and collective action for specific land use changes. The word "strategy" rather than "technology" seems more appropriate because it implies the possibility, and indeed likelihood, of defeat in efforts to achieve these discrete initiatives and of failure of achieved reforms to meet their objectives.

In yet other cases, we witness the commodification of land deployed by corrupt bureaucrats and elected officials as a tactic of rent seeking, as state actors use specific and targeted regulatory and administrative tricks to created windfall profits for politicians and their accomplices in the private sector. In reality, we can in some instances witness all three logics—commodification of land as a technology of governing, as a strategy of accumulation, and as a tactic of rent seeking—playing out in the same city at the same time. The conceptual distinction between these three logics of state land management, I argue, is a useful heuristic for understanding both the differences in the motivations behind urban development strategies and the strategies themselves. This typology obviously also raises the question of why we see one of these logics play out in any given case.

Finally, the literature on neoliberalization and urban policy has recently witnessed important works by a number of scholars, notably Jennifer Robinson (2011), that question whether neoliberalism is a useful framework for understanding cities of the Global South. In her earlier work, Robinson (2006) called on scholars to transcend the view of Western cities as defining the meaning of urbanity and fundamentally shaping and anticipating urbanism everywhere. She argues for a need to move beyond categories of cities as developed or underdeveloped, global or not global, and instead to view all cities as "ordinary," meaning they are all "dynamic and diverse, if conflicted, arenas for social life" (Robinson 2006, 1). In an article specifically addressing the concept of neoliberalism, Parnell and Robinson (2012) argue that the tendency of Anglo-American researchers to "tend to their own backyards" in theorizing urban change has led to the hegemony of this concept even though it simply may not be that important in the context of cities of the Global South. They argue that the theoretical constructs that have drawn the attention of scholars of neoliberalism in the American and English contexts—urban regimes, gentrification, and formal urban renewal—may be of less importance in the "global South where traditional authority, religion, and informality are as central to legitimate urban narratives as the vacillations in modern urban capitalist public policy" (Parnell and Robinson 2012, 596).

While it is indeed critical to avoid assumptions about parallels between the experiences of cities of the anglophone world and elsewhere, the empirical material presented in the chapters that follow indicates that the either-or framing implied by the above quote, between neoliberal and non-neoliberal spaces and realms of social activity, is not borne out by the weight of evidence. Communities like the morning glory farmers of Boeung Kak may exist in spaces defined by "informality," by customary tenure, and by social and political arrangements that have roots in deep historical and cultural practices, but these systems inevitably interact with larger economies and with the politics of neoliberalization. It is therefore important to understand them as subject to processes of neoliberalization, even if we agree that they are not defined by these processes. One (literally) concrete example of such interaction, which will be discussed at greater length in chapter 3, is the *kampungs* in many periurban areas of Jakarta that have been walled in by developers of the elite new towns that are being built around them. Although they are largely self-regulating settlements that have customary tenure rights to the lands they occupy, their daily reality is shaped by these concrete barricades that delineate them as residual and temporary spaces awaiting full commodification and indeed already increasingly transformed by this process.

The *kampungs* are emblematic of all communities that exist within nations and cities where neoliberal trends in governance are under way. While their agency and the non-neoliberal logics that have shaped these communities are critical to the story of the contested and not inevitable process of neoliberalization, such communities must nonetheless be understood in the light of the transformations that are taking place around them. Nevertheless, while this book focuses on urban real estate megaproject developments and on the web of changes to politics, economy, and society they are a part of, the insights of Robinson (2011), Roy (2011), and other scholars working within postcolonial frameworks have reminded me of the dimensions of these phenomena that I have not focused attention on. Much more research is needed on the lifeworlds of people experiencing and contesting change and on the varied logics that shape urban transformations.

At the center of the debates summarized above are questions of agency, questions of who is able to shape agendas of urban development, and of the extent to which local social and cultural norms and historically formed institutions may continue to shape cities in the face of the incursion of neoliberal logics. Is neoliberalization foisted on local and national politicians and bureaucrats through international rule regimes, political indoctrination, and the cooptation of state actors by global corporate elites, creating a landscape of misery, dispossession, and conflict? Or can state actors effectively deploy neoliberal frameworks, and position themselves at the center of economic processes, to achieve goals of state building, political control, and economic growth? What are the possibilities for movements that resist trends toward neoliberalization.

The view taken in this book is that neoliberalism should not simply be seen as taking hold through a universal logic of ideological succession, but neither should it be viewed as but one among any number of modes of social and political organization that communities can choose freely to adopt. Rather, understanding processes of neoliberalization requires us to analyze the specific points of interaction between the global and the local and to analyze the incentives and pressures that local actors perceive in their push to create and exploit markets. Global economic processes have introduced economic logics that present state and corporate actors with new opportunities and incentives to exercise power through the cultivation and exploitation of markets. The main dynamic explored in this book is the simple logic of increasing land values, which presents new avenues for state economic influence and rent seeking. The growing role of land markets in urban policy should therefore be understood from an actor-centered perspective, which focuses on how particular urban actors (elected officials, bureaucrats, developers, corporate heads, community leaders, and others) respond to the impacts of rising land values on the field of urban political power. At the same time, questions of land and property have evolved historically through the formations of institutions, policies, and social norms. They are therefore often infused with conflicting and overlapping logics of bureaucratic control, resource management, modernist ideals of master planning, and long-standing and politically rooted extralegal and communal claims.

Hence this book focuses on land management and property rights as one critical arena in which new contestations have emerged with global economic change. As both a site of the production and consumption of commodities, and as a valuable and scarce resource in its own right, developable urban land has become increasingly central to the agendas of capital accumulation of both domestic and international corporate actors, as well as state actors. In an era of increasing flows of international trade and investment, and of speculative flows of international finance, the potential wealth to be generated from urban land has increased dramatically. Yet the ability of powerful interests to capitalize on these possibilities is shaped in important ways by institutions of property rights, patterns of land ownership, and popular norms about claims to space. These same institutions and norms also shape the terrain on which communities, vendors, small workshop industries, and numerous others who face pressure for displacement seek to stake out and protect their claims to urban space in the face of powerful competition.

Stated succinctly, the central argument of this book is that the proliferation of urban real estate megaprojects, a change that has led to the privatization of urban space, has nonetheless emerged in large part through state action. Such projects embody one way in which state actors have sought to maximize their control over land markets and use them as mechanisms for state empowerment and legitimation by mediating the allocation of the massive profits to be realized from real estate development. Critical to the ability of both national and local state actors to realize these possibilities is their capacity to monetize urban land, to use their regulatory and sometimes coercive power to assert control over the massive potential profits to be gained from land value increases. They use this power to directly tap into land development as a source of revenue for the state or to direct the profits from land development to key allies of the state. This trend toward *land monetization*, and the increasingly acquisitive and speculative eye with which states have viewed land markets, constitutes what the title of this volume refers to as the "real estate turn" in urban policy in Asia.

The idea of land *monetization*, as used in this book, overlaps with but is distinct from the idea of land *commodification*. The latter term refers to the process, widely analyzed in the literature on neoliberal urbanization, through which land is increasingly treated by state and corporate actors primarily as an object of exchange and accumulation, rather than of everyday use. The term land monetization as used in this book refers to the use of state powers to enable the state itself, or its corporate allies, to capture revenue streams from land. This term is intended to highlight the agency of particular actors—mayors, heads of state, governors, legislators, and bureaucrats—in deploying specific strategies of land commodification in the deliberate pursuit of the interests of state actors and their politically influential allies.

The book further argues that this real estate turn has been a central dynamic in shaping the policies of national governments, particularly with respect to property rights, state rescaling, and state–civil society relations. Yet this common push toward land monetization takes shape very differently based on patterns of land ownership and state powers of land management, factors that may enhance or constrain state actors' ability to influence the terms under which corporate investment shapes urban development. Hence an examination of state practices of land management around urban real estate megaprojects, and of the political conflict and negotiation these practices engender, may tell us more about the actual impacts of these developments than an analysis of the architectural or urban design schemes for the projects, which in any case are rarely fully carried out. In fact, one hypothesis supported by the case studies examined in later chapters is that the fantastic imagery of the architectural renderings that uniformly attend these projects often serve a primarily promotional purpose, to justify the financing, regulatory changes, and changes in land ownership needed to unlock land for development. As will be apparent from the examples provided throughout this study, these renderings are quite often cast aside or changed almost beyond recognition as projects break ground and move toward completion.

Two aspects of the Boeung Kak case help to elucidate this central argument concerning the importance of land in state political strategies with respect to urban development. The first is the Municipality of Phnom Penh's aggressive use of powers to reclaim land, which seem to have been deployed in this case to distribute patronage to a powerful political actor. As will become clear in the chapters that follow, state actors almost always play a key role in the realization of urban real estate megaprojects, particularly at the stage of land acquisition. Governments deploy a variety of powers of land acquisition and management to realize these projects, including state powers to take land through eminent domain; the sale or lease of government land; the use of state regulatory powers, such as the issuance of land development permits or the rezoning of land; the development of infrastructure to open up new lands for development; and, as in the case of Boeung Kak, land reclamation. In fact, these projects generally represent a close intermingling, and indeed sometimes a fusion, of state and for-profit corporate interests in land. In a world where hedge fund managers cast their eyes about the globe in search of nine- and even ten-figure real estate investments, state actors use their leverage over land both as a powerful tool to shape urban development and as a means to control the revenue that development generates.

In this context, shared interests between state and corporate actors have fostered new forms of governance that institutionalize the intersection between state and corporate interests. These include public-private partnerships in land development, parastatal organizations tasked with transferring land to corporate developers, and state-owned enterprises venturing into commercial land development. In the case of Boeung Kak these interests were embodied in the person of Lao Meng Khin, a figure who straddles the state/corporate nexus. Elsewhere, this nexus may be constituted by the development of for-profit state-owned corporations (as in China's state capitalist model) or in the growing influence of private-sector corporate leaders in state and civil society mechanisms of governance (as in the corporate-state alliance embodied in the Bangalore Agenda Task Force and its organizational antecedents).

Because of this fusion of profit orientations with state interests, urban real estate megaprojects foster a tension between state objectives of political legitimation and corporate objectives of profit maximization and risk management. In this context, questions of urban politics—the mechanisms of political accountability to the public—become critical to the question of whose interests are represented in these developments. Boeung Kak is a case of a particularly egregious and rapacious grasp for land. Later chapters will reveal a number of factors—the prevalence of state land ownership and the political accountability of state land use managers being two—that lead to quite different models of land acquisition, with different outcomes for affected communities and for relations between communities and the state.

The second aspect of the Boeung Kak project that helps to illustrate the central argument of this book is simply that it is stalled indefinitely, its future uncertain. Only a proportion, perhaps a minority, of urban real estate megaprojects proposals are actually built, with many others scuttled by public protest, political maneuvering, and the vicissitudes of high finance. The specific elements of the controversy over Boeung Kak—the evocation of questions of property rights, housing rights, and social justice—resonate through many of the cases that will be discussed throughout this volume. Such large-scale acts of land acquisition often necessitate a renegotiation of well-established property relations that are deeply rooted in political and social institutions. As urban real estate megaprojects are often formulated to appeal to the interests of corporations and the relatively wealthy, and frequently result in evictions of significant numbers of people, these projects also appear to contradict state claims as arbiters of social justice and developmentalism. This is particularly true in cities where large segments of populations, sometimes substantial majorities, occupy land in various degrees of illegality or with customary claims that are under attack in the relentless push toward land commodification. Hence urban real estate megaprojects often become central to increasingly fraught debates over property rights and rights of access to urban space. This book will explore how the real estate turn in urban policy has shaped state-community relations in the areas of urban land use planning, property rights, housing, and infrastructure.

The central aspects of the Boeung Kak case and of other stories that will be related in the pages that follow—the exploitation of land development by the politically powerful, state interests in real estate, and people's fight for a place in the city—resonate with recurring themes in political economy analyses of cities under capitalism. Harvey (2003) illustrates these conditions in his account of Haussmann's reconstruction of Paris in the mid-nineteenth century, which was financed through the city government's acquisition of land and the use of land value gains resulting from redevelopment. Here the city government consciously took the place of private enterprise, positioning itself to "recapture the betterment values derived from its own investment, thereby becoming, as critics complained, the biggest speculator of all" (Harvey 2003, 133). In New York during the 1860s and 1870s, Boss Tweed and other members of the Tammany Hall machine that ran New York City capitalized on mass transit and other infrastructure investment by enriching themselves through large-scale property investment (Burrows and Wallace 1999). In contemporary times, seminal works on the political economy or urban development have placed state interests in the commodification of place at the center of debates about urban politics in capitalist societies (notable examples include Harvey 1989 and Logan and Molotch 1987).

Yet the cases in this book are not simply new chapters in an old story. The fundamental common thread that links all these historical and contemporary experiences together—that urban politics in capitalist societies is shaped fundamentally by the politics of land—plays out in dramatically different ways in the cases examined in this volume. The cases reveal the ways key differences in institutional and historical contexts—for example in legal definitions and social norms of property rights, political institutions, and historically formed patterns of land ownership—lead to quite different experiments with urban development that are resulting in different models of urbanity. Given how much of humanity is living in and shaping these new urban sites, it is critical that social scientists and public policy makers begin to analyze the implications of these experiments for Asia's urban future.

Framing Urban Real Estate Megaprojects as a Land-Management Strategy

This book uses the term "urban real estate megaproject" to delineate a certain category of urban development project: large, integrated, master planned, and commercially driven real estate developments that seek to fundamentally transform the urban fabric. I choose to deploy this new and somewhat unwieldy terminology because it captures a particular type of project that distills some of the key issues of concern to this study. These include the growing direct interest of state actors in commercial land markets and the mixing of state and corporate interests in whole-cloth urban transformations. The term "urban real estate megaproject" overlaps substantially with what have been referred to in popular parlance and academic studies as "new town" projects (Phillips, Yeh, and Kim 1987). The terms diverge, however, in that many new towns have historically been state-built, with commercial considerations secondary. Moreover, many of the projects examined here function more as new urban districts than as stand-alone new towns. The term "urban megaproject" likewise overlaps with the projects examined in this book, although this term has been applied to a broader range of projects, including single-use real estate developments, for example tourism enclaves or government centers, and large urban infrastructure projects.

Urban real estate megaprojects in Asia share a strong kinship with large urban redevelopment projects in the United States and Europe; London's Docklands and Battery Park City in New York are two prominent examples (Fainstein 2001). These projects, like the cases examined in this book, represent efforts by governments to play an active role in channeling corporate-led development in ways that achieve state goals. Studies of European and American urban megaprojects have traced their lineage to postwar efforts to battle urban blight and disinvestment, such as the

U.S. federal government's efforts to stimulate urban renewal in the 1950s and 1960s by clearing "slum" areas and decaying commercial districts in central cities to make way for corporate investment that sometimes never arrived. According to the literature on these European and American cases, the emergence of these projects marks an entrepreneurial turn in urban governance that has seen local states play a more active role. States have acquired and transferred land, financed development, and sometimes partnered with private developers to realize strategic, high-profile developments focused on positioning cities as major sites of investment within global corporate and tourism economies (Swyngedouw, Moulaert, and Rodriguez 2002; Orueta and Fainstein 2008; Siemiatycki 2013). In the context of trends toward austerity in governance and the retreat of national states from programs of redistribution and social welfare, these projects are indicative of a more general trend of the rescaling of state action to the metropolitan scale and the consequent focus of local state action on economic development and the generation of property tax revenue.

One important difference between urban real estate megaprojects in European and American cities and those in Asian cities is that the latter are built in contexts not of urban decline but rather of population growth, economic expansion, and dramatic expansion of the consumer class (Orueta and Fainstein 2008). As a result, they are often framed by government backers as a new approach to city building, a means for cities to achieve infrastructural modernization and economic growth while meeting the demands of rapid urbanization. These contexts of rapid growth also mean that the potential wealth to be generated from land monetization is that much more significant in relative terms and provides that much more of a lure to pursue massive projects.

Recent years have seen a growing numbers of studies looking at urban real estate megaprojects in Asia, but these studies have pursued different lines of inquiry from those on European projects. Researchers have focused attention on two related questions concerning the impacts of globalization and modernization on urban form: the question of whether cities are experiencing a convergence of urban form with the West and the social implications of the privatization of urban space and governance. In one early and important contribution to this debate, Dick and Rimmer (1998) argued that the growth of privately built "new town" projects in Southeast Asia reflects growing social polarization in Southeast Asian cities. They argue that economic restructuring with globalization has led to the rapid expansion of a consumer class that has sought to escape the congestion and perceived dangers of central cities dominated by the poor. They and others further argue that developers have anticipated market demand by looking to the West for models of suburban development that have become familiar through travel, television, and Hollywood. The result has been a proliferation of new towns modeled explicitly on American "edge cities" and planned suburbs, integrated in a manner that allows consumer class families to circulate and meet most of their needs (shopping, work, housing, services) within a planned urban environment (Cowherd and Heikkila 2002; Hogan and Houston 2002; Kusno 2004). Subsequent studies have questioned this hypothesis of convergence with the West. Some, for example, have pointed to the influence of other, non-Western cities, such as Singapore and Shanghai, that increasingly act as regional and global models of urbanism (Marshall 2003; Bunnell and Maringanti 2010; Ong 2011). In both perspectives, however, there is a pervasive concern about the impacts of privatized new town development: the wholesale privatization of urban space, the destruction of existing communities, and the creation of spaces of exclusion of large urban majorities who do not belong to the consumer class.

The focus of this volume on land-management politics and policy is not intended to supplant these important debates about the origins of the urban design and architectural models for urban real estate megaprojects. Rather, focusing on the role of state actors in land acquisition helps to shed light on a different set of issues presented by these projects. The first is the question of the displacement and eviction that accompanies these developments, and the broader related questions of what these projects mean for rights to exist in and use urban space. The processes of land acquisition and development by both state and private actors that have accompanied the push to monetize land have come with massive population dislocation that is rewriting the social meaning of cities. The scale of this displacement is difficult to quantify, but in China alone, Hsing (2010) estimates that between sixty and seventy-five million people were evicted as a result of urban development from 1990 to 2007. In Metro Manila, state estimates of population displacement that would take place with planned urban development and infrastructure projects totaled more than one million in the late 2000s (Shatkin 2008). In New Delhi, according to Bhan (2009), forty thousand homes were demolished from 2004 to 2007 in the development that occurred in the run-up to the Commonwealth Games.

But the impact of displacements goes beyond their direct impacts on urban geography; contestations over evictions foster political change as well. State complicity in evictions of communities and local economies is often perceived to be in jarring contradiction with values states have themselves posed as central to their legitimacy. These include social equity, universal citizenship, and (especially in periurban areas) food security and the sanctity of agriculture. Where people have established legal claims to land and access to urban space, as was the case for many Boeung Kak residents, displacement without due process also contradicts state claims to be the arbiter and protector of the rule of law. The resulting political conflicts have on occasion led to the fall of governments. In the state of West Bengal, for example, efforts by the state government to take land from hundreds of small farmers in the district of Singur outside Kolkata for the development of an automobile manufacturing plant and supporting township contributed directly to the electoral defeat in 2011 of the Communist Party of India-Marxist, which had held power for thirty-four years. Hence the violence of displacement, viewed by governments as necessary to achieve large-scale land monetization, creates a fraught political situation in which politicians and bureaucrats are forced to constantly improvise their positions and approaches to dealing with displaced communities. This process can be complicated by the lack of a clear developmental rationale for projects that the public often sees as gifts to developers.

One issue that requires particular attention if we are to understand contestations over emergent state roles in land acquisition and development is the question of property rights. This question has proven particularly vexing to the realization of urban real estate megaprojects because in so many cases the state itself has enabled the creation of splintered property rights regimes. There is often a division between land that is titled and therefore subject to transfer through market exchange and land that is occupied without title, under customary forms of tenure, or often illegally or with ambiguous legality. In Indonesia, for example, only about 30 percent of land is registered with the National Land Agency and therefore subject to government regulations regarding titling, market exchange, and real estate development (Kusno 2012a). On the remaining lands, corporate developers have no legal rights to develop, and existing users either reside illegally or are subject to various forms of customary land tenure. In Delhi's National Capital Territory, according to Bhan (2009), only about 24 percent of the population resides in "planned colonies," with the remainder residing in slums, "authorized" and "unauthorized" colonies, urban villages, and various other areas where rules of titling, government regulation, and market exchange are much more unevenly applied. This active encouragement of informal patterns of land occupation has led Roy (2005) to characterize the prevalence of "informality" as a mode of governing, a means through which state actors can manage urban populations by confining them to spaces of exception, where they can be moved around or subject to regimes of regulation as suits the requirements of the powerful. In this volume, I follow Leaf (2005), in referring to this not as an issue of "informality"—for the use of this term obscures what are sometimes solid legal and institutional foundations for alternative property rights—but rather one of a dualism between land that is titled and therefore subject to exchange within the market and land that is occupied without title, either through customary forms of tenure or through illegal occupation by "squatters," vendors, or other users.

Terminology aside, the question that confronts governments in many instances is: How can land be titled, and therefore subject to market exchange, so that it can be transferred to corporate developers for large-scale urban development and infrastructure projects? Across the cases examined in this book, this question has driven a wave of innovation in law and politics aimed at developing a new social contract around land that will quell political opposition to large-scale development while enabling the release of land for megaprojects. These innovations have varied from weakly implemented efforts to shift the agenda of corporate-driven growth down-market to consolidate the urban poor at a higher density in legal settlements, to efforts to enhance the coercive power of the state to engage in summary eviction, and to insulate public authorities from accountability to affected communities (Goldman 2011; Kusno 2012a). Governments have also sought, in rarer instances, to formulate procedures for eviction and implement measures to ensure due process, and to create mechanisms to redistribute some of the benefits of development. One question that motivates the comparisons of the cities in this book is: When and why does the political influence of those displaced by urban real estate megaprojects make a difference in shaping this new social contract around land and in avoiding some of the more violent and unjust forms of eviction such as occurred in the Boeung Kak case?

A focus on state land management also helps to elucidate the question of the distribution of the benefits and costs of urban real estate megaproject development. Benefits of these projects include not only the tremendous wealth generated by the surge in land values they create, but also access to the amenities within them, such as green space and infrastructure. Perhaps more important for low- and moderate-income groups is access to the economic opportunities created by the clustering of new economic activities and consumers within these developments. Costs are extensive and varied, including increased burdens on infrastructure systems, ecological damage, and considerable amounts of traffic and congestion. Some attention has been paid to ways governments can redistribute the financial benefits of real estate development, for example by selling or leasing state land and using the revenue to provide public goods, or using land grants to infrastructure development corporations as a means to finance infrastructure (Peterson 2009; Peterson 2013). Governments can also finance infrastructure through "value capture," for example by levying taxes or fees on developers who benefit from increases in property values resulting from new infrastructure, or by entering into partnerships with developers to engage in property development around a new infrastructure investment such as an airport. Yet other mechanisms include generating government revenue through the sale of development rights to urbanize rural land or to increase floor area ratios. Governments can also deal with some of the negative externalities of developments through the requirement of exactions, or public goods to be provided by the developer, or through inclusionary zoning, a term that refers to requirements for the inclusion of affordable housing within a development (Peterson 2009). They can also ameliorate negative environmental impacts of a development simply through the rigorous application of environmental and land-use regulations.

While the technocratic literature on this topic is rich with ideas and case studies, two critical questions remain. The first is: When and why do governments have the autonomy, incentives, and political will to enact some of these ideas, all of which can cut into the revenue streams of both private and state-owned enterprises and state agencies? As will be discussed in greater detail in chapter 2, the prevalence of state land ownership is a critical mechanism through which some countries, notably China and Singapore, have gained sufficient control of land-based revenue to engage in massive public investment through land monetization. In other cases, even modest efforts at the redistribution of project revenue can face stiff resistance. Second, what are the political calculations involved in the assertion of state influence on the distribution of the benefits and costs of land development? On the one hand, if the central arguments of this volume are correct, then the fusion of state and corporate interests around land development raises considerable obstacles to the capacity and will of the state to exact concessions from developers. On the other, the capacity of state actors to directly draw on land-based financial windfalls creates tremendous incentives for graft and abuse of power that raise yet another set of troubling political concerns. Indeed, the possibility of rent-seeking behavior on the part of state actors looms across all the case studies discussed in this volume, and it appears to have played a role in the case of Boeung Kak. Instances of graft are of course difficult to document, although they occasionally do come to light through instances of litigation and through investigative journalism. The issue of state motivation and behavior with respect to land monetization once again boils down to the politics of land and property, and specifically to the question of what institutional and legal mechanisms provide state, corporate, and community actors with the capacity to shape decisions about property development.

Finally, the focus on the political economy of land and property helps us to unpack a central question of concern in contemporary literature on neoliberal urbanization, that of the rescaling of state action. Research has extensively documented a shift away from a system of "spatial Keynesianism," in which national governments position themselves as arbiters of interregional equity, and toward efforts to rescale power and responsibility downwards to urban and metropolitan governments (Brenner 2004). In contexts of intense competition for global corporate investment, this broad trend toward the decentralization of powers and responsibilities signals an effort by national states to re-engineer local states into entrepreneurial agents of economic growth by providing them the incentives and means to cater local economies to the needs of capital.

A focus on state practices of land management places the politics of this shift, and the intrastate conflicts it produces, into sharp relief. With the rapid spike in land values that many Asian countries have experienced, many national governments have provided local state actors with enhanced abilities to intervene in land development and property markets, tools they need to exploit the financial potential of land development, and have incentivized them to utilize these powers to their greatest potential. Cambodia represents an extreme case of such a strategy. The Cambodian People's Party appears to have empowered the Municipality of Phnom Penh to act as an agent of a small cabal of individuals straddling the corporate-state nexus who enriched themselves through state-facilitated land development. Elsewhere, national governments have provided more meaningful local autonomy, for example by providing municipal governments and parastatals with powers to lease state land (as in China), or incentives and legal authority to formalize land tenure and thereby enable land acquisition by state and corporate actors (as in India) (Ding 2007; Shatkin and Vidyarthi 2013). Yet providing local state actors with such a direct stake in land can also be a double-edged sword, for it may encourage corrupt and predatory behavior that undermines the legitimacy of both the local and the national state. Land development also emerges in the cases examined in this volume as weapon in a high-stakes conflict between different political interests with vested interests in urban development, including municipal governments, state and provincial governments, national ministries, state-owned corporations, and others. In China, for example, Hsing (2010) argues that urban politics in contemporary China center around competition for land between municipal governments and what she calls "socialist land masters," large state-owned enterprises, military units, and other central government entities.

In sum, this project focuses on land development, and specifically on the monetization of land through the realization of massive real estate developments. This focus helps explain some of the central issues of emergent urban conflicts over social inequality and exclusion, democracy and political participation, state rescaling, and access to urban space. It also sheds light on some of the important levers of change that are at the center of these conflicts: questions of property rights and rights to use urban space, the rescaling of state action, and the administrative and electoral mechanisms through which people outside the state, be they communities or corporations, gain influence over the state.

Interpreting the Spatial and Temporal Logic of Urban Real Estate Megaproject Development

In addition to the question of the impacts of the real estate turn in urban policy, this book also seeks to understand when such a turn takes place and how this turn plays out in urban spatial change. The embrace of urban real estate megaprojects has taken place at different junctures in different parts of Asia. Such projects first became prominent in Southeast Asian cities in the late 1980s, particularly in Jakarta, Bangkok, and Manila. In China, the development of urban real estate megaprojects began in earnest in the late 1990s, while India saw a sudden burst of proposals for real estate megaprojects between 2003 and 2007. Urban real estate megaprojects also emerge in different parts of urban regions, on the urban periphery, in central cities, and occasionally in far-flung exurban regions. They emerge on state-owned land, on land held by smallholders, and on reclaimed land. This spatial and temporal variation has important implications for understanding the opportunities and threats that compel state and private-sector actors to push forward with urban real estate megaproject strategies and for understanding the modalities of their policy strategies.

Neil Smith's rent gap theory presents a simple framework for interpreting spatial and temporal patterns of urban real estate megaproject development, for it cuts to the very center of the incentives that state and corporate actors face during real estate booms. The theory seeks to explain when and why land prices surge upwards, providing opportunities for speculative investment by real estate developers and investors, and how the behavior of these actors in turn shapes the spatial development and politics of cities. For Smith (1996), the rent gap is constituted by the difference between the capitalized ground rent, or the amount of rent the current landowner is extracting from a piece of property, and the potential ground rent that could be realized if the land were redeveloped to its "highest and best use." Smith's classic 1996 study on gentrification was written in the context of the wave of growth in financial services and other high-end service industries in certain American and European cities in the late twentieth century. He argued that the physical and social deterioration of lower-income central city neighborhoods suppressed capitalized rent, even as growing demand for space in such centrally located areas from consumers and corporations caused an escalation of potential rent. The widening gap between capitalized and potential ground rent created opportunities for windfall profits, motivating urban policy change and speculative activity by real estate developers and driving a processes of conflict-ridden and sometimes violent displacement of existing residents and businesses.

The specifics of Smith's analysis of gentrification in the United States and Europe are of limited relevance in much of urban Asia. Underlying market conditions, economic development dynamics, and pre-existing spatial patterns are fundamentally different. To be useful in these settings, therefore, the rent gap concept must be decontextualized from the European and American settings and understood simply as the gap between capitalized and ground rent. Doing so provides useful insights into the opportunities and threats that Asian governments have faced in the past three decades. Cities throughout East, Southeast, and South Asia have experienced surging property values with population growth and increases in foreign investment and international trade, although the periodicity of these surges has differed as different cities have become the focus of international trade and finance at different junctures. Rapid economic growth has brought both increased demand for high-end residential, commercial, and office development and an increased supply of finance through an influx of investment capital that inevitably seeks an outlet in property development as land and property prices rise.

As will be elucidated in the next chapter, at the early stages of a real estate boom, even as rapid urbanization and economic change place upward pressure on land values, legal and political restraints on foreign investment and land development place constraints on the large-scale commodification of urban space. The result is the buildup of massive rent gaps that come to constitute a significant potential source of windfall profits for government and corporate actors. Such emergent rent gaps have motivated moments of coordinated policy reform in many countries in Asia, as governments have enacted reforms to liberalize financial service industries and to reduce restrictions on property ownership and investment in an effort to consummate massive urban development. The resulting waves of investment in real estate have caused further explosive increases in demands for land, widening rent gaps still further. These transformations have occurred at different junctures in different countries according to changing trends in international finance and investment. They have further reflected differences in prevailing patterns of land use, legal and political contexts of land ownership, and political structures.

Rent gap theory also helps explain *where* new development emerges by focusing attention on the factors that have suppressed capitalized rents and those that have led to a dramatic increase in potential rents. Three factors stand out as particularly worthy of examination.

First, and most significant, is the massive spatial expansion of cities in rapidly urbanizing countries. Urban expansion creates tremendous upward pressure on land values even as prices are suppressed by regulatory restrictions on the development of lands designated for agricultural or rural use and by the lack of urban infrastructure. Based on a detailed analysis of changes in the built-up area of cities using Landsat imagery, Angel, Parent, Civco, and Blei (2012) document a near doubling of the urban built-up area of the Bangkok Metropolitan Region between 1994 and 2002, a 70 percent increase from 1993 to 2002 in Metro Manila, and about a 250 percent increase in the urban land area of Guangzhou from 1990 to 2000. Such growth presents tremendous opportunities to unlock value through infrastructure development and regulatory machinations at the periurban fringe.

Second, large-scale state land ownership has acted as a significant constraint on the capitalization of potential rents. While state land ownership is particularly prevalent in postsocialist societies, in almost all major cities state functionaries—port, airport, and railway authorities, national government departments and agencies (such as ministries of defense), and state-owned enterprise—control significant landholdings (Peterson and Kaganova 2010). These lands present alluring opportunities for the enrichment of the state, and of state functionaries, through sale or lease to private developers or the formation of public-private partnerships in their redevelopment.

Third, the prevalence of dualistic land rights regimes discussed earlier also constrains the commodification of urban space and the realization of land rents. As noted previously, the occupation of land and the use of urban space outside of property rights regimes defined by transferable title persist in part because they are often accorded some recognition from elements of the state. Political support for customary tenure arrangements and extralegal occupations of urban land creates a space for social negotiation of the terms of rights to urban space that can act as a significant obstacle to the schemes of developers and governments. It is this obstacle that motivates urban policy reforms aimed at titling land.

The concept of the rent gap renders government urban development strategies legible. An understanding of the constraints on the monetization of periurban, state, customary and extralegal occupations of land helps to unpack the varied strategies that states have pursued, which include land use and regulatory change, infrastructure investment, the creation of parastatal organizations tasked with selling or leasing land, political reform aimed at weakening the political base of urban poor communities, and land reclamation. These varied strategies present different challenges to states that endeavor to use them and to communities that seek to deflect the forces of displacement. The case studies will explore the spatial and political implications of these strategies in the diverse contexts of the cities examined in this book.

Why Study Contestations over Property Rights and Urban Space?

This is a book about the politics of land and real estate markets. It did not start out with this focus. My initial focus was on the form and functioning of urban real estate megaprojects themselves, on the social and political implications that their spatial impacts were having for cities. The seeds of this project lie in an earlier research effort focusing on the growing role of private developers in shaping urban form in Metro Manila (Shatkin 2008). Eager to delve into this topic in greater depth, I initially framed a research project examining the design and spatial planning strategies of developers. My initial hypothesis was that a process I framed as "the privatization of planning," the transfer of powers and responsibilities for planning, development, and regulation of urban form to private developers, was leading to new dynamics of sociospatial exclusion and segregation. This focus shifted gradually as I engaged in field investigations and explored the literature on these projects.

The insights that led most directly to the shift in focus of my analysis came from a series of field visits between 2007 and 2011 to numerous urban real estate megaproject developments and from discussions with developers, government officials, and academics familiar with these projects.[2] Over the course of these visits I came to expect the often jarring disjuncture between the representation of these projects and their reality on the ground (although China was strikingly different in the extent to which master plans were actually implemented). Indonesian new towns presented themselves as fragmented, low-slung landscapes, an incomplete vision of a new model of urbanism. At Kolkata West International City, a project touted as a major urban imposition had ground to a halt after the completion of a row of model units. Muang Thong Thani represented one audacious example of a developer who, in the heady days at the height of the disastrous Bangkok property bubble of the mid-1990s, had pushed forward with the development of some eighty thousand housing units. The bursting of this bubble, however, left a visually striking legacy of abandoned thirty-story condominium towers with lobbies that had become overgrown with impenetrable weeds. Outside of China and rare examples like Muang Thong Thani, urban real estate projects had rarely come remotely close to meeting their projections for eventual population and form.

The designs produced by the developers of these projects also proved to be a moving target. The developers of many of the projects I visited during this period had hired illustrious architecture and planning firms, usually firms based in the United States and Europe, to develop master plans. Yet it soon became clear that these high-profile documents often bore little resemblance to the projects that were eventually built. On more than one occasion local architects, planners, and real estate professionals who worked for developers openly stated that the plans for these projects had consciously been solicited for political purposes, to sell the project to government officials and a skeptical public. In the move to implementation, however, the final plans often required significant adjustment to realize commercial imperatives, sometimes in ways the developer had anticipated and other times in unexpected ways. For example, plans produced by the San Francisco–based firm HOK suffered such a fate in the cases of Bonifacio Global City in Metro Manila and Calcutta Riverside in Kolkata.

As the design of urban real estate megaprojects emerged as a more muddled, complex, and contested story than was originally anticipated, the questions for this study turned to the question of how to explain such variation. At the same time, the question of the role of the state came more sharply into focus as it became apparent that the course of urban real estate megaprojects was shaped by particular moments in the process of land acquisition, dispossession of existing users, and transfer to developers. It also became abundantly clear that these moments emerged very much through the agency of state actors. As the question of land came into focus, so too did an entire constellation of transformations in political representation, property rights, finance, and other realms of politics. The plans and designs that had originally constituted the focus of the study now seemed part of a larger story of urban land monetization that was wrapped up in broader processes of political and social change.

This shift in focus led to a change in the choice of case studies. From January to April of 2010 I embarked on research on the Kolkata case while on a Fulbright Senior Research Fellowship. By this stage I had begun to think of Kolkata as a classic case of a deeply pluralistic model of urban politics in which the state was struggling to exert greater control over land through new innovations in public-private partnership and transformations in practices of land management. In the emergent framework for this volume, it therefore occupied a similar space to Metro Manila, which I had originally intended to include as an important case study of developer-driven urban planning and design. The shift in focus to land management led me to focus instead on Suharto-era Jakarta, a highly contrasting case of an authoritarian state shifting toward dominance of urban land as a linchpin of a strategy of urban political and economic control. The choice of Jakarta was also opportune because the distance provided by seventeen years of postauthoritarian analysis and scholarship allowed for a critical, arms-length analysis of Suharto-era policy that would not be possible, for example, in the comparable case of Hun Sen's Cambodia. Finally, China presented itself as an obvious candidate for analysis, both because of its quantitative importance and because of its salience as a model of state capitalist urban planning. The selection of Chongqing as a case study came about through discussions with colleagues who were experts on China and through contacts with academics who were based there. It proved a fortuitous choice, as Chongqing was to emerge as a major flashpoint in debates on China's urban development model. This made it an ideal case to explore the contradictions in China's path of urban development, and it also provided the benefit of allowing me to track the substantial scholarship and popular debate that emerged on Chongqing over the course of my research, particularly in the immediate aftermath of the fall of Chongqing party secretary Bo Xilai. These studies helped to make up to some extent for the inevitable shortcomings of my research for the China case study: my lack of access to the behind-the-scenes debates around the highly contentious politics of land in the city at the height of Bo's power.

In total, this book represents the culmination of eight years of research on this topic. During this time, I have undertaken site visits to more than two dozen urban real estate megaprojects in eight countries: China, India, Indonesia, the Philippines, Thailand, Cambodia, Singapore, and Malaysia. In each of these countries I have had the opportunity to discuss these projects with informed individuals from varied walks to life: real estate developers, public officials, academics and others. I have also conducted more than 120 formal interviews with architects, urban designers, planners, real estate agents and investors, bureaucrats, elected officials, academics, and representatives of nongovernmental and community organizations representing those who face displacement as a result of these projects. I have also collected data from a number of sources, including government and nongovernmental organization reports and datasets, urban plans, architectural renderings, annual reports and promotional materials of developers, academic studies, and newspaper and other media accounts.

In this way this study employed a process that I believe answers Robinson's (2016) call for a "comparative practice" of urbanism. Robinson (2016, 2) refers to an approach of "comparative practice" as one that focuses not on testing preset hypotheses through rigid methodologies and efforts to control for variation, but rather an approach that focuses on "finding shared features across cases, or working with 'repeated instances' (Jacobs, 2006) distributed across numerous urban contexts and produced within shared and interconnected processes." It may be that the model of comparative practice that Robinson refers to requires the kind of time-consuming, grounded, and exploratory approach undertaken in this project. None of the cases examined in this book is usually identified as a paradigmatic model of urbanism. Yet I will argue in this volume that taken together, they tell us something coherent and important about the recent trajectory of urban development in Asia and beyond, and that each represents a model of urbanism that is important to our understanding of contemporary cities everywhere.

Organization of the Remainder of the Book

The chapters that follow will first explore the historical factors that have shaped the environment in which urban real estate megaprojects have emerged as a predominant state strategy and will develop a theoretical framework to assess the varied ways in which this strategy has been pursued. Chapter 1 will begin by addressing the question of why governments have embraced the concept of urban real estate megaprojects at varying junctures. The chapter traces the origins of the real estate turn in urban policy in Southeast Asia to the mid-1980s, and particularly the period after the signing of the Plaza Accord of 1985, which unleashed a flood of Japanese foreign direct investment in Bangkok, Jakarta, and Metro Manila. It was in these three cities that some of the earliest examples of urban real estate megaproject development emerged, in each case preceded by a similar set of reforms in urban policy and the financial sector and a similar set of transformations in the real estate development sector. These same trajectories of change emerged later in India and China during the middle to late 2000s. The chapter then provides brief descriptions of the three case-study cities—Jakarta, Chongqing, and Kolkata—outlining implications of the emergent land monetization strategies of these three cities for issues of spatial exclusion, the politics of property, and the politics of state rescaling. Chapter 2 explores the different political and spatial outcomes of urban real estate megaproject development and of the real estate turn in urban policy more generally. It develops a typology of three models of land monetization: those defined by a politics of land grabbing, a politics of state capitalist urban planning, and a politics of what the urban scholar Solomon Benjamin (2008) has called "occupancy urbanism." It further argues that the case studies in this volume—of Suharto-era Jakarta, Chongqing, and Kolkata—fit roughly into these three categories.

Chapters 3 through 5 deploy this analytical framework to analyze urban real estate megaproject development in the three case-study cities: Jakarta,

Kolkata, and Chongqing. These chapters examine similarities and differences between the three case studies with respect to questions of spatial exclusion, property, and state rescaling. The conclusion will provide some final thoughts on the implications of this analysis for urban theory and urban policy.

1

ORIGINS AND CONSEQUENCES OF THE REAL ESTATE TURN

> A company is a country. A country is a company. They are the same.
> The management is the same. It is management by economics. From
> now onwards this is the era of management by economics, not
> management by other means. Economics is the deciding factor.
> —THAKSIN SHINAWATRA, QUOTED IN PASUK 2003, 8

The quote above, from Thailand's former prime minister Thaksin Shinawatra, is a particularly clear and direct expression of an idea that began to shape political discourses in Asia during the 1990s, that of political leaders as chief executive officers (CEOs). While seldom expounded upon in detail, the idea of a CEO politician expresses a certain kind of aspiration to power. First and foremost, it expresses a desire for the extent of authority and autonomy of action enjoyed by a corporate CEO. It further expresses the idea that, if it is to be sustained, this capacity to act must be used to financially empower the state, and by extension the nation, by exploiting the commercial value of its land, labor, and natural resources. It calls for a new role for the state as a market actor that achieves goals of fiscal strength and national economic growth (increasingly seen as the primary measures of state legitimacy) through the market delivery of goods and services. Such explicit references to countries as corporations and to political leaders as CEOs have become common in the popular press, in academic analyses of the changing role of the state, and in the pronouncement of Asian government leaders themselves (see for example Low 2002; Kalbag 2011; Economic Planning Unit 2013).[1]

This chapter contends that urban land has come in many contexts to be a central focus for this explicit market orientation of governments, and that the politics of land has consequently come to fundamentally reshape relationships between government, business, and citizens. Urban land has, of course, always been subject to political struggle. Land management forms the basis for place making and consequently for state projects of political and social engineering. Being fixed in place, land is also relatively easily subject to state control, surveillance, regulation, and taxation, and therefore becomes central to the nation-building projects of governments. As property values have exploded in much of Asia since the 1980s, however, governments have increasingly viewed urban land differently. Long-standing state interests in political control and the creation of symbolic space have come to be overlaid with a speculative interest in potential windfall financial gains to be realized through the monetization of land. The question of how states might capitalize on this new potential source of wealth, either by directly tapping into land as a source of revenue or by using powers of land management to allocate this wealth to political supporters, has arisen as a major focus of state-directed urban redevelopment and urban governance reform. What has resulted has, in many cases, been an unprecedented meeting of the minds and marriage of the interests of state and real estate actors. This meeting of minds has sometimes led to a dramatic transformation of urban space, and where it has not it has at least redefined debates about what cities should look like and what criteria should be applied to the right to use urban space.

These changes are a critical part of the story of the embrace of urban real estate megaprojects throughout Asia that is the central focus of this book. These massive projects represent a marriage of two state objectives: the creation of symbolically powerful landscapes of development and the release of massive amounts of value that can be captured by the state and its allies in the corporate sector. Hence the flashy architectural renderings of imposing new skylines serve a dual purpose; they are both a reflection of a nation's development and a vehicle for a new model of urban governance.

As this new business orientation of the state has taken shape, however, it has also implicated both state actors and their business allies in new processes of dispossession and displacement, as developers and state actors seek to delegitimize and systematically undermine (and sometime reconstitute in new, market-friendly form) people's existing claims to neighborhood and livelihood. And these processes of dispossession and displacement have in turn instigated a new moral politics of citizenship, as those displaced by redevelopment—low- and moderate-income communities, markets, street vendors, small manufacturers, and others—have raised questions of the fairness and legitimacy of these new state roles. That these communities are themselves often critical centers of production for both domestic and international markets raises the issue of how and why the production of corporate entities is included in the accounting of national development, while the production that occurs outside corporate spaces is not (Simone and Rao 2012). In their reach to transform urban space, states have revisited long-contested questions of property rights and have launched controversial new initiatives aimed at displacing entrenched claims to urban space and in some cases at integrating the poor into commercial property markets. Yet communities have, in many instances, successfully turned the tables to question the legality and political propriety of state interventions in real estate markets. This market-oriented shift in governance is therefore a part of a larger reshaping of the political and social landscape of cities that has played out as much in political contestations as in physical space.

The shifts in the politics of land development discussed in this chapter unfold against a backdrop of the changing relationships between national and local governments in urban planning and development, or what Brenner (2004) has discussed as the rescaling of state action. As cities have emerged as critical centers for economic growth within international networks of trade, Brenner (2004, 3) argues, they have consequently emerged as "key institutional sites in which a major rescaling of national state power has been unfolding."

One aspect of this rescaling revealed in a focus on land management is a "real estate turn" in national urban policy, as national governments have proactively sought to capitalize on the economic, fiscal, and developmental opportunities presented by the escalation of land prices. They have been motivated to do so by the political gains to be had from growing urban economies, from the cultivation of powerful new interest groups like corporate leaders and a growing consumer class, and from the fiscal gains to be had by tapping into the new power of real estate markets. They have also been spurred to act, as powerful agencies like the World Bank and global consulting firms like McKinsey have increasingly emphasized the importance of large, extended urban regions as economic drivers. As it has become clear that national governments are often the only entities with the inherent interests and geographic scope of authority to capitalize on the potential of sprawling and rapidly expanding urban regions, they have increasingly concentrated the thrust of their political will on the management of the political economy of urbanization. They have done so with great variety in their capacity to achieve their aims. Nonetheless, the past three decades have seen creative efforts to develop new legal and institutional vehicles for state land acquisition, for the creation of public-private partnerships in land development, and for the sale or lease of state land to corporate developers, among other measures. Many national governments have also rolled out reform agendas—liberalization of the financial sector, reforms to urban land-use planning frameworks, fiscal decentralization, and others—that are explicitly intended to empower local governments and prod them toward a more commercial orientation in their land management. In some instances, national government actors themselves have gotten into the game of real estate, formulating commercial developments in which national agencies are key partners.

Despite this commercial thrust of public policy, the analogy of the "state as corporation" implicit in Thaksin's quote will, of course, never fully be realized. A nation is not a commercial enterprise, and the logic of state political power and legitimation does not equate to the simple logic of corporate profitability. Particularly in electoral systems, politics reflect the simple fact that societies embody competing interests and that the institutionalization of these interests necessarily requires that government institutions will not cohere to a unitary set of goals. The analogy particularly breaks down when we consider the role of citizens in a commercially oriented state. Are they shareholders in this corporation? Consumers of its products? Or are they instead providers of labor and their communities' raw material, to be exploited to maximize profit for a much smaller set of shareholders? Or are their demands for space and livelihood simply an obstacle to corporate and government efforts to maximize their power and profitability through the gradual commodification of everything? In fact, in varying circumstances and to varying degrees, citizens play each of these contradictory roles, sometimes in combination. What they are in every instance is vulnerable, as their political interests are increasingly subject to reassessment in light of a new set of criteria for citizenship and social and economic inclusion. States posing as corporations face thorny contradictions and questions. Can the state's drive to capitalize financially on urban development, and the dispossessions that necessarily result, be reconciled with its role as an arbiter of national citizenship? Can governments be held accountable, and can the impulse to reward allies and exploit nonallies be reined in, within the framework of a commercially oriented state? Can the financial benefits of urban development be allocated equitably and fairly? And even if they can, do citizens deserve the right to retain ways of life and livelihood that do not fit neatly into a corporate paradigm?

Many of these issues were apparent in the case of Thaksin himself. A multibillionaire telecommunications and information technology entrepreneur who was prime minister of Thailand from 2001 to 2006, Thaksin was unseated in a coup following allegations of corruption. While in office Thaksin combined efforts to seek new sources of state revenue with proposals for the most ambitious spending program on infrastructure megaprojects and grassroots economic development initiatives in Thailand's history. These policies constituted an effort to pump prime the economy and stimulate economic growth in the aftermath of the Asian financial crisis of 1997–1998. His model for doing so came to be known as "Thaksinomics," referring to an approach to managing the economy in which an activist and entrepreneurial state uses policy and public expenditure to exploit opportunities for economic growth while also maximizing its fiscal capacity (Pasuk and Baker 2004). In practice this meant pump priming and retooling the economy through the aggressive use of state financial institutions to finance infrastructure megaprojects and economic development schemes, while simultaneously encouraging state enterprises to be entrepreneurial in exploiting their assets for commercial gain (Pasuk 2003; Charoen, 2004; NESDB 2005; *The Nation*, January 13 and September 1, 2006, Internet edition).

One specific strategy promoted by Thaksin's government, which had precedents in the pre-Thaksin era, was the promotion of real estate megaprojects intended to exploit state landholdings as a source of revenue. This was often to be achieved by crafting public-private partnerships initiated by state-owned enterprises or government ministries.[2] One such project, conceived in the pre-Thaksin era but which gained traction while he was in office, was the National Housing Authority's (NHA's) Din Daeng Redevelopment Project. The initiative was planned for three proximate 1960s public housing complexes covering a total of one hundred hectares of land. While once a garbage dump at Bangkok's edge, the area around Din Daeng had transformed over the decades into a vibrant commercial area that the NHA increasingly viewed as an alluring development opportunity. In 1999 a team of Thai and multinational consulting firms issued a preliminary redevelopment master plan for the site that included hotels, office buildings, serviced condominium units, a shopping mall and other retail spaces, a convention center, and a theater (Attaporn 2005). This concept gained some momentum in the early to mid-2000s, but the project foundered on controversy over the displacement of forty thousand existing public housing residents, the vast majority of whom were not slated to be rehoused on site. To the seeming surprise of the NHA, the residents valued both the community ties they had developed in Din Daeng and the access to jobs and amenities that its centrality provided. To the distress of NHA officials, they proved quite adept at asserting their interests in the popular press and in countering government-promoted images of the housing complex as dangerously derelict and socially dysfunctional. The intensity of the conflict engendered by this particular project and the incapacity of entrenched bureaucratic cultures to adapt to new modes of public relations and political action, ensured the failure of the Din Daeng Redevelopment Project. Other proposed developments in Thailand have similarly foundered on controversies over social displacement and over competing bureaucratic and political interests.

In the pages that follow I will argue that the central tensions of the Din Daeng case—the moral quandaries and political contradictions inherent in reframing questions of rights to the city involved in this new state/ developer nexus—resonate through many contexts in Asia. The chapter will begin by reviewing the historical circumstances that have led to the surge in property development that has fostered fundamental changes in the political economy of urbanization in different Asian cities. The following section will then discuss three common categories of issues that have emerged wherever urban real estate megaprojects have been pursued: the politics of state rescaling and questions of what state actors should shape land development; the spatial politics that emerge around the enclosures, displacements, and exclusions associated with large-scale land commodification; and a new moral politics, as debates over rights to housing and livelihood, and over questions of formality and informality, legality and illegality, have become increasingly central to questions of state legitimation, citizenship, and social justice. Finally, the chapter will preview the three case studies that are the focus of this book (Jakarta, Chongqing, and Kolkata), examining how these three issues have played out in urban development in three Asian cities.

Real Estate Booms and Megaproject Development: A Brief Historical Review

One intent of focusing attention on the monetization of land in this book is to take a step toward the development of stronger, more empirically rooted comparative frameworks for analyzing the political economy of urban development in Asia. The development of such frameworks has proven a persistent challenge. One approach to addressing Asia comparatively has been to ask whether Asian cities are experiencing spatial change akin to that found in the globalizing and neoliberalizing cities of the West, such as the emergence of gated communities, the privatization of urban space, and the rote translation of Western architectural and urban design forms to other contexts (Wu and Webber 2004; Glasze, Webster, and Frantz 2006). Yet this idea of convergence has been subject to critique on both theoretical and empirical grounds.

From an empirical perspective, the idea of convergence does not appear to capture the diversity of urban form evident in Asia's new master-planned urban spaces. An exhaustive discussion of typologies and models of urbanism in urban real estate megaprojects is beyond the scope of this volume and has been the subject of other excellent books and articles (see for example Marshall 2003). A quick comparison of commercial and residential typologies in several developments, however, is useful to illustrate their diversity of form. Figures 1.1 through 1.4, which contains examples drawn from Shanghai, Jakarta, and Bangkok, is intended to illustrate some of this diversity.

Some urban real estate megaprojects have indeed borrowed directly from architectural and urban design models originating in the West. Many

Figure 1.1. Villa in Lippo Karawaci, Jakarta Metropolitan Region. Source: Author.

Figure 1.2. Songjiang City in Songjiang Province near Shanghai. Source: Author

Figure 1.3. Xintiandi, Shanghai. Source: Author

Figure 1.4. Muang Thong Thani, Nonthaburi Province near Bangkok.
Source: Author.

of Jakarta's new towns are designed by Southern California–based architecture and design firms and include prototypical auto-oriented, elite "gated community" suburban subdivisions containing rows of single-family houses designed in a pastiche of architectural styles (see figure 1.1). Yet the example of high-rise housing Shanghai's Songjiang New Town, in figure 1.2, illustrates a typology resembling Singapore's new towns. Such projects are planned for transit orientation, with streets intended as pedestrian thoroughfares connecting high-rise structures to schools, shopping centers, and other facilities located within the residential complex. The example of Shanghai's Xintiandi development, in figure 1.3, is akin to other global experiments in new urbanist planning in its focus on the scale of development, pedestrian orientation, and mix of commercial and residential land uses (He and Wu 2005). Yet its architectural motif is intended to remain consistent with the distinctive and architecturally significant *shikumen* style of the original neighborhood, the French Quarter, which contains historically important sites. Finally, the low-cost condominiums that characterize a substantial portion of Muang Thong Thani in Bangkok, in figure 1.4, illustrate a distinct typology that emerged from the Australian architect's interpretation of the mix of residential, commercial, and recreational space that typifies Thai working-class urban settlements (Marshall 2003). The result is a block of functionalist, medium-rise residential cubes, each with rows of small shops occupying their ground floors, fronting on broad sidewalks that are intended as spaces of leisure and everyday commerce.

These examples illustrate the mix of logics that inform the choices of designers and developers in shaping these places beyond the impulse to copy from models of "global city form." Perhaps they are primarily influenced by the economics of land acquisition and consumer demand in a given place. In many cases, and most certainly in the examples of major Chinese and Indian cities, land prices dictate high density, leading to the allure of models of Singapore or Hong Kong. Developers may also face pressure from state or community actors to shape space according to existing historical, social, and ecological contexts, as in the case of Xintiandi. And finally, the imaginations of architects and urban designers seeking to formulate new models of urbanism are often also at play, as evident in Muang Thong Thani.

Theoretical critiques of the idea of convergence mirror the observed diversity on the ground. Postcolonial critics, most notably Jennifer Robinson (2011), have argued that the proclivity of anglophone scholars to reproduce theoretical concepts originating largely in the United States and England creates a substantial danger that distinct logics of urbanization may be overlooked and that urban theory may become locked in a degenerative path dependency. Recent studies have argued that the spatial, social, political, and cultural logic of urban development in Asian cities must be understood within the unique historical logic of specific societies. Hogan et al. (2012), for example, argue that the implied nostalgia for an idyll of a "public space" in the critique of the privatization of space seems out of touch with the reality of most Southeast Asian cities, where, they argue, a strong public role in the management of streets, neighborhoods, and other nominally "public" spaces never fully took hold and urban space therefore historically remained privately controlled. Yet other commentators have questioned the assumption in much of the Western-generated literature on "gated communities" that gating is a fundamentally new phenomenon. They point out that Chinese cities have a long history of gated residential enclaves in the Maoist era and deep into the country's imperial past (Webster, Wu, and Zhao 2006). In all of the above cases, the common complaint is that comparison is too often framed around normative categories emerging from Western academic studies instead of the empirical reality of Asian cities.

This chapter adds to critiques of theories of convergence, but approaches this question from a quite different angle. It argues that the varied forms of urbanism witnessed in different settings reflect in large part differences in the politics of land. The chapter focuses on one particular variable—government policy responses to massive potential land value increases—as an empirical window into state practices of neoliberalization and spatial change. It argues that one key factor that unifies many of the disparate contexts and histories of urban political and spatial change throughout Asia is the increasingly commercial orientation of state actors toward urban land and their growing affinity to corporate real estate actors. This commercial orientation has emerged as governments have, in a context of rapid increases in land values, developed strategies to create new political coalitions around land development.

This focus on land management helps to crystallize the issues of social inequality, political contestation, and spatial change that are occurring across so many contexts. It helps to unpack the particular political contradictions that emerge as the displacements wrought by land commodification have seemingly contradicted long-standing state narratives of citizenship and social equality. It also points to new tensions within Asian states as the political fallout from aggressive state development initiatives at the local level has bled upwards to local state relations with higher levels of government. Yet it also points to the important role of factors specific to each city—histories of government and private-sector land development practices, patterns of land ownership, the functioning of political institutions, and the prevalence of grassroots political mobilization—in shaping contests around these land-management practices and their outcomes in urban spatial change. It therefore provides a useful conceptual tool for understanding how processes of neoliberalization have interacted with local contexts in shaping urban spatial outcomes.

The history of the massive appreciation of land values, and the push toward land commodification that occurred in its wake, has unfolded in different cities at different times, according to differences in the proclivities of international capital and the uneven trajectories of economic and political reform in different countries. Some of the immediate drivers of this process are well understood. One is population growth and the growing scarcity of centrally located urban land. According the United Nations, the combined urban population of East, South, and Southeast Asia increased by about a billion in the thirty years from 1980 and 2010, reaching about 1.67 billion by 2010, and was projected to increase by almost another billion in the following twenty years to 2030 (United Nations Population Division 2012). This urbanization has coincided with an explosion of manufacturing and service sector foreign direct investment (FDI), rising from about US$200 billion in 1980 to more than US$4 trillion in 2010 (UNCTAD 2013). These transformations have contributed to the rapid spatial expansion of cities. This economic and spatial expansion has created new opportunity in the formal, corporate real estate sector through the rapid growth of corporate investment and spending by a growing consumer class. The consulting company McKinsey argues in a major report on urbanization that "600 million (consumers) will live in only around 440 cities in emerging markets that are expected to generate close to half of global GDP growth between 2010 and 2025" (McKinsey & Company 2012).

While all these forces have contributed to the story of land price escalation and large-scale development in many Asian cities, they are but a part of it. This shift has also been driven by policy decisions undertaken at the international, national, and local levels that have enabled developers and land speculators to tap into international and domestic finance and gain access to new sources of land. As will be explained later in this chapter, international investment in real estate emerged as a transformative force in much of Asia through the explosion of Japanese foreign direct investment in real estate in the late 1980s, which at this early stage impacted Southeast Asian countries most profoundly (Renaud 1995). At the national and local levels, governments have in many instances actively facilitated the emergence of rent gaps by deregulating financial sectors, building infrastructure, and reforming land management to encourage the commodification of land. It is in the context of these broader economic and policy changes that many governments have focused intense planning and policy attention on the development of lands that have historically been viewed as residual spaces: land at the urban fringe, exurban villages, informal settlements, fading industrial districts, public housing complexes, military bases, ports, and other state-owned land. Some governments have also developed aggressive campaigns to create new lands through reclamation and to encourage the urbanization of lands far beyond the urban fringe as a way to overcome the constraints posed by claims of existing occupants and users on the development of the existing stock of urban land.

In many countries where it has occurred, this emergent real estate turn in policy has accompanied a remarkable synchronicity in changes in the property sector. First in Southeast Asia, and later in India, a variety of changes took place in a short time frame that led to a fundamental change in the relationship between the state, the corporate sector, and citizens in shaping urban development. These changes—the listing of real estate companies on stock exchanges, the spinning off of real estate companies from larger conglomerates, major efforts at land acquisition by the private and public sectors, significant legal reforms regarding land transfer and ownership, the initiation of major new master-planned developments— signified the mobilization of new interests and the formation of new partnerships between government and corporate interests. Waves of change are also evident in China, although the details have differed because of the very different relationship between state and economy there, specifically, the strong role of state-owned enterprises in property development and finance.

In each case this meeting of minds of state actors and corporate real estate actors was encouraged by an exogenous stimulus. Southeast Asia saw this change first with the exogenous force coming from the gradual growth of manufacturing foreign direct investment in the region during the 1980s. The truly transformative moment was the signing of the Plaza Accord on September 22, 1985, in which the US and Japanese governments agreed to depreciate the US dollar relative to the yen in an effort to boost US exports. The immediate and less directly intended consequence was a period of Japanese dominance of world financial markets as Japanese investors sought new outlets for investment, and manufacturers sought lower costs of production. Japanese foreign direct investment rose from US$5 billion in 1984 to US$144 billion in 1994 (Mera and Renaud 2000). During the early 1990s, FDI inflows to Asian countries from Japan averaged US$56 billion annually. While this investment initially focused on the manufacturing sector, profit rates in manufacturing began a steady decline in the late 1980s, driven downwards in large part by increasing competition from China and other countries that could provide lower-wage labor (Glassman 2004). As Bello (1998) explains:

> This massive inflow found its way not into the domestic manufacturing sector or agriculture, for these were considered low-yield sectors that would, moreover, provide a decent rate of return only after a long gestation period of huge blocks of capital. The high yield sectors with a quick turnaround time that foreign money inevitably gravitated to were the stock market, consumer financing and, in particular, real estate.

The publication of the World Bank's 1993 report titled "The East Asian Miracle" signaled the arrival of Southeast Asia as a major global growth story, stimulating further waves of investment from banks and pension funds in the United States, Europe, Japan, and increasingly also emergent capital exporters like South Korea, Singapore, Hong Kong, and Taiwan.

As a consequence of this chain of events, the period after 1985 was one of explosive economic growth in Southeast Asia, with that growth

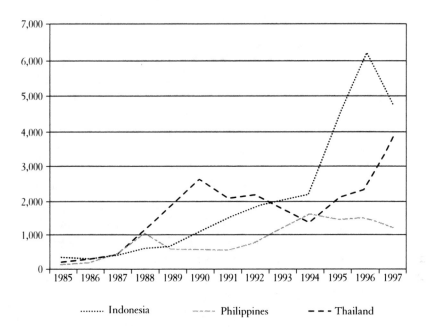

Figure 1.5. Annual inward and outward foreign direct investment flows into Indonesia, the Philippines, and Thailand, 1985–1997 (millions of US dollars). Source: Figure produced with data from UNCTAD (2013).

increasingly driven by the property sector. This larger story of economic transformation played out most dramatically in the explosion of the real estate sectors of three large Southeast Asian metropolitan regions—the extended metropolitan regions of Jakarta, Bangkok, and Metro Manila—that emerged as major targets for investment, initially from Japan and later from other parts of the world. The initial wave of manufacturing investment in the mid-1980s was accompanied by Japanese loans to build the transport, power, and other infrastructure needed to transform those metropolitan regions into industrial powerhouses. By 1997 the three cities that had received the most money in soft loans from the Japan Bank for International Cooperation were Bangkok, Jakarta, and Manila, and Bangkok's total of 328 billion yen was the highest in the world (Webster 2000). These three rapidly growing mega-urban regions came to be seen as favored destinations for international manufacturing investment by Asian, European, and American investors.

The period from 1988 to 1992 stands out as a juncture in which a number of critical changes occurred in the politics of urban land in Jakarta, Bangkok, and Metro Manila. This was a period of dramatic increases in land values. In Bangkok, for example, studies conducted by a real estate consulting firm indicate that between 1987 and 1992, land values increased about five times in the central city and twenty-five times on the urban fringe (Sheng and Kirinpanu 2000). Rising land values accompanied changes in the structure of the real estate industry that signaled the rise of a powerful new set of real estate actors. The biggest players in the development of the massive urban real estate megaprojects that began to emerge in these regions—Ayala Land Incorporated in Metro Manila, Bangkok Land Incorporated, and PT Tunggal Reksakencana in Jakarta—were formed respectively in 1988, 1989, and 1990. The former two listed on their respective stock exchanges in 1991 and 1992. In all, Pasuk and Baker (1998) note, during the late 1980s, thirty-six real estate companies floated on the Bangkok stock exchange alone. In 1989 the Ciputra Group ramped up development of Bumi Serpong Damai (2,500 hectares) in southwest Jakarta, which was to provide a template for subsequent large new town developments. In 1990, the year Bangkok Land began the construction of Muang Thong Thani, a 640-hectare project master-planned for about 700,000 people, Ayala Land initiated its Ayala South initiative with the purchase of 412 hectares of land for the creation the Laguna Technopark and a housing estate. In 1992 Lippo Land Development, an offshoot of the Lippo Group of Mochtar Riady, a major Indonesian conglomerate, launched two new town developments, Lippo Karawaci (2,630 hectares), and Lippo Cikarang (5,500 hectares). In 1993, the year construction of Lippo Karawaci was initiated, Ayala Land purchased the rights to develop the 1,300-hectare Canlubang Sugar Estate.

These machinations in the real estate industry were actively supported and facilitated by public policy. Many of the major projects of this era were made possible by government assistance in land acquisition and redevelopment. In the case of Indonesia, which will be discussed at length in chapter 3, policy changes in the land-permitting process were instrumental to land acquisition for the major projects in the Jakarta Metropolitan Region, particularly during the mid-1980s to the mid-1990s. In 1992 the Philippine government stepped up its direct stake in urban land markets by forming the Bases Conversion Development

Authority, with the primary objective of realizing the redevelopment of major military facilities, notably Fort Bonifacio in central Metro Manila, Villamor Air Base, and Clark Air Base (Bases Conversion Development Authority 2013). This led in the subsequent decade to the sale or lease of large tracts of urban land in Metro Manila and the surrounding region. It was also during this period that the Thai government began to formulate massive new urban development projects, few of which were to be developed. It was in 1992 that initial plans to redevelop the Din Daeng area were developed (Attaporn 2005). The Rama III New Financial District, a 730-hectare project planned for land owned by the Port Authority, was also conceived in the early 1990s (Douglass and Pornpan 2006).

Perhaps as important to the urban land development push as state strategies of land management, however, were reforms in the banking sector. When combined with reforms in legal and policy frameworks for land acquisition and titling, reforms to the banking sector allowed major corporate actors in many cities to engage in large-scale land speculation, as property became a mechanism to tap into the massive amounts of equity flowing into Asian markets. In Indonesia the banking sector had consisted of five government-controlled banks prior to 1988. In that year, however, deregulation opened the sector to private investment and created a relatively loose licensing system (Fischer 2000). The result was an explosion in the number of banks and bank branches and a rapid influx of equity into Indonesia, with much of this equity going into the real estate market (Winarso and Firman 2002). In Thailand, where the banking sector has historically been dominated by a select number of private banks, deregulation initiated in 1990 allowed these banks access to international financial markets. In 1992, the creation of the Bangkok International Banking Facility allowed commercial banks to borrow abroad in foreign denominations and then reinvest in the Thai economy. This was a significant factor in the tripling of loans from commercial banks to property developers between 1993 and 1996 (Herring and Wachter 1998; Kawai and Takayasu 1999). Reforms in the Philippines likewise eased restrictions on bank licensing and branching and eased entry into the market by foreign banks (Pasadilla and Milo 2005). The result was the same as in Thailand and Indonesia: a multifold increase in lending from banks and other financial institutions in the early to mid-1990s, with much of this lending going to the property sector.

The surge in speculative property investment in the region did not, of course, end well. During the peak of the real estate boom many Asian countries experienced during the mid-1990s, the soaring value of property encouraged a ratcheting up of real estate investment for two main reasons. First, the increased value of the property holdings of real estate developers allowed them to use these properties as collateral for additional loans, a practice that was to be subject to extensive criticism in the aftermath of the Asian financial crisis as a contributor to excessive real estate investment (Mera and Renaud 2000). Second, the wealth effect created by profits from growth in the finance and real estate industries carried the boom in property prices forward, encouraging additional property investment by real estate developers and speculative buying of property by investors. Eventually, however, the underlying fundamentals of the economy fell behind the rapid pace of property development; in Thailand, this first became apparent as vacancy rates in commercial office space rose sharply in 1997, reaching 40 percent by 1998 (Mera and Renaud 2000). As rents and property prices fell across segments of the property market, developers and property owners had increasing trouble servicing their debt. As trouble mounted in the banking sector, foreign lenders withdrew their investments. This led in turn to downward pressure on the value of local currencies, which were pegged to the US dollar, as these funds were converted from local currencies. The subsequent devaluation of currencies increased the value of dollar-denominated debt, leading to a deepening of the downward spiral of the financial sector. This spiral, which led to the collapse first of the Thai and then of the Indonesian financial sector, led to a broader withdrawal of bank, portfolio, and foreign direct investment across Asia as investors increasingly perceived risk in Asian economies. The consequence of this downward spiral was the Asian financial crisis, and by the end of 1997, the Philippines, Thailand, and Indonesia had all received rescue packages from the IMF that enforced deepened liberalization and painful austerity measures.

The history of the real estate explosion of the late 1980s has largely been written from the vantage point of the Asian financial crisis and has focused on the question of what caused the meltdown. As a major event in a series of international financial crises rooted in part in real estate bubbles, the Asian financial crisis has emerged as a critical case for addressing important questions: Did lax regulation allow the tail of foreign currency inflows to wag the dog of real estate investment, leading to a wave of speculative investment? Was the prevalence of moral hazard, bred by corruption and nepotism in the financial sector, in turn responsible for the lack of regulation of the banking sector and of international capital inflows? Did the IMF's rescue package actually exacerbate the crisis by imposing austerity and forcing bank closures when economies needed stimulus through continued investment?

Of greater interest to the current discussion, however, is the question of how the real estate boom impacted urban politics and the spatial development of cities. In each of these three cases, the explosion of the real estate sector played an important role in state strategies to retain power by developing new class coalitions around a changing political economy of national development. These emergent strategies were not complete breaks from the past; they played out in a context of long-standing relations between state and capital that had formed over decades. In each case the "real estate shift" in urban policy was part of a broader shift toward the empowerment of metropolitan-based economic actors through the expansion of corporate manufacturing and service sectors in extended urban regions. The increasing role of real estate interests in politics were particularly apparent in Thailand and Indonesia, which experienced economic shifts during this period that destabilized established relationships between the state and powerful economic actors and that fostered an imperative to open up new opportunities for profit, in many cases for long-standing business allies of the state. A similar shift was also apparent in the Philippines, although here political leaders were focused more on the basics of public security, consolidation of political power, and democratic transition in the period after the fall of the dictatorship of Ferdinand Marcos in 1986. As a result, the real estate shift in urban politics and policy unfolded more gradually in the Philippine case. In each case, however, while real estate development initially slowed in the aftermath of the Asian financial crisis, the hallmarks of this boom era have remained firmly in place. To date, the alliances of government and real estate developers, the rollout of aggressive new roles for government in real estate markets, and the allure of the ideal of massive, transformative master-planned developments have all remained firmly in place in these three countries, and indeed through much of Southeast Asia.

In Thailand, the real estate turn in urban politics took place in a context of growing contestation between the military, the bureaucracy, and

Bangkok-based business interests. An increasingly influential business class had attempted to assert greater political power as their economic influence grew in the 1980s and 1990s, a trend that has continued into the twenty-first century. For much of the period of since the institution of the constitutional monarchy in 1932 until the late twentieth century, the Thai military dominated politics and ruled through a highly centralized system of governance in which national ministries and state-owned enterprises controlled the lion's share of state resources and decision-making power (Pasuk and Baker 1995). Beginning in the early 1970s, however, Bangkok-based Sino-Thai business families sought to expand their influence (Hewison 1989; Suehiro 1989). Their efforts to assert independent political power by supporting elected politicians, along with the emergence of a middle class calling for greater transparency in government, were the primary forces behind the cycle of prodemocracy demonstrations and coups that defined Thai politics from the early 1970s into the 1990s (Hewison 1989; Pasuk and Baker 1995).

The period of rapid economic growth from the late 1980s on, and the growing dominance of Bangkok in the national economy, led to the political ascendance of Bangkok-based business interests. This led to a political dynamic that Pasuk and Baker (2004) term "state capture by tycoon politicians" who effectively employed patronage and vote-buying to dominate electoral politics. With this shift:

> (T)he nature of corruption changed. Classic bureaucratic squeeze—charging informal fees for public services—became less important. Meanwhile conspiracies between bureaucrats, politicians and businessmen to make superprofits from the manipulation of government rules, budgets and mechanisms enjoyed a boom. (Pasuk and Baker 2004, 14)

In Bangkok, these "conspiracies" have included efforts by real estate developers and large landowners to influence the direction of infrastructure development, to employ government assistance in obtaining land, and to gain other forms of state support. Thaksin Shinawatra's rule represented an effort to consolidate the power of business elites. By developing an ambitious political platform, including the development of new government social welfare programs, Thaksin sought to develop a broad political base that would cut into the support of the entrenched coalition of the military, bureaucracy, and monarchy. Yet the continued political influence of powerful national government ministries and state-owned enterprises, and the drawn-out political conflict that has occurred in response to Thaksin's agenda, helps to explain why so many megaprojects have been conceived while so few have progressed.

Jakarta similarly experienced a shift in political power from the 1970s to the 1990s toward city-based economic interests. In this case the shift largely benefited a select group of powerful family-based conglomerates with close connections to Suharto and his immediate family (Winarso and Firman 2002). As will be explained in greater detail in chapter 3, the massive transfer of land through the land-permitting process beginning in the middle to late 1980s came on the heels of a steep drop in oil prices during the early to mid-1980s and corresponded with a decline in the profitability of manufacturing investment in Thailand that presaged the decline in Indonesia. This new mechanism for land transfer, combined with the rapid expansion of the nexus between land and finance during this period, opened up new paths to profitability for many of the same large conglomerates that were active in these other business areas.

In other parts of Asia, the temporality of the real estate shift in urban policy has unfolded differently, in response to differences in the timing of surges in international investment and trade and different domestic political dynamics. In each case, however, the central elements of the story remain the same. Exogenous stimuli—a shift of capital flows toward urban markets—instigate a process of financial deregulation and economic liberalization. This wave of investment and reform creates rapid increases in land values that attract additional investment, leading large private corporations, state agencies, and state-owned corporations into the fray. The state-corporate coalitions that emerge as a result then develop political strategies to establish administrative and regulatory mechanisms to consolidate large plots of land in the hands of developers.

In the Southeast Asian countries that have more recently joined the Association of Southeast Asian Nations (ASEAN), and which were slower to incorporate into the global economy, these changes have occurred later. In Vietnam and Cambodia, the real estate turn in planning and policy has occurred particularly as South Korea, Taiwan, Singapore, Thailand, Malaysia, and Indonesia have emerged as major capital exporters and have looked to these markets for new outlets for investment in real estate, in addition to manufacturing, resource extraction, and other sectors. In Vietnam, plans for major urban real estate megaprojects began to emerge in the late 1990s, enabled by a 1993 land law that expanded land rights of households and organizations and by the expansion of state powers of compulsory land acquisition (Marshall 2003; Labbe and Musil 2013). These reforms were characterized by a more central role for state action. Labbe and Musil (2013) focus particularly on the land for infrastructure mechanism, in which local government agencies barter grants of land for commercial urban development to enterprises in exchange for the development of infrastructure. This mechanism has resulted in an explosion of land development; between 2001 and 2009, "over 1 million hectares of agricultural land across the country were mobilized for urban functions, regional infrastructure and other public facilities (Labbe and Musil 2013, 2)." As discussed in the introduction, a very different model of land monetization is unfolding in Phnom Penh. Here state actors are engaging in the large-scale leasing of lakes, marshes, and wetlands, both in the central city and the periurban fringe, to be filled and developed by commercial real estate developers.

In the Chinese and Indian cases, which will be discussed in greater detail in chapters 4 and 5, the temporality of the emergent politics of property unfolded in response to yet other distinct combinations of external stimuli and domestic political economic conditions. In India, urban land development became a major thrust of public policy during the mid-2000s, as financial sector reforms, an influx of FDI primarily in information technology, and economic growth led to dramatic increases in land values. The property sector has subsequently transformed through an iterative process of reforms in land management and finance, major surges in private-sector investment, and ambitious national government efforts at governance reform and infrastructure development aimed at breaking down some of the barriers to large-scale land development embedded in the contemporary governance framework. The critical years here were from 2005, the year of the initiation of the national government's ambitious Jawaharlal Nehru National Urban Renewal Mission (JNNURM), to 2009, when the impacts of the world financial crisis were felt, initially modestly, in the Indian real estate sector. These years witnessed a cascade of FDI in the Indian real estate sector, such that by the 2009–2010 fiscal year the US$2.84 billion in investment in housing and real estate represented more than three times the amount of investment in computer hardware and software and was the second largest category of investment

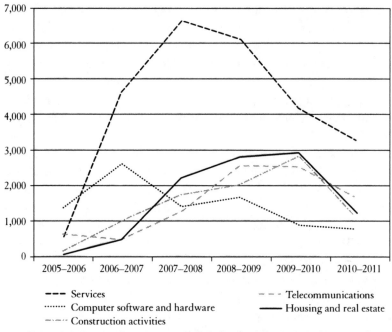

Figure 1.6. Foreign direct investment in India, five largest sectoral recipients between 2005 and 2011 (millions of US dollars). From a minuscule proportion when first reported in the 2005–2006 fiscal year, housing and real estate and construction emerged as the second and third largest sectoral recipients by 2009–2010. Source: Figure produced with data from the Department of Industrial and Policy Promotion 2008, 2010, 2011.

in India after the broad category of services (Department of Industrial and Policy Promotion 2011).

A spate of major real estate companies went public during this period of rapidly escalating FDI in real estate. This was highlighted by the listing of DLF, a major developer, which was valued at US$25 billion by 2006, making it the third largest company in India and placing it among the top five listed real estate firms worldwide. Stories of massive new town developments and real estate initiatives were regularly featured in the press during this period. In 2007, for example, the Delhi Development Authority unveiled a plan to engage private developers in developing five new towns around the city to accommodate 7.3 million people (Das Gupta 2008). One prominent news outlet estimated in early 2008 that two hundred "integrated townships" were in various stages of planning and development throughout India, although this figure seems low in light of the fact that DLF alone, according to another report, had plans under way to build seventy townships of three to five hundred acres each in fifty cities (Karmali 2006; Singh 2008). Few of these plans were realized, however, and the global economic downturn of 2008–2009 cast doubt on the short- and medium-turn prospects for the further rapid expansion of the Indian real estate market.

In China, state strategies of property development have unfolded more deliberately, and the resulting spatial transformation has been more sustained and dramatic. This is largely attributable to the state's unusual degree of control of both the land market and the financial sector, which has allowed it a greater degree of leeway in manipulating the pace and direction of property development to cater to its own objectives of governance and economic development.

While the aftermath of the Asian financial crisis left a legacy of abandoned structures and bankrupt developers in Thailand, Indonesia, and the Philippines, it is clear in retrospect that it did not mark the end of the ideal of urban real estate megaprojects, but rather a turning point in government roles in their realization. Indeed, as the experience of projects like the Din Daeng initiative in Thaksin-era Thailand reveals, governments have in some cases become even more aggressive in attempting to deploy such projects as a means to finance state action in the areas of economic and infrastructure development. Similarly, the early 2000s also saw the Philippine government seek to enjoin a consortium of private developers to build the LRT-7, a twenty-two-kilometer light rail line, in exchange for rights to develop a real estate megaproject on several hundred hectares of land in a periurban area outside Metro Manila. Here too, property development held allure as a source of revenue and infrastructure development (Shatkin 2008).

Governments have also in some cases revealed a new purposiveness and focus in the period after the 1997–1998 economic crisis, attempting to tether property development to specific state goals. As competition for labor-intensive manufacturing investment from China, Vietnam, and elsewhere has intensified, governments have sometimes sought to develop real estate megaprojects as a means to draw on the resources of international and domestic business interests in developing what Glassman (2007) has termed a "high road spatial fix." This term refers to efforts to transform the urban built environment to enable a shift away from labor-intensive manufacturing by creating spaces for the production of higher-value-added products and services and for research and development. In Thailand, for example, the State Railway of Thailand's planning of the Makkasan Redevelopment Project, a proposed redevelopment of 130 hectares of rail storage facilities, centered on the development of convention and office space catering to the fashion industry, which the Thai government had identified as a major target growth industry for the country (TEC/DCA 2005). In Metro Manila, the seventeen-hectare Eastwood City development contains a cyberpark, designated by the Philippine Economic Zone Authority as an approved IT center, that has emerged as a major center for business process outsourcing. Master-planned developments have also emerged as a mechanism to realize other goals, such as sustainability and hazard resilience, and climate change adaptation. In Jakarta, the National Capital Integrated Coastal Development Plan, released in 2014, proposed financing a massive seawall and giant pumping stations, meant to protect the city from sea level rise and storm surge, through the development of a new town on land reclaimed on either side of the wall (Government of Indonesia 2014).

In sum, the real-estate-driven creation of new urban space has emerged as a central tool for the achievement of development goals, a hammer that has led governments to view a variety of economic development and sustainability problems as nails. Land management has consequently become more central to the political economy of urban governance. The next section will discuss some of the contradictions inherent in this real estate turn in public policy and will explore some of the diversity in models of land management, and in the specific issues that result from these models, through a preview of the Jakarta, Chongqing, and Kolkata case studies.

Interpreting the Politics of Urban Real Estate Megaprojects: Jakarta, Chongqing, Kolkata

Thus far the discussion in this chapter has focused on the historical circumstances that have fueled dramatic growth in land values across Asia and that have drawn governments to see real estate markets as a strategic realm in which to build regimes and legitimize their rule. This section turns to questions about the politics of this strategy: How does the growing nexus of government and real estate interests affect relationships between government, corporate actors, and citizens, especially those citizens whose foothold in the city is tenuous? How does it affect the relations between different state actors, who have varying interests in urban development? The section will begin to address these questions through an examination of land management around real estate megaprojects in Jakarta, Chongqing, and Kolkata. While they embody very different paradigms of urban governance, I will argue that state interventions in land markets foster common categories of issues in all three cities, and that these issues have come to be defining features of urban politics across much of Asia. Specifically, three categories of issues are particularly pertinent to an understanding of the politics of urban real estate megaprojects.

First, the real estate turn in government policy often accompanies efforts to purge existing uses (and users) of land and replace them with users who will maximize the potential for revenue generation by corporations and the state. This effort to foster a whole-cloth transformation of access to rights to urban space leads to a *spatial politics of exclusion*, centering on the contentious question of who should have access to urban space, for what uses, and under what circumstances. These questions become particularly pointed when the realization of large projects, the development of the infrastructure to support them, and the broader processes of land commodification of which they are a part, lead to large-scale dislocations of existing populations. Beyond direct displacement, real estate megaprojects also raise questions of who benefits from the economic opportunity that they create. Being conceived as self-contained urban entities focused on "attracting and circulating custom" (Dick and Rimmer 1998, 2312) by creating clusters of malls, office buildings, high-end residences, golf courses, and other uses, these projects are usually deliberately designed to limit access to those with a capacity to consume. Their spaces are also usually managed and policed to restrict possibilities for appropriation by small vendors and producers. Many urban residents, in most cities substantial majorities, therefore find themselves excluded from the social and political opportunities afforded by these spaces. This often includes not only the very poor but also more middle-income communities that are significant centers of manufacturing and service production (Benjamin 2008; Simone and Rao 2012). The displacement and exclusion of communities and economies that are central to the global economic aspirations of political leaders evokes the question of whose production "counts" and why (Simone and Rao 2012).

Second, the deployment of aggressive new state strategies for large-scale land acquisition for commercial developers is necessarily founded on an effort to delegitimize alternate claims to land by substantially reframing questions of land ownership and tenure. As such, it is associated with an attendant shift in the *moral politics of property*. This politics emerges notably around the disjuncture between previous state practices in adjudicating what allocation of rights is just, fair, and equitable and practices that emerge with the agenda of land monetization. Where households do hold recognized legal status on the land they occupy, such as in the case of Chinese "nail households" that resist demolition for large-scale redevelopment efforts, moral claims are often based on this previous legal recognition and on claims to livelihood and community rooted in place (Hsing 2010; Shin 2013). In other cases, moral questions center around the prevalence of extralegal occupations of land or the question of "informality." As Roy (2009) and others have convincingly argued, the proliferation of informal uses of space is itself often a deliberate outcome of government policy, such that it has become, in her words, a "mode of regulation" of the economy, of land, and of citizens. With the push to monetize land, however, there has been a shift in the moral stance of state actors toward informality. This shift is clear, for example, in Bhan's (2009, 132) analysis of the treatment of the poor by the Supreme Court of India. He contrasts court rulings in the middle to late 1980s that emphasize the "humble and honorable" claims to livelihood of slum dwellers and the legitimacy of their claims to housing with a shift in the 2000s toward an equation of slums with criminality and immorality. This tendency toward criminalization and stigmatization of land claims of the poor plays out in many parts of Asia, and it attends a shift in debates on the legal and political basis of claims to urban space that has had important implications for urban development policy.

Finally, the emergence of new modes of state intervention in land markets leads to the potential for conflict between state actors at different levels, who inherently have different interests in urban development. This leads to a third category of issues related to the *politics of state rescaling*. As is clear from the discussion of shifts in land-management strategies in the preceding section, national governments have often been complicit in, if not active drivers of, the expansion of real estate markets and the displacement of nonmarket-based claims to land. National governments have also often implemented reform agendas aimed at incentivizing and empowering municipal governments to play new roles in acquiring land for, and sometimes directly partnering in, real estate megaprojects. Yet such reforms inevitably elicit questions about how the spoils of development should be allocated between state actors, which must be resolved through political competition or outright conflict. Hsing (2010) argues that in China, contemporary urban politics is defined in part by competition for land between municipal governments and what she calls "socialist land masters," large central government state-owned enterprises, military units, and other entities. In addition to this competition over resources, the push to unleash entrepreneurial action in land management at the local level also holds the risk that local state actors may abuse newfound powers to pursue personal interests. How can governance reforms avoid tendencies toward rent seeking and wholesale dispossession that undermine the economic vibrancy and political legitimacy of the resulting system? Finally, governance reform may meet resistance from state actors whose interests are aligned with those who stand to be displaced by redevelopment. This dynamic is apparent in India, for example, where the substantial majority of voters whose livelihood depends on extralegal uses of urban space renders efforts by government actors to use tools of land expropriation highly contentious.

Analyzing the politics of state interventions in property markets through the perspective of these three issues—the politics of urban space, of property relations, and of state rescaling—provides a basis for comparison across different cities that avoids the danger of analytical overreach inherent in deploying pre-existing frameworks and normative assumptions. As noted earlier, comparative analyses of urban change in Asia that focus on specific spatial outcomes, such as the "privatization of public space" or the emergence of "gated communities," have been subject to critique as being rooted more in the anxieties and presumptions of Western scholars than in the reality of Asian cities. This perspective is most clearly expressed in a recent article by Hogan et al. (2012), who argue, in seeming contradiction with the focus of scholarship on the privatization of urban space, that most Asian cities have historically been built and managed largely by "private" actors. If this is true, then the implicit question is:

Why should the privateness of contemporary development stand out as a matter of concern? They also question whether contemporary trends in urban development in Asia fit the dystopic narratives of much of the Western-generated literature. They note, for example, that the emergence of "gated communities" in China may represent an advance in personal liberty through the creation of spaces of relative freedom from state surveillance and control rather than a degeneration of social life through the decline of public space.

The perspective presented here seeks to move beyond any assumptions about change rooted in predetermined frameworks or normative assumptions. Instead, it seeks to understand the context-specificity of processes of land-use change, the distinct distributional issues that emerge as a consequence, and the particular political contestations that result. Focusing on the issue this way provides a stronger understanding of the context-dependent meaning of spatial change than do debates about the meaning of the publicness or privateness of space. It also roots normative questions in the historical norms and discourses of the cities in question rather than imposing norms externally. As a consequence, this focus helps shift attention to the choices that governments and communities face as they undertake wrenching transformations in their own historical trajectory from established social compacts and aspirations for urban space to emergent visions of urban transformation based on a corporate-driven development of urban space.

The following brief treatments will examine how these issues have played out in the three case study cities, previewing the longer treatment of these cities in chapters 3 through 5.

Jakarta: Rent Seeking and the Politics of Land-Management Reform

As with other large capital cities in Southeast Asia, particularly Bangkok and Metro Manila, Jakarta sits at the center of a massive and rapidly growing urban region that, as the political and economic epicenter of its country, has significant symbolic and developmental influence on the rest of the nation. The city of Jakarta, with a population of 9.6 million in 2010, sits within a larger Jakarta Metropolitan Area (JMA) that contained a population of twenty-eight million in that year (Firman, Kombaitan, and Pradono 2007; United Nations Population Division 2012). This region has expanded rapidly; Hudalah and Firman (2012) estimate that more than ninety thousand hectares of land were converted from mostly agricultural to built-up land uses in the period from 1992 to 2000 alone, an area about 20 percent larger than that of the city of Jakarta itself. The development of new town megaprojects has been a significant driver of this expansion.

The narrative of the urbanization of the JMA since the 1980s, and particularly the narrative of the development of the new towns, is often written as a case study in the Westernization of urban form. Scholars have deconstructed the garish mimicry evident in much of the architecture and urban design in the new towns, often modeled explicitly on the West, and have pondered the parallels between new town developments outside Jakarta and the phenomenon of "edge cities" in the United States (Dick and Rimmer 1998; Hogan and Houston 2002; Kusno 2010). This narrative of Westernization is captured vividly in Cowherd and Heikkila's (2002, 199) meticulous accounting of the influence of Southern California–based architecture and planning firms on development on the JMA's sprawling edge:

> The significant number of architectural, engineering, and planning firms located in Southern California employed by Indonesian developers makes the Indonesian real estate industry in many ways an extension of the Southern California real estate industry. The 770-hectare Alam Sutera housing estate was planned by SWA group in Laguna Beach, Orange County. The 3,000-hectare Citra Raya new town developed by Ciputra is based on a master plan and architectural designs of RNM Architects of Newport Beach, Orange County. The 30,000-hectare Bukit Jonggol Asri series of new towns employed the same planners as the 35,000-hectare Irvine Ranch, which constitutes over one-fifth of Orange County.

While the emulation of Western models of architecture and urban design have shaped the region's development in important ways, however, state efforts to monetize land have perhaps exerted a more important and fundamental influence. The planning of the new towns that have been subject to such architectural critique were only possible as a result of land-management reforms during the authoritarian regime of President Suharto, who ruled from 1965 to 1998. Through these reforms the Suharto regime sought to consolidate its base of power by exploiting the massive periurban rent gaps that emerged during the real estate boom of the 1980s to distribute patronage to powerful corporate allies.

The primary mechanism through which the Suharto regime accomplished this was the land-permitting process, which enabled developers to acquire development rights to large parcels of land. The permitting system is rooted in a colonial-era dualism between registered state and freehold property rights, and unregistered but legally recognized claims held under customary tenure and usership rights. The permitting system, as developed during the Suharto regime, allowed developers to apply for permits that provided them sole rights to purchase and develop large parcels of land. Customary tenure holders whose land was being expropriated only had recourse to adjust the terms of compensation through an appeal system that was time-consuming and quite frequently ruled in favor of developers. The land-permitting system reached a crescendo during the explosion of the Jakarta real estate market during the late 1980s and early 1990s. Between the mid-1980s and 1995 the National Land Agency (Badan Pertanahan Nasional or BPN) issued permits for more than eighty thousand hectares of land—an area larger than New York City—in the Jakarta Metropolitan Region provinces of Bogor, Tengerang, and Bekasi (Firman 1997).

As Winarso and Firman (2002, 500) demonstrate, the land permits issues during the late Suharto period largely went to a handful of Sino-Indonesian business groups who shared close links "through cross-shareholding and shared directors, joint ventures among conglomerates and family links such as marriages among major business families' members." These families were usually further linked to the immediate family of President Suharto and to Suharto himself, thus creating a closed loop that fused corporate and state power and facilitated lobbying for land acquisition and necessary regulatory changes to allow developments to progress. This system was, of course, prone to abuse. Pamuntjak (1990) relates the story of a group of developers who persuaded a top official, recently returned from a visit to the celebrated Tsukuba Science City in Tokyo, to provide them with permits to replicate this project near the National Research Center outside Jakarta. Upon receiving the permits, the developers purchased the land, installed basic infrastructure, and quickly sold it at one hundred times their purchase price.

Viewed through the prism of postindependence Indonesian history, the emergence of the land-permitting system as a powerful tool for patronage appears to mark one aspect of a critical pivot in President Suharto's "New Order" regime. Suharto, a general who had come to power in the aftermath of communal violence and a consequent massive government crackdown in 1965, had founded his rule on a power base of state bureaucrats, military officers, and business groups who were accorded a privileged role in the economy. During the 1970s the regime had sought to deepen industrial development by regulating foreign capital penetration in key sectors, through regulatory support to privileged corporate groups through the provision of credit and licenses, and by granting monopolies in key sectors (Robison 1988, 1990). But with the dramatic decrease in oil prices during the early 1980s and the decline in the manufacture of exports of Southeast Asian countries, the Suharto regime turned to urban land as one new mechanism to distribute patronage. Shifts in permitting practices accompanied complementary reforms to the banking sector in 1988. These reforms, which opened up the banking sector to private investment and loosened restrictions on bank licensing, enabled many of the interlocking corporate groups who received favor in land permitting and who were involved in land development to tap into domestic and international sources of capital by branching into financial markets (Fischer 2000).

Silver's (2007) account of the development of Bumi Serpong Damai (also known as BSD City), one of the earliest new towns and a model for many of the projects that were to come later, sheds light on the institutional mechanisms and political processes that enabled the massive spate of permitting during the late Suharto period. The plan brought together several prominent corporate allies of the Suharto regime. It was backed by Sudono Salim, head of the Salim Group, who had become the wealthiest person in Indonesia through his close association with Suharto. It was the brainchild of Ciputra, a major figure in the Indonesian real estate industry and founder of Real Estate Indonesia (REI), membership in which was required for access to government development permits. Suharto's cousin Sudwikatmono was appointed as chief executive advisor to the project. Slated to house a population of 600,000 to 800,000 on six thousand hectares of land, the project was ostensibly formulated and rationalized as a part of a regional planning process aimed at providing a counterweight to the development of Jakarta. Yet some twenty years later, in 2004, only about a tenth of the planned houses were built, still a significant intervention at fifteen thousand units, but much less transformative than the plans that had been used to sell the project.

The BSD City case reveals both the technocratic rationale and modernist imagery that have been used to lend legitimacy to a process that has contributed to the fragmentation of the JMA's urban form: sprawling, auto-centric new towns built overwhelmingly for the elite interspersed with derelict agricultural land and clusters of low-income housing. This outcome has occurred in part because, given the oligopolistic nature of land ownership fostered by the land-permitting process and by the lack of effective land-use controls, much of the land that was permitted has become what is referred to as "sleeping land," held speculatively and undeveloped to this day (Firman 2004). The land-permitting process continues to encourage this kind of speculation, as the benefits of maximizing the amount of permitted land far outweigh the low cost of holding these permits.

In the aftermath of Suharto's fall from power in 1997 following the onset of the Asian financial crisis, debates about the land-permitting system, and about the state's role in land markets more generally, have unfolded in the context of a changing polity and changing social relations. While many developers continue to hold permits issued under Suharto, their capacity to develop these lands is increasingly subject to negotiation by local governments and communities politically empowered by democratization and decentralization (Monkkonen 2013). Intensified social negotiation over land development has in turn instigated national government reforms intended to bring new lands to market by resolving the issue of unregistered land that still, by some estimates, constitutes 70 percent of all land in Jakarta (Kusno 2012a). Efforts to bring these lands under the sway of the market have included the formulation of affordable housing projects that in fact function primarily to enable the transfer of previously informally held land to private developers (Kusno 2012a). Such initiatives, fragmentary as they are, are one element of broader contestations around land development that continue to shape urban politics.

Chongqing: Land-Based Financing and the Developmental State

China's drive toward a complete rescripting of urban space has captivated the attention of observers in both academia and the popular press. The country has realized historically unprecedented infrastructural and urban development that has underwritten its explosive economic growth. Understanding the models of land monetization that have emerged in Chinese cities over the past two decades helps explain how China has come to be a coveted model of urban development in many parts of the world. In contrast with the blunt manner in which the Suharto regime exercised authoritarian power to distribute the spoils of land development to cronies, the Chinese Communist Party's (CCP's) ability to exploit land monetization as a tool for state fiscal empowerment and legitimation based on a property-centered economic development strategy stands apart (Lin 2010; Hsing 2010). Perhaps the most important factor in the CCP's ability to pursue this strategy is the state's dominance of land ownership; since 1982, the constitution has stipulated that the state owns all urban land. This allowed the CCP in 1988 to establish a land leasehold system through which state owners of urban land lease it for private development (Lin 2010; Hsing 2010). In 1994 the government established a new tax-sharing system that strongly incentivized local governments to seek new off-budget sources of revenue, and since then local governments have engaged in a wave of innovation, creating new institutional vehicles for financing urban development and infrastructure based on land leasing (Wu 2002; Sanderson and Forsythe 2013).

At the same time, however, the central state has sought constantly to exert control over municipal governments, both to ensure that local state practices of land leasing and acquisition of rural collective land adhere to national state interests, and to rein in local government corruption and rapacity. The CCP maintains control over local governments primarily through its power to appoint and promote officials at the municipal and provincial levels, including mayors, governors, district leaders, secretaries of local party branches, and others, through the Central Organization Department (COD) (McGregor 2010). The COD also influences local development through its power to appoint heads of the major state-owned enterprises, some of which are major players in real estate and infrastructure development.

Finally, the CCP has been able to pursue land monetization as a strategy of growth through its control of the banking system, which is dominated by five state banks. Since reforms to the tax code in 1994, local governments have come to rely heavily on state banks to finance urban development and infrastructure projects (Sanderson and Forsythe 2013). They have done so largely through the creation of local government financing vehicles that have used state-owned assets, notably including land, as collateral for state bank loans to finance infrastructure and commercial property development. These state banks have emerged as an important mechanism through which the central state directs urban and infrastructure development. In the aftermath of the 2008 financial crisis, for example, much of the central government's fiscal stimulus program was enacted through state bank loans to local government financing vehicles.

In sum, the Chinese model of urban development has been driven largely by local governments that are empowered to draw down massive amounts of state bank financing to capitalize on land value appreciation as a means to realize an agenda of infrastructure and real estate development and economic growth. Under this system, as Hsing (2010, 9) states, "urban land-use planning has replaced economic planning as the main vehicle of state intervention in the local political economy." This model has led to the formulation of increasingly ambitious state-sponsored, commercially developed new town projects. Both the economic activity generated by the construction boom, and the investment that has been stimulated by the resulting development of urban space and infrastructure, have been central to municipalities' achievement of GDP growth objectives set by the CCP.

At the same time, however, the contradictions in the land-based financing model have led the CCP to assert increasing control over local state actors in recent years. The development incentives facing local and national state actors have led to waves of dispossession of inner-city residents and periurban villages that have bred increasing social discontent. Extremely rapid urban growth has also bred growing ecological problems and raised concerns about the loss of arable land and potential issues of food security.

In this context, Chongqing emerged in the late 2000s as a laboratory for new models of urban development aimed at addressing some of these contradictions. The city's current borders were formed out of a 1997 merger with three neighboring districts and encompass a large footprint of more than eighty-two thousand square kilometers, about thirteen times the size of Shanghai. The city's population stands at thirty-three million, but only about ten million are classified as urban dwellers. Chongqing has been actively promoted in national policy as a growth center, providing it access to central government assistance intended to draw investment inland from the coast (Cai et al. 2012). Since 2007 in particular the city has witnessed an explosion of foreign direct investment and urbanization, largely in manufacturing, and it emerged for a period as the fastest growing urban economy in China, with growth of 14 percent in 2008. Its position as a major new growth center and the assignment of a prominent and audacious leadership team headed by Chongqing party secretary Bo Xilai led to a wave of policy experimentation from 2007 to 2012.

Urban development in Chongqing has largely been realized through urban development investment corporations, local development financing vehicles that are each allocated responsibility for the development of specific categories of infrastructure (World Bank 2010b). The Chongqing Municipal Government allocates lands to these companies—there were eight such entities in the late 2000s—as a mechanism to finance the municipality's infrastructure priorities. The companies then use land as collateral for loans from the China Development Bank, other central state banks, and other sources both to build infrastructure and to develop the

Figure 1.7. Jiangbeizui central business district model. China's ownership of urban land has enabled cities like Chongqing to plan and implement massive developments like the Jiangbeizui plan. Source: Author.

granted land on a commercial basis. Ideally, these loans are to be paid down using revenue streams from commercial land development.

What makes the Chongqing experience distinct, however, is the ways the city has used this land-based financing model to pursue innovative new models of social-welfare-oriented development. Notably, Chongqing has pioneered new programs for equalizing access to state services and assistance between rural dwellers and holders of urban *hukou* registration. Drawing on profits from state-owned enterprises and land development, the Chongqing Municipal Government has created programs to provide affordable rental housing to migrant workers and has equalized access to services like health care, retirement benefits, and education (Huang 2012). Hence Chongqing's distinctive model for capitalizing on the monetary value of state landholdings has played an essential role in a broader effort to build new models of state legitimacy in Chongqing and beyond by facilitating economic growth and creating new social programs that address some of the most vexing social issues facing the country.

Yet the Chongqing case also illustrates some of the contradictions inherent in China's model of state-driven land commodification. First, as questions about the potential bursting of a speculative bubble in the Chinese real estate industry have mounted, so too have concerns about Chinese state bank exposure to the property sector. While it is difficult to determine exactly how much debt state banks have on their books, some estimates place the amount at around US$2 trillion (Schuman 2013). Second, as highlighted by the spectacular fall of Party Secretary Bo following the murder of a British business associate and his subsequent conviction on charges of corruption and bribery, the Chinese urban development model is troubled by a distinct lack of popular accountability. Indeed, local government corruption, particularly in land deals, is the subject of much popular frustration. In this particular case, the prominence of the Chongqing model, and of the actors involved, meant that these frustrations posed a threat to the structure of power within the CCP's central leadership.

Thus the Chongqing model demonstrates the contradictions of the Chinese model of a state that places itself at the center of the dynamic yet potentially destabilizing and destructive economics of real estate. On the one hand, this model serves to consolidate state power through the state's extraction of value from land and the achievement of developmental goals.

On the other, the centrality of the state itself to processes of land monetization places the state at the center of the political contestations that inevitably emerge around displacement, ecological damage, and market instability.

Kolkata: A Decentered Politics of Gradual, Halting Land Commodification

While the ambitions for urban real estate megaproject development in Indian cities have certainly shared the scale of those in China and Indonesia, their realization has not. Throughout India, plans for new towns and special economic zones have often stalled as communities of farmers and less-well-heeled urbanites have parlayed their political capital with local elected officials and street-level bureaucrats into potent forces of opposition. Yet the allure of large projects remains powerful, as increasing inflows of FDI and demands for housing reflecting new lifestyle aspirations of a growing consumer class have created possibilities for massive wealth creation. The spike in land values has also created possibilities for new sources of revenue and patronage for government as well. Where the Indian case is most revealing, therefore, is in the halting, fragmentary, and often unsuccessful political machinations of local, state, and national government actors in engineering new modes of governance and land management that will enable land monetization. These efforts reveal much both about the goals of governments in pursuing urban development and the contradictions that such re-engineering involves.

Perhaps nowhere has this dynamic of reform and contestation played out with more irony than in Kolkata, which sits at the center of India's third largest urban agglomeration, with a population of more than fourteen million. Kolkata's liberalization push was fronted until 2011 by the Communist Party of India-Marxist (CPI-M), a party that historically had based its legitimacy on the distribution of land to urban and rural poor communities. The party's fall, however, was precipitated by controversy over the inequities involved in its vigorous pursuit of heavily populated farmlands for two abortive industrial new town projects on Kolkata's periurban fringe, at Singur and Nandigram. The intensity of the politics around land in Kolkata highlights the fundamental urban political change that is under way in India and the indeterminate nature of that change.

India presents a sharp contrast with China in terms of land governance, and this contrast helps to explain many of the obstacles to the large-scale commodification of urban space in Indian cities. Whereas the CCP exercises strong control over municipalities in the China case, the governance of Indian cities is defined by much less central state control and much less-well-defined structures of municipal authority. This looseness is rooted in India's postindependence constitution, which, reflecting a perception that local politics are inherently riven with corruption, nepotism, and the legacies of caste and class bias, made no mention of city or village governance (Weinstein 2009). Instead, it placed most responsibility for infrastructure, housing, economic development, and other matters of municipal governance in the hands of state governments, which under Nehru's model of state socialism hewed to national government guidelines and five-year plans that set the agenda of physical planning and economic, urban, and infrastructure development. In most states, executive authority over urban development at the municipal level has historically been held by municipal commissioners, who are Indian Administrative Service (IAS) civil servants appointed by state governments. Elected mayors have largely played a much weaker role. Given that most state politicians have overwhelmingly rural electorates and IAS bureaucrats do not have direct accountability to either citizens or business, this arrangement helps explain in part why there has been less coordination between the state and business interests than in the Indonesian and Chinese cases. It also helps to explain why there have been less state resources and political will applied to urban development issues.

The Indian case also contrasts with that of China in the area of land management. While the Chinese constitution provides the national state with strong legal authority to manage land as it sees fit, in India both legal and political practice has rendered land-management authority subject to much greater social negotiation. Policy initiatives rooted in social welfare concerns have frequently contributed to the legal ambiguity of land ownership claims. For example, regulatory measures intended to improve access to housing, such as the imposition of ceilings on urban land ownership under the Urban Land Ceiling and Regulation Act, or ULCRA, of 1976, have bred myriad evasive measures (such as not registering land sales or renting off the books) that have contributed to the pervasive informalization of land claims. There are numerous other ways in which government interventions in slums have contributed to the opacity of land claims. Bjorkman (2013), for example, documents the case of Shivajinagar Bainganwadi, a government-sponsored resettlement area that has gradually been "reslummed" in bureaucratic discourse. This has occurred in part through what she terms "the politically-mediated deterioration and criminalization of its water infrastructure," which has forced residents to resort to illegal practices such as installing pumps on water taps and illegally tapping pipes (Bjorkman 2013, 210).

The flood of investment in real estate that ramped up in the 2000s, therefore, unfolded in contexts where the interests of elected politicians inclined toward the protection of extralegal claims that are often deeply rooted in bureaucratic practice and where in any case many key officeholders are appointed from above. As a result, there have been few actors with much power who have the incentives to think of themselves as the "CEO political leader" evoked at the beginning of this chapter. Central government reforms have certainly encouraged large-scale land-development schemes. Reforms in the real estate sector legalized foreign direct investment in townships in 2002, allowed venture capital fund investment in real estate in 2004, and provided new incentives for the development of special economic zones in 2005 (Searle 2014). More recently, the Indian government has taken more direct steps to monetize state land by setting up a Public Sector Land Development Authority responsible for leasing to private developers lands currently occupied by ports, railways, and public-sector enterprises (Tiwari 2012). Yet in this context where structures and cultures of governance are the main obstacle to the commodification of space, it is the central state's push for local governance reform and the formalization of land markets that represent perhaps the most fundamental and potentially transformative shift in urban political and spatial change.

The passage of the 74th Amendment in 1992, which led to a significant decentralization of authority to urban local governments, was the first such shift in India's local governance paradigm. The amendment defined urban local bodies for the first time, devolved significant powers, responsibilities, and sources of revenue to them, and created a democratic and decentralized governance framework in which they should operate (Weinstein 2009). The Jawaharlal Nehru National Urban Renewal Mission (JNNURM), initiated in 2005, injected large amounts of infrastructure and local government capacity-building funds into selected Indian cities. It also imposed a number of conditions on states receiving grants that were focused on strengthening local governance and enabling urban redevelopment, including the modernization of accounting systems; improvements in property tax collection efficiency and in land registration and cadastral systems; movement toward full cost recovery in service delivery; more effective implementation of the 74th Amendment; and repeal of the ULCRA (Mahadevia 2006). The focus of JNNURM on property registration has been supported by other national reform efforts, including the National Land Records Modernization Program (NLRMP), launched in 2008, which seeks to regularize land titles by computerizing land records and the land-registration process, and by resurveying land ownership (Government of India 2013). The JNNURM was clearly intended not only to improve urban infrastructure, but also to change the political economy of land development in Indian cities. By regularizing land title, tying land development more strongly to local government revenue generation, and augmenting the process of decentralization, the reforms seek to overcome legal and institutional barriers to development and incentivize local political actors to pursue large urban development projects.

In its implementation, many of the conditionalities attached to the JNNURM fell victim to the realities of patronage; the JNNURM monies were spent, but often not according to the letter of the program and absent the broader reform agenda. Nevertheless, efforts at urban land reform are ongoing. These efforts are pushed along by aggressive and more immediately impactful initiatives to free up land for large-scale development by state and local governments. Most notably, many states have aggressively used the Land Acquisition Act of 1894, a colonial-era act that allows the government to take land for public purposes. The use of this antiquated law, which does not adequately address questions of compensation or relocation of those displaced, has met with widespread protest that has stopped many development projects in their tracks. In an effort to overcome some of this local political opposition, the Land Acquisition and Rehabilitation and Resettlement Bill, which was passed by the Lok Sabha in August of 2013, seeks to regularize procedures for establishing compensation to people displaced by government land acquisition. While its impact is yet to be determined, this law itself has been subject to criticism from all sides. Advocates of the poor argue that it remains inequitable, while advocates of government development efforts argue that it will still allow multiple land claimants to slow the progress of development.

As the national legislative and programmatic reform agenda has unfolded slowly and unevenly, state governments have frequently proven willing to engage in contentious and sometimes violent efforts to dispossess the poor to achieve economic growth goals and to realize new sources of revenue and rent seeking. In Kolkata, the development of the three-thousand-hectare New Town project at Rajarhat (one example of several such projects in the city) has proceeded through the government of West Bengal's creation of a special purpose vehicle, the Housing Infrastructure Development Corporation (HIDC), tasked with assembling land, building infrastructure, and leasing land on a commercial basis (Mitra 2002; Sengupta 2006). This development is one example of a trend across India of state governments using the Land Acquisition Act of 1894 as a mechanism to acquire land for large-scale periurban development projects.

Yet these efforts have been particularly politically fraught in India's context of political pluralism and state narratives of justice and social equity. In the cases of Singur and Nandigram, political fallout from efforts to acquire land for these developments led to sustained protest, initiated

Figure 1.8. Calcutta Riverside. While billboards for real estate megaprojects are a common sight around Indian cities, on the ground urban change occurs slowly and fitfully. Source: Author.

by local farmers but eventually expanding into a larger campaign that gained participation from some segments of the Indian elite. In the Singur case, the government of West Bengal attempted to acquire about four hundred hectares of land through the Land Acquisition Act to transfer to the Tata Corporation to develop an automobile factory and associated township (Ghatak, Mitra, Mookherjee, and Nath 2013). The effort met with vehement opposition from local farmers, who argued that the terms of compensation were inadequate. The protests turned violent, and after two years the planned acquisition was finally scrapped.

In West Bengal itself, the fallout from the Singur and Nandigram cases has hexed other government efforts at real estate megaproject development. Subsequent efforts to reinitiate the push toward large-scale land acquisition for master-planned development have for the most part proven politically infeasible. This reflects the reality across India that the aspirations among politicians and corporate elites to transform India's cities remain largely unfulfilled.

Variegated Processes of Urban Change

The preceding examination of the three case study cities, to be expounded on in greater detail in chapters 3 through 5, reveals the significant differences in urban change that have resulted from the real estate turn in urban politics. These differences are evident in very different patterns of spatial development: massive planned urbanization in the China case, a highly fragmented and disjointed pattern of development in Jakarta, and sporadic and piecemeal development in Kolkata. These preliminary sketches illustrate how an understanding of the politics of land helps interpret these differences. They point to the important question of *who* undertakes to neoliberalize urban space, the actors who stand to benefit from changes to property and real estate, the tools they use to achieve their objectives, and the actual brick-and-mortar strategies that emerge from their machinations. Chapter 2 will undertake a more sustained discussion of a comparative framework for understanding differences in models of land monetization across very different contexts of governance and urban development in Asia. Suffice here to conclude with a few observations concerning what these three cases tell us about the politics of state rescaling, spatial exclusion, and property that were discussed at the beginning of this section.

The first observation concerns the role of national state actors in seeking to extend state power by using powers over land as a means to rescale state action. National governments have sought in each case to encourage local state actors to pursue entrepreneurial strategies of land development as a means to empower the state. These cases therefore help to illustrate an important means through which states pursue state rescaling. In Brenner's (2004, 3) influential formulation, state rescaling has involved not a dissolution of national state power. Rather, national state power is reformulated as "national state institutions continue to play key roles in formulating, implementing, coordinating, and supervising urban policy initiatives, even as the primacy of the national scale of politico-economic life is decentered." The discussion in the preceding pages reveals the importance of land and real estate markets to this agenda.

Yet these cases also reveal some of the significant paradoxes involved in this national state push toward land monetization. There is a fundamental contradiction between national state efforts to enable local state entrepreneurship and the need to ensure that these local states do not act in ways that undermine state legitimacy and stability. How can state power be deployed in ways that allow state actors and allies to benefit from capital accumulation without the resulting tendencies toward rent seeking and wholesale dispossession that could undermine the political legitimacy of the resulting system? This paradox is evident in the example of the Din Daeng Redevelopment Project discussed at the beginning of this chapter. In this case, the push to entrepreneurialize the National Housing Authority led to a proposal that, to those affected and many external observers, clearly violated a well-established social contract between the state and its citizens. In this and other examples, the use of land management to empower the state pulls the politics of spatial exclusion and property rights close to the heart of questions of state-society relations. This plays out in very different ways in different contexts.

In the Chinese case, the state seems to have been extraordinarily successful in overcoming any contestation surrounding the politics of scale, spatial exclusion, and property, and it has consequently been able to cultivate local entrepreneurialism as a powerful basis for state legitimation through sustained economic growth. Yet this very success in turn appears to be intensifying the resulting contradictions surrounding issues of the scale of state power, exclusion, and property rights. Even as the CCP has come to rely heavily on creative local state strategies of property development to maintain a growth-driven agenda of state legitimation, the deprivations and abuses of power by local authorities, along with massive social displacement, have increasingly undermined the CCP's claims of legitimacy. As a consequence, the contradictions inherent in the local state's taking on a role of market actor, a role that sometimes contradicts directly with its purported function as an arbiter of the public interest, has "bled up" to color popular perspectives of the CCP itself.

The CCP clearly recognizes the threats posed by this contradiction and has actively sought to address them. The idea of "coordinating rural and urban development," which includes dealing with property rights disputes on the urban fringe, preserving agricultural land, and ensuring greater equity in urbanization processes, has emerged as a major policy thrust in recent years (Ye and LeGates 2013). And indeed the state's power in China provides it a unique ability to force questions of equity and justice onto local state agendas. At the same time, however, the national state is compelled to promote its commodification-driven urban-development paradigm by its need to maintain growth as a central element of its legitimacy. It is increasingly clear that it envisions the logical conclusion of its drive toward land-financed urban development as the full urbanization of China's human settlements. As this model reaches deeper into the rural hinterland, however, debate has grown over the extremes of social dislocation, cultural loss, and ecological damage that have resulted (Johnson 2013a).

Advocates of urban governance reform in India face a different set of contradictions. Here the central state has struggled to formulate a governance agenda that can overcome obstacles to urban development and land-financed economic growth. Moreover, its efforts to do so, which to date have achieved relatively modest results, have raised concerns about a fundamental reformulation of urban political economies that would upend deeply entrenched power relations. The reality of the historically embedded social negotiations around land claims means that efforts to bring land more centrally under the control of markets portend massive dislocation of communities and a shift in political authority from the ward and neighborhood level upwards to municipal, state, and national government. Central state efforts to strike a social bargain around such a change by distributing some of the material benefits to those dispossessed have as yet met with little success.

In the Jakarta case, when the Suharto regime was stable, the contradictions imposed by the manipulation of the land-permitting process were arguably less urgently felt by the national state, simply because the state ruled as much through coercion as through a developmental agenda. The Suharto government's claims to legitimacy were staked on the promise of political stability, security, and a limited developmentalism rather than on any broader promise of political inclusion or economic empowerment of the masses. When the regime itself became less stable, however, the underlying injustices of the regime led to an explosion of protest that sealed its fate. As Sidel (1998) has argued, Suharto's regime was founded on "logics of circulation and accumulation," the continuous reproduction of networks of powerful supporters in the corporate sector, military, and bureaucracy whose support was ensured and whose power was perpetuated through the use of state power to create new mechanisms for capital accumulation. Once the creation and circulation of capital and the cultivation of power networks could no longer be sustained—an outcome of social and political change but also of economic crisis, to which the real estate bust contributed—popular political movements soon overwhelmed the regime. The postauthoritarian Indonesian government has been struggling ever since to seek a new paradigm of urban governance. These debates have centered on ways the continued political primacy of the real estate industry can be reconciled with an urban reality in which most people access shelter and economic opportunity in unregistered settlements and through informal economies that exist outside the corporate built environment.

Conclusion

This chapter has argued that the monetization of land has become a driving imperative of urban politics in much of Asia in a context of fiscal austerity, increasing competitive pressure to develop new urban space, and the allure of wealth generation through land development. It started by providing an overview of the geoeconomic and political contexts in which countries throughout Asia began to experience increasing land values and began to respond with reforms intended to capitalize on this trend. The chapter then reviewed the cases of Jakarta, Chongqing, and Kolkata, attempting to explain why these settings experienced very different processes of land monetization and very different political, social, and spatial outcomes. This review has taken an initial step toward explaining the varied spatial and social outcomes of market-oriented reforms in different contexts by unpacking the particular context in which these reforms take place, the actors who pursue these reforms, and the institutional context in which they do so. Chapter 2 will pursue this line of analysis further by developing a conceptual framework for understanding three distinct models of neoliberalization of land management.

COMPARING STATE AGENDAS OF LAND MONETIZATION

Magarpatta City, located outside the emerging information technology center of Pune in the Indian state of Maharashtra, is an unusual success story of urban real estate megaproject development. Spanning 160 hectares, Magarpatta has emerged as a major business hub, one of the few projects of such a scale to be completed in India. The project is home to about fifty thousand residents and contains the offices of several multinational and domestic information technology, engineering, and consulting firms (Sami 2013). What makes Magarpatta City stand out among all major real estate developments in India, however, is that it was developed not by a major real estate development corporation, but rather by a collective of farming families. As Pune expanded in the late 1990s, the 120 families residing in this area, all members of the Magar clan, came to realize that urbanization would inevitably engulf their community, rendering farming unviable. The community formed the Magarpatta Township Development and Construction Company, with shares allocated among farmers in proportion to their landholdings. In a further remarkable detail, household members of the corporation sought training in construction and development, and they formed companies that contracted for much of the actual development of the project.

A close examination of the Magarpatta case reveals that it is not a David and Goliath story of poor peasants overcoming the power of the state and global capital. In fact, the community has long been politically influential through its strong role in Pune's sugar cooperatives, historically an important font of power. In addition, the Magarpatta project would almost certainly have been unsuccessful had it not been led by Satish Magar, a major landholder in the area and member of a politically powerful family; his grandfather had been Pune's mayor. Nonetheless, the Magarpatta City case provides a stark counterexample to the much more common story of the collusion of corporations and government officials in appropriating land value increases and dispossessing farmers.

Is the Magarpatta model replicable elsewhere in Asia, or even in other parts of India? Probably not. In China, for example, farmers would face insurmountable obstacles in any effort to gain control of development: opposition from politically dominant state-owned enterprises, strict land-use restrictions, and most importantly the Chinese state's constitutional monopoly on ownership of urban land. In Cambodia, farmers face the dominance of powerful politically connected corporations in land development. Even elsewhere in India, for example in Mumbai or Delhi, the heat generated by massive property price increases has attracted powerful economic and political interests that would likely restrict the space for political maneuvering by even a relatively well-connected clan like the Magars.

These contrasts raise the central question that motivates this chapter: How do we understand the differences between nations, cities, and communities in the political contestations over, and the actual physical and redistributive outcomes of, urban real estate megaprojects? What differences in the legal and political histories help to explain the strategies of state, corporate, and community actors and their likelihood for success? The introduction has argued that an examination of state efforts to transform institutions, norms, and politics of property rights and land-use management that attend the push to monetize urban land, and the spatial transformations that result, can help us give substance to recent theoretical calls to understand the neoliberalization of urban spatial production as a "variegated" process (Brenner, Peck, and Theodore 2010). That chapter posited a heuristic model for differentiating between approaches state actors might take in attempting to re-engineer land markets to enable access by market-oriented actors: deploying these efforts alternately, and sometimes simultaneously, as a "technology of governing" (a la Ong 2007), as a "strategy of accumulation," and as a "tactic of rent seeking." The introductory discussion of the case study cities in chapter 1 has further provided insights into the different powers, incentives, and contexts confronting state actors in Jakarta, Chongqing, and Kolkata, the specific tactics pursued by various actors, and the spatial and political outcomes that resulted. The task of this chapter is to provide a theoretical framework for further analysis of the case studies in the chapters to follow that will help to interpret the institutional, political, and social factors underlying these differences.

The examples already presented in this book illustrate what is at stake in such an analysis. Urban real estate megaprojects universally present a façade of glossy renderings and slick marketing material, but behind them lie a range of motivations and terms of engagement. When are these projects undertaken as a predatory attempt to dispossess communities and small businesses of their livelihoods and shelter and reallocate rents to politicians and politically connected businesses? When, instead, are they relatively "developmental," focused on legitimizing and empowering the state through infrastructure and economic development, social control, and the propagation of an ideology of modernization? And when do states have to engage in meaningful negotiation with forces pushing different agendas of urban development, including communities and economies that face displacement?

Given the social, cultural, and political complexity involved in rural-to-urban transitions and state-market relations in all cities, it is not possible for any framework to fully unpack variation between cases. Every city is unique in its historically formed patterns of property ownership, its property rights regime, its legal and political frameworks, and its social and cultural norms around the use of urban space. Nevertheless, this chapter develops a simple framework that, I will argue, helps to develop a basic typology of land monetization outcomes. This typology will in turn help to interpret some of the variation that will become apparent in the extended examination of the case studies that follow.

This framework focuses attention on two variables, representing two key factors that may constrain or enable government intervention in land markets and property development. The first is the state's ability to exert direct control over land markets, most significantly through state land ownership. The second is the autonomy of state authorities responsible for the planning and management of urban land against the influence of nonstate social actors. Neither of these variables is dichotomous, for each city exists along a theoretical continuum. Moreover, these two variables interact in important ways. State land ownership in itself provides state actors a great deal of autonomy in shaping land use. The autonomy of state land managers also allows state actors greater powers to accumulate land. It is the interaction between these two factors that, I will argue, shapes the politics of urban development in important ways. Indeed, throughout Asia and much of the rest of the world, these two variables represent important areas of state reform in the drive to monetize land. Political coalitions are in many cases undertaking a two-pronged push both to expand government land holdings and monetize existing state lands, and to insulate land-management authorities from external social influences that are not allies in the push to monetize land. Hence it is important to understand that what appears be a neoliberalization of land management does not necessarily result in a retreat of the state or reduction of the power of state actors. Rather, what often emerges is a state-directed construction of particular types of market mechanisms that enable new forms of state power.

This chapter will examine the implications of these two variables for our understanding of state strategies in navigating the real estate turn in urban policy. After discussing the variables in greater depth, the chapter will use them to develop a typology of state strategies of urban real estate megaproject development.

State Control of Land Management

State control of land markets is perhaps the most readily apparent factor shaping state strategies of land monetization, for it has a direct bearing on state capacity to enable and benefit from the commodification of land. The critical mechanism of such control in many cases is state land ownership, which allows state actors to directly extract revenue from land and to exert greater persuasive and coercive power over land development.

Near one end of the spectrum of state control of land markets is China, where the state's monopoly of land ownership in cities creates the basis for a model of urban governance founded on land monetization. The state's land ownership, and its development of mechanisms to appropriate periurban land held under communal ownership, have allowed it to appropriate land price appreciation as a tool to finance infrastructure and economic development and to reward state functionaries and allies. In some cases, it has also resulted in significant investments in social spending (Lin and Yi 2011; Huang 2012). The resulting capacity to deliver material improvement for much of the population has been central to state legitimation. The propagation of a model of party-driven modernization, backed by strong state powers to shape urban development, has further helped to create a sense of corporate identity and allegiance within the Communist Party. State land ownership also gives the state a powerful tool in shaping urban development to meet its social agenda. In countries where state land leasing constitutes the primary means through which land can be acquired for commercial development, states can use lease covenants to control how and by whom land is developed and to control the physical characteristics of urban space to meet their social and political objectives (Kotaka and Callies 2002). State land ownership also provides the state more direct opportunities to play a role in land development through government agencies and state-owned enterprises.

At the same time, however, the wholesale dispossession of communities that has resulted from large-scale redevelopment in China has not gone uncontested. Forms of protest have ranged from the passive, such as refusal to pay rent in relocation apartments, to more active forms, including public acts of protest (Hsing 2010). As noted in chapter 1, however, the contestations in the Chinese case that have the greatest consequence for urban development are between state institutions themselves. These contests over the spoils of land development specifically play out between municipal governments and central government and military units that own urban land (Hsing 2010). Hence the model of land monetization premised on state land ownership leads to the internalization of power conflicts over land within the state and places the state at the center of community-based grievances over dispossession.

There are parallels between China and other states that enjoy significant control over land markets. Most notable is Singapore, where, through a muscular agenda of land acquisition, state ownership of land rose from about 31 percent in 1949 to 80 percent in 1992 (Han 2005). The ruling People's Action Party has used this control of land as a powerful means to finance infrastructure, housing, social welfare, and public space (Chua 1997; Shatkin 2013). The state's leasing of land to private developers has become an important source of state revenue, accounting for about a fifth of the national budget in the late 2000s. The national government also generates revenue through land development, and it exerts influence over this development through its significant stake in the country's two largest developers, CapitaLand and Keppel. Perhaps most importantly, the Singaporean government has utilized its control of land to fundamentally shape the city-state's spatial development and dominate its housing market through the development of public housing new towns, which house more than 80 percent of Singapore's citizens. The Housing Development Board's (HDB) new towns have become the linchpin of the People's Action Party's claim to legitimacy, providing high-quality housing and services at prices that are affordable to residents, through a model of development that is essentially subsidized by the state's compulsory below-market acquisition of land.

India and Indonesia are closer to the other end of the spectrum. In these cases land ownership is highly diffused among a myriad of private and state landowners. Moreover, both cities are characterized by the prevalence of "informal" or unregistered claims to land. In Jakarta, an estimated 70 percent of land is unregistered with the National Land Agency, rendering its commercial development technically in contravention of the law (Kusno 2012a). In these and other cases of weak state roles in land markets, reform efforts that seek to enable land monetization have often focused on enabling land acquisition by private actors. Examples of such reforms include efforts to clarify land titles and subject them to the forces of the commercial land market, to sell state land or issue land permits to private developers, and to develop housing projects ostensibly for the poor that involve the transfer of previously informally held land to private developers (Kusno 2012a; Shatkin and Vidyarthi 2013). State actors have also sought in some cases to undertake large-scale compulsory acquisition of land. In India, for example, many state governments, in the aftermath of economic liberalization, sought to make more extensive use of the colonial-era Land Acquisition Act of 1894. Such large-scale government appropriation of land, however, is often politically controversial, if not infeasible.

It is important to note that cities occupy a range of positions on the spectrum of state control of land markets and that their place on the spectrum represents a tug of war between the state and other social forces. All municipal and national governments own land, often in substantial quantities, and in most of Asia as in the rest of the world it seems these lands are increasingly being sized up for commercial exploitation.[1] For example, Peterson (2013) documents about one hundred thousand hectares of land deemed "excess" and developable held by India Railways, the Airports Authority, the Major Ports Trust, and the Ministry of Defense. The Indian government has expressed increasing interest in developing many of these lands, with the explicit objective of "monetizing" them as a way to strengthen the state's capacity to manage urban growth (Tiwari 2012).

The Autonomy of Land Managers

The second variable in the framework developed in this chapter, stated broadly, is the ability of a national state and its local state counterparts to use their powers over land to shape urban space to their desired image. This is largely contingent on the presence or absence of institutional or legal mechanisms through which nonstate actors are able to influence the decisions of state land managers. State autonomy of action may be constrained by community groups who can use institutionalized opportunities for public input into policy, or legal protections against summary removal, to contest state and corporate projects. It may also be constrained by the ability of the wealthy and powerful to exploit state weaknesses to pursue developments that contravene state goals or to oppose state-sponsored projects. The permeability of the state to external interests should thus not be equated with any normative sense of the state's "accountability" to its population. The question is rather one of whether the state is able to shape the agendas of social actors (be they wealthy or poor) to its own intentions, or whether instead social actors capture the state for their own interests.

This variable exists along a theoretical spectrum. At one extreme is an authoritarian state land-management system in which a highly centralized state formulates a nexus with capital that allows the state to direct the benefits of land development in ways that extend state power. At the other is a land-management system in which decisions are uniformly open to nonstate influence and contestation. Land claims are always socially negotiated to some degree; even in China and Singapore nonstate actors violate state-defined norms of land use. There are, however, certain circumstances that push matters of land management more centrally into the realm of social negotiation.

The first of the circumstances is the presence of elected officials who have significant power over land management. In democratic, decentralized political systems, there is a greater likelihood that those who claim land through customary land tenure or extralegal appropriations will organize and aggregate into sufficiently large collectivities to constitute a significant electoral force. This reality has been summarized succinctly by Benjamin (2008, 719) in the concept of "vote bank politics," in which people lay "claim to public investments in basic infrastructure and services via a ground-up process focused on land and economy in return for guaranteed access to voter lists in municipal elections." Such a politics pushes questions of land and property "beyond discipline by 'the rule of law' or by 'structured civil representation'" and into a domain marked by messy and deeply ambiguous negotiation between government, corporate groups, and the poor (720). Benjamin coins the term "occupancy urbanism" to capture the kind of spatial development that results, which is shaped more by the political capacity of a group to occupy space than by any overarching objectives of state modernism or corporate-driven commodification. In India in particular, an extensive literature has focused attention on this space of negotiation between the poor, elected officials, petty bureaucrats, and corporate actors (Chatterjee 2004; Anjaria 2011). Hence the preponderance of illegal claims to land creates a situation in which state institutions are shot through with informality, and much of the day-to-day bartering over claims to space takes place through rent seeking by street-level state functionaries. The police, whose livelihood and authority flow from their capacity to extract bribes, and local politicians who collect votes from slum communities, form a powerful countercurrent against state aspirations to monetize land and plan space.

As Benjamin has clearly articulated in his discussion of occupancy urbanism, vote-bank politics is notably not only the politics of the poor. It does indeed provide a space in which the poor can gain valuable state recognition for their claims, which they can sometimes parlay into protection against eviction and even into some legal recognition of their land-use rights. Electoral influence can also provide a forum for calls for greater remuneration in cases of dispossession. Yet vote bank politics also creates a space for the influence of money on electoral politics and therefore may subject land-management decisions to manipulation by the powerful. Weinstein (2008) provides a cogent example of this in her discussion of land development in postliberalization Mumbai, where criminal syndicates utilized their allegiance with the powerful Shiv Sena Party, along with bribes and intimidation, to emerge as major players in the explosive growth of Mumbai's real estate development industry.

Where local elections are not the norm, or where dominance of a single party means that they are not actively contested, state bureaucracies and institutions enjoy greater autonomy of action in their efforts to displace existing users of space and transfer land to commercial developers. In the case of Suharto's Jakarta, for example, land-management decisions were largely made by highly centralized state bureaucracies and were supported by provincial governors, many of whom were retired military officers loyal to Suharto and his military high command (Sidel 1998). Likewise, during the period of rapid development in Chongqing, a powerful secretary of the Chongqing branch of the Chinese Communist Party was able to pursue his land-development plans with the full backing of the Chinese state. While legal mechanisms exist for citizens to express grievances and appeal cases of eviction, in China they are generally weak, and local officials hold most of the cards in negotiations.

The second factor that shapes the extent of social negotiation over large developments is the legal framework of property and housing rights and urban planning. This includes the extent of protection of both legal and extralegal claims to land by individuals and the extent of state rights and powers to take land and develop it for what it defines as the public interest. This framework is shaped by certain institutional factors. One of these is the treatment in national constitutions of property rights, rights to housing, and government rights to take property. One comparative study of ten countries in the Asia-Pacific region found that most constitutions contain wording that protects individual property rights (Kotaka and Callies 2002). It also found that constitutions of "most countries make broad statements of public purpose as justification for the exercise of compulsory purchase powers" (Ibid., 6). Yet countries vary in the extent to which constitutions articulate the limitations to this power and rights to compensation and due process in the case of compulsory purchase. These differences do not correspond perfectly to the strength of private property rights more generally, and in fact protections of property rights are sometimes spelled out most strongly in constitutions and in statutory law in cases where state land ownership predominates. For example, in China, where the state owns all urban land, there are significant formal restrictions on the taking of land from collectives. Australia, on the other hand, provides weak protection of property rights in case of compulsory acquisition, and the state is not bound to provide any compensation (Alterman 2010). Why this might be the case is an interesting topic for speculation. Perhaps in those countries where private property rights are stronger, governments feel compelled to spell out their right to take land more clearly and forcefully in order to justify the use of such powers.

Rights to housing can provide another potential argument against eviction and for requirements dictating adequate compensation or relocation. In a survey of 204 countries, Oren, Alterman, and Zilberschatz (2013) find that most constitutions contain some language defining rights to housing. These statements vary widely from weaker, general statements of citizen's rights to acquire and own housing, to much stronger articles that define a specific standard of housing to which every citizen has a right, and specific institutional, financing, and legislative measures that the state must take to ensure that this standard is met. Where housing rights are stated strongly in constitutions, this may strengthen the arguments of communities occupying land illegally. Such provisions can potentially be used to call for restrictions on eviction, or for adequate compensation, on the basis that dislocation without alternatives is likely to leave the displaced without adequate shelter.

Yet another factor that might affect the degree of social negotiation over property rights is the type of legal system in place. In common law systems, case law may emerge as an important arena of contestation over questions of property rights, housing rights, and government rights to take land (Kotaka and Callies 2002). In fact, the courts are emerging as important agents in shaping urban development agendas in some contexts, with varied outcomes. In India, for example, Bhan (2009) and Ghertner (2008) point to the shift in court discourses toward a more punitive stance toward poor communities, driven both by shifting judicial philosophy with regards to property rights and by public interest litigations (PILs) brought by middle-class communities against vendors and poor communities.

As is clear from the above discussion, legal and planning frameworks shaping land development are not determinative and are often subjugated to political considerations. As Alterman (2010) finds in an international comparative study of practices of compulsory acquisition, constitutional protections and legal institutional frameworks only go so far in explaining the degree to which the law protects property claims or compensation. Indeed, the law itself is often contradictory, and in many instances both state- and private-sector-driven evictions violate both its letter and intent. Legal frameworks are nonetheless important, if for no other reason than that they can be deployed as powerful arguments for or against a particular act of land acquisition. For groups facing displacement, codifications of rights to housing, urban space, and economic opportunity have been used in many cases to resist dispossession, albeit with varied success. Yet the urban poor have also found themselves displaced when the law has been used to deem their appropriations of land as criminal, as a nuisance, or as a threat to the environment.

In examining the role of the law in shaping the politics of land development, therefore, the review of cases that follows will treat the law not only as a set of institutions that set the rules of the game, but also as an arena of contestation in and of itself. A growing literature has begun to understand land law in this way. Much of this literature has focused on India, where public interest litigations (PILs) brought by organizations of the wealthy have driven a range of actions, including the displacement of communities and the relocation of small industries. While the courts have traditionally been regarded as as "a site of justice for the poor and marginalized" (Bhan 2009, 133), rulings have increasingly redefined the public interest in ways that are punitive of groups that occupy urban space in violation of the letter of the law (Baviskar 2003; Ramanathan 2006; Ghertner 2008). In contexts where extralegal and common property claims have historically been recognized, these court cases represent a push by property owners to seek new legal grounds for the displacement of uses they characterize as an aesthetical, environmental, and economic drag on the city.

The two variables highlighted in the preceding discussion—state control of land markets and autonomy of state land managers—help to contrast differences in outcomes for urban development in varying Asian contexts from the outcomes that might be predicted by the most influential theory of urban politics, urban regime theory. Developed in the context of American cities, regime theory argues that in the context of interjurisdictional competition for footloose capital in America's post-Fordist urban landscape, a primary function of urban political leaders (notably mayors) has been to "develop policies in concert with those who have access to capital" (Fainstein 1995, 35) in the pursuit of shared goals of economic growth and increased property values. Urban regimes, when they come together, are characterized by governing coalitions in which "public bodies and private interests function together in order to be able to make and carry out governing decisions" (Stone 1989, 6). Municipal leaders engage in a delicate negotiation between the realm of democratic politics and the interests of capital, such that the challenge of growth-oriented urban politics emerges as:

> the creation of preferences and the translation of those choices into policy. There is a sophisticated recognition that policy is not simply the imposition of preferences by an economic elite but rather the shaping of public opinion by upper class groups. Thus, ideology or public values become crucial to an understanding of what government of the third sector can or should do. (Fainstein 1995, 36)

Emerging as it did from the American context, regime theory is founded in assumptions that are distinct to that case. Stone (1993, 2) identifies two key such assumptions:

> One is a set of government institutions controlled to an important degree by popularly elected officials chosen in open and competitive contests and operating within a larger context of the free expression of competing ideas and claims. Second, the economy of a liberal order is guided mainly, but not exclusively, by privately controlled investment decisions. A regime, whether national or local, is a set of arrangements by which this division of labor is bridged.

The discussion of variations in state autonomy and state roles in land markets obviously highlights many potential departures from the assumptions of the regime theory model, and it invites a consideration of how these departures might shape differences in the politics of urban development. First, in settings characterized by a relatively strong state, and particularly in authoritarian settings, the role of both municipal and higher-level governments may extend well beyond bringing representatives of capital into decision-making processes. In such settings state actors can, and generally do, use their dominance of the legal and political realm to manipulate the economy in the interests of the state. This may be accomplished by allocating control of important economic functions to state-owned or state-controlled enterprises, as in Singapore and China. It may also be accomplished by distributing economic opportunity to cronies or relatives of political leaders, as in Suharto's Indonesia or in contemporary Myanmar, where the centers of gravity of the economy lie at the nexus of executive power, the military, and a select group of politically connected business interests. In both cases, economies cannot be said to be shaped primarily by "privately controlled investment decisions." Indeed the distinction between the state and the private sector becomes unclear, as does the market versus political logic of urban development. Contrarily, political systems in which results can be contested provide opportunities for the wealthy to exercise political influence that may undermine or contradict state goals, while simultaneously allowing the dispossessed to exercise agency in urban development processes.

The diversity of state roles in land markets further indicates that states may play a much more direct role in fostering economic growth than simply shaping preferences and defining policy choices, and they may benefit more directly from land value increases than simply reaping eventual property taxes. Rather, such states have an opportunity to more directly shape urban form and to gain immediate access to the financial benefits of urban development. National governments are likewise able to more deeply embed goals of corporate profit maximization within state planning objectives regarding urban development.

These two variables also interact with each other in important ways. The autonomy of state institutions gives them greater capacity to extend their control over land markets. Extensive state landholdings also provide state actors stronger legal and political claims to shape land development, thus accentuating their autonomy. For states that aspire to control land markets and use the rents that emerge from commercial land development to extend their legitimacy and political control, therefore, realizing these two objectives simultaneously appears to present a virtuous cycle. The section that follows will examine the intersection of these two variables in greater detail, using these intersections to develop a comparative framework for analyzing state urban real estate megaproject strategies.

A Comparative Framework for Understanding Land-Monetization Strategies

Figure 2.1 places the two variables described in the previous section into a simple two-by-two matrix. It does so to raise the question: How do the interactions between these two variables shape the strategies of urban

	Less state control of land markets	More state control of land markets
More autonomy of state land managers	**Type A** Political economy of the land grab	**Type B** Political economy of state capitalist urban planning
Less autonomy of state land managers	**Type C** Political economy of occupancy urbanism	**Type D** ?

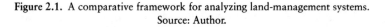

Figure 2.1. A comparative framework for analyzing land-management systems.
Source: Author.

development pursued by state actors? As the two variables are not dichotomous, no country will fall neatly into any one of these four boxes. But the
matrix provides a useful framework for considering the distinct challenges
and opportunities faced by varying "ideal type" land-management regimes,
and it frames how the various cases discussed in this book might relate to
these types. Because no Asian societies appear to resemble the lower-right
quadrant—where states have strong control of land markets but land managers are subject to strong social control—this quadrant of the matrix is left
empty. This section draws on observations from a number of cases throughout Asia to pose hypotheses about the implications of this framework for
urban politics. These hypotheses will be examined at greater length in the
case studies of Jakarta, Kolkata, and Chongqing to be examined in the
chapters that follow. The sections are titled according to the hypothesized
model of politics that emerges in each "ideal type" scenario.

Type A: Urban Politics and the Land Grab

The first model I will examine is that of countries that gravitate toward
the upper left-hand quadrant of the matrix, where the exercise of state
powers of land management is largely unchecked (a condition most notable in authoritarian political systems) and where state actors have relatively little direct control of land markets. The cases discussed thus far in
this book that most closely match this model are contemporary Cambodia
and Suharto-era Indonesia, both one-party states in which land ownership
is dominated by nonstate actors. In such a circumstance, the state's political dominance provides it the means to assert greater influence over urban
development and real estate, while rapid increases in land values and the
emergence of massive urban and periurban rent gaps provide powerful incentives to do so. This confluence of means and motive helps to explain
the commonalities in their approaches to land management. In each case,
state actors used their coercive power to forcibly take land from existing
users and to appropriate scarce public lands for private development in
order to distribute the benefits of land monetization among actors who
operated at the nexus of the state and the corporate economy. In such settings, therefore, land monetization is more likely to be driven by discrete
goals of accumulation and rent seeking.

The results in each case are acts of wholesale dispossession of existing
landholders, with relatively little effort to ensure justice in the distribution

of benefits. In the Indonesian case, a highly centralized administration used a regulatory mechanism—the land-permitting process—to transfer development control of massive amounts of land to family-based corporations with direct contacts to the Suharto regime. In the Cambodian case, it appears from circumstantial evidence that land reclamation has emerged as a means for the central state to use its hegemony over local politics to realize a large-scale transfer of developable land to actors with ties to the ruling Cambodian People's Party.

Recent years have seen a growing literature concerned with the politics of "land grabs" that, while largely focused on rural contexts, is nonetheless relevant to the discussion of urban and periurban development (see for example Borras et al. 2011 and other contributions in the associated special issue of the *Journal of Peasant Studies*). While often left undefined, the term "land grab" generally refers to large-scale acquisitions of land for transfer to corporate users that are "involuntary or otherwise unfair" (Hirsch 2011, 1). This broad definition appears to fit many of the cases examined thus far in this book, but the cases of Cambodia and Suharto-era Indonesia stand out for the degree to which displacement has occurred on a large scale with relatively little recourse to due process or state action to address distributional concerns. Land transfers in these cases appear "grabbier" than those in cases with more permeable politics and greater state capacity to appropriate benefits in the name of the public interest.

Furthermore, the cases of Cambodia and Indonesia under Suharto's New Order regime point to interesting observations about the implications of land monetization on governance that contrast with some of the central contentions of the literature on rural land grabs. Sassen (2013, 26) has argued that the massive land acquisition in rural Africa by foreign actors (global corporations, sovereign wealth funds, wealthy country governments) is one facet of a trend toward the disassembling of national territory that is "producing massive structural holes in the tissue of the sovereign national state." State sovereignty and community agency, she argues, have atrophied as decision making has shifted to "opaque transnational networks that control the land" (Sassen 2013, 26–27). The meaning of neoliberalization in such contexts, according to this view, is the imposition through the disciplining regime of fiscal austerity of a gradual disassembling of the authority, rights, and the very territory of the nation-state. Yet in the Cambodia and New Order Indonesia cases, the global façade of urban real estate megaproject developments—the starchitect designers, the multinational tenants of the resulting spaces, the foreign investors—masks a strong role for domestic actors, notably domestic real estate development interests and the state. Urban real estate megaprojects in these cases are actually used as a tool to exploit state control over land and development in the interests of the state. This is a different kind of governance shift than that described by Sassen, one in which corrupt and nepotistic one-party states extend their power by placing the state astride the process of commodification of land and of the national economy more generally. The results are paradoxical for state actors, because seeking enhanced authority and territorial control through land commodification subjects state influences to the uncertainty of the shifting currents of the global economy. That Suharto's eventual fall was precipitated by a financial crisis that had its roots in a property bubble highlights the risks associated with such a maneuver.

Type B: Urban Politics and State Capitalist Urban Planning

The second model that emerges from the matrix in figure 2.1 is that of states that trend toward the upper right-hand quadrant, those that are relatively autonomous and also have significant control over land markets. The cases that most fit this description are those of Singapore and China, both one-party states that control dominant shares of urban land markets. In both cases, states have also used their political pre-eminence to gain a central role in the corporate economy through such measures as cultivating state-owned enterprises as central economic actors, investing in private enterprise through sovereign wealth funds, and using state-owned banks as a key tool in shaping financial markets. This combination of a monopoly on political power and control over land markets allows these governments to utilize land markets to legitimize and empower ruling parties (the Communist Party in China and the People's Action Party in Singapore) in several ways. They can use the revenue from land development to enact social welfare, housing, and infrastructure initiatives as tools for political legitimation. They can also directly use urban design and planning as tools for political control, and they can distribute patronage to key political actors, notably state functionaries and members of ruling parties. The presence of this extremely powerful tool for infrastructure development, urban master planning, and economic development allows states to craft narratives of state legitimacy based on modernization, expansion of economic opportunity, and redistribution of some of the revenue generated by state-driven real estate development.

Elsewhere I have discussed a similar strategy in the case of Singapore as one of "urban planning under state capitalism," a condition in which, to paraphrase Bremmer (2010), the state plays a leading role in urban real estate markets and uses its control of these markets for political gain (Shatkin 2013). It is this model of the congruence of state and market power that has enabled the dramatic periurban transformations witnessed in Chongqing and Singapore, where land monetization financed the planned expansion of these cities and ambitious agendas of infrastructure and housing construction. Yet this model also poses challenges, for it places ruling parties at the center of the contradictions of market-driven development. Problems of deepening social inequality, of development-induced displacement, and of corruption emerge as major issues that undercut state discourses of developmentalism. Moreover, the state capitalist model places pressure on the state to ceaselessly generate new opportunities for real estate profit, thus casting the state as the central protagonist in the dynamic of "creative destruction" described by Schumpeter. This imperative to constantly reinvent and commodify life spaces threatens to drive the state to reflexively and relentlessly destroy and reshape social and economic relations, and therefore to risk alienating citizens.

Type C: Urban Politics and Occupancy Urbanism

The third model is that of states that gravitate toward the lower left-hand quadrant, in which the state's exercise of land management authority is subject to greater negotiation and where the state has a less direct stake in land markets. Of the cases discussed thus far, India and the Philippines most closely resemble this description. It is in such contexts that the dynamic of occupancy urbanism identified by Benjamin plays its strongest role, as the ability of both wealthy and poor claimants to urban space to access some degree of political influence ensures that contestations over competing claims become the norm in urban politics. It is also in such contexts that politically motivated validations of land tenure claims tend to create multiple, overlapping land tenures.

While creating significant obstacles to the commodification of urban land, the pervasive dualism between land that has clear title and land that does not creates a significant land supply constraint that merely widens urban rent gaps. This provides strong incentives for the state to wade into the highly politicized realm of land markets and attempt to acquire land and transfer it to commercial developers. Constrained as they are by the potentially tumultuous politics that attends efforts at large-scale land acquisition, states in such situations tend to engage in multiple strategies to monetize rent gaps. One such strategy is to sell or lease what state-owned land is available and is relatively unencumbered by alternate claims. This strategy is evident, for example, in the Philippine government's efforts to redevelop former military bases in both urban and peri-urban areas (Bases Conversion Development Authority 2013). Another strategy is to forge a new social contract around urban land by providing stronger incentives for landowners to part with their land or undergo land readjustment.

Another strategy that state actors in such contexts pursue is to attempt to engineer a fundamental change in the underlying political economy of urbanization in ways that push cities upwards and rightwards on the matrix in figure 2.1. In other words, many governments have seen concerted reform efforts focused on two goals: first, to increase state control over urban land markets; and second, to insulate state land managers from the influence of those who contest large-scale land commodification. In some cases, these efforts have been directly modeled on practices in China and Singapore. Examples of such reforms include the creation of parastatal land-development agencies that are insulated from public participation processes, the formation of new governance structures that shift authority away from neighborhood or ward-level political authorities, and the passage of laws to facilitate state land acquisition. Within prevailing governance frameworks and patterns of land ownership, however, such reforms cut to the very center of established political cultures and state legitimation narratives. They therefore tend to open new frontiers of political conflict, the resolution of which can only be realized with fundamental changes in state-society relations.

Conclusion

The framework presented in this chapter is intended to explain the broad institutional and political factors confronting state actors as they seek to capitalize on rising land values, and the capacities and constraints they experience. There is much that this framework does not explain. For example, it does not explain the particular sets of social relations and political networks the Magar clan exploited in realizing its development goals in the Magarpatta City case, or the particular political idiom they deployed in negotiations with state actors. It does, however, provide us with a set of analytical tools to make legible how and why this project was able to move forward in the Pune context when it would have been difficult to achieve in other settings. Thus this framework provides a basis for analyzing the kinds of variation we might expect to find in both government and community strategies of negotiation and conflicts over questions relating to property rights, claims to urban space, and distributional issues surrounding these projects. The framework also indicates that governments might under different circumstances be more or less likely to progressively redistribute the benefits and costs of urban real estate megaproject development.

The following discussion will explore these variations more deeply in the cases of Chongqing, Jakarta, and Kolkata. In doing so, it asks how the politics of property differs between three cities representing the three models of political economy identified in this chapter, and it explores how these differences in politics have shaped the spatial and social development of these cities.

3

Planned Grab

Capitalizing on Land Dualism in New Order Jakarta

> There must not be any forceful eviction of local families. If evictions
> cannot be avoided the evicted people must be made more prosperous.
> —President Suharto quoted in the *Jakarta Post*,
> December 19, 1996

President Suharto made the above pronouncement in 1996 as he signed his approval to plans for Bukit Jonggol Asri, a master-planned new town located fifty kilometers southeast of Jakarta in the province of Bogor. Even by the standards of the massively ambitious new town projects that cropped up in the years before the end of Suharto's New Order regime in 1998, the Bukit Jonggol Asri scheme stood out in its scale and audacity. At thirty thousand hectares, the proposed new town was nearly half the land area of Jakarta itself. Located in an area protected by law as a water catchment area for the region, Bukit Jonggol Asri was to have been the location of a string of developments modeled on suburban communities of Southern California (Cowherd 2002). The consortium that proposed the development was headed by Suharto's son, Bambang Trihatmodjo, lending the project more than usual suspicions of cronyism. There was even some discussion that the Indonesian capital might relocate to the development (Silver 2007). Ultimately, the plan was abandoned, and the presidential proclamation creating the project was canceled in the aftermath of Suharto's fall (Firman 2004). To date, however, much of the land that was originally slated for development remains under permit, the development rights since sold to Sentul City, a major developer of townships in contemporary Jakarta (Cahyafitri 2013; Nurfiyasari 2013). In 2014 Sentul City itself became embroiled in a corruption controversy over allegations that it had bribed the regent of Bogor to issue development permits on protected forest lands lying in the original Bukit Jonggol Asri site (Halim 2014).

The Bukit Jonggol Asri plan is the most audacious example of the surge in land permitting undertaken by Indonesia's National Land Agency beginning in the late 1980s, what approached at its crescendo a feeding frenzy of permitting in the early to mid-1990s. Between 1985 and 1995 the National Land Agency issued location permits to private developers for rights to develop more than eighty thousand hectares, or eight hundred square kilometers, in the Jakarta Metropolitan Region alone (Firman 1997). In 1996, the year before the approval of the Bukit Jonggol Asri plan, there were twenty-two different residential development projects of five hundred hectares or more documented by Winarso (2000), with twelve of these more than a thousand hectares and five more than three thousand hectares. This massive transfer of land occurred in the context of an authoritarian regime that brooked little opposition. Indeed, contrary to Suharto's pronouncement, land permitting was indeed accompanied by instances of coercion and violence.

This chapter will explore Suharto-era Indonesia as one case of what was referred to in the previous chapter as a political economy of the land grab. It will trace the response of an authoritarian regime that based its power on the patronage of an economic oligarchy as urban land emerged as an important economic and therefore political resource. The previous chapter argued that such circumstances present state actors with strong incentives to engage in large-scale coercive land takings as a means to maintain oligarchic economic and political control. At first glance this chapter's epigraph appears to belie this argument; it expresses a seemingly earnest intention to seek an equitable and developmental approach to new town planning. Indeed, the planning of Jakarta's new towns took place within a spatial planning framework that ostensibly deployed the latest thinking in architecture, urban design, and regional development. Yet during the peak of the "land rush," pretenses of technocracy and fairness were sublimated to the impulse to seize control of the financial and ultimately political power to be gained from control of land. Technocracy and the rhetoric of the formation of a newly modern urbanism came to be deployed as mechanisms to legitimize a massive politically and spatially transformative transfer of control over the development and use of land to a handful of corporate backers of the authoritarian regime. The result was a systematic subversion of the core principles that ostensibly lie at the heart of contemporary planning practice, including principles of rationality, equity, and ecological sustainability.

The paradoxes of the Indonesian state's dual push to create an aura of technocratic rationality and its bid for a monumental land grab parallel the paradoxes of Suharto's New Order regime more generally. Political scientists have characterized the Suharto regime as an oligarchy, a regime in which political power evolved at the nexus of state and corporate power. Central to this oligarchy was Suharto's use of state regulatory and police power to distribute economic opportunity to a handful of individuals with close connections to political power, including his own family (Sidel 1998; Winters 2011). Yet the Suharto regime also took care to cultivate its claims to broader legitimacy, both by building a competent technocratic bureaucracy and by fostering the growth of state-guided civic and cultural organizations. The Suharto government thus "encompassed a highly organized system of social power not easily explained in terms of universally random and opportunistic predatory practices" (Robison and Hadiz 2004, 42). This social power included a scrupulous effort to embed state planning within technocratic ideals, of the famed "Berkeley mafia" economists on the economic front, and of skilled and highly trained planners and developers on the urban front.

As land prices surged beginning in the late 1980s, the state-corporate nexus took increasing interest in urban development as a source of patronage, and the system of location permits gradually came to be exploited for this purpose. Location permitting exploits a distinct aspect of Indonesia's property system: a dualism in the land-tenure regime between registered land, held by freehold owners or government, and unregistered land, held by myriad smallholders who hold no title and consequently cannot gain development permits or project financing to undertake large-scale development. These subordinate, limited land claims mean that vast swaths of land in Jakarta and at its periphery, in unregistered *kampung* settlements, are excluded from the commodified property-development market,

Figure 3.1. Jakarta skyline, with *kampung* in the foreground. Source: Author.

suppressing their value and creating massive rent gaps. Within a system defined by the power of a small economic oligarchy, the existence of these subordinate land claims recommended itself to just the sort of magical bureaucratic transformation represented by the land-permit system, which could be used to bring unregistered land into the corporate fold. The location permit allowed developers to claim the rights to purchase, register, and develop vast tracts of unregistered land in the name of modernizing urban space and infrastructure. Even as the planning of new towns like Bukit Jonggol Asri played out in discourses of regional planning, urban design, and the creation of global spaces, they also served to bring land strategically into the commodity fold, allowing politically connected families to realize windfall profits.

Hence the Jakarta case provides one notable example of Roy's (2005) argument that "informality"—the institutionalized legal marginality of economies and claims to space—should be treated not as an aberration or a failure of state power, but rather as a state of exception that is produced by a suspension of legal order by the state:

> The planning and legal apparatus of the state has the power to determine when to enact this suspension, to determine what is informal and what is

not, and to determine which forms of informality will thrive and which will disappear. State power is reproduced through the capacity to construct and reconstruct categories of legitimacy and illegitimacy. (Roy 2005, 149)

Putting aside the question of whether the term "informal" applies to the case of Jakarta's unregistered lands (which have legal although subordinate status), Roy's formulation certainly resonates in the Indonesian case, where the privilege of registering land, and therefore reaping the windfall of land commodification, was allotted in ways that enriched a few while subjecting established communities to insecurity and deepened marginality.

The form of the Jakarta Metropolitan Region—the ecological and social injustices and irrationalities that mark the region to this day—can only be understood in the context of the spatial and political path dependencies that the location permitting system created. The massive permitting of periurban land has accelerated the suburbanization and fragmentation of the Jakarta Metropolitan Region. This sprawling of Jakarta was quantified in one post–New Order study comparing the spatial distribution of urban populations, which found the Jakarta metropolitan area to be at a much more advanced stage of suburbanization that the comparison cases of Bangkok and Metro Manila, a jarring finding considering the relatively modest rates of car ownership in Jakarta relative to these cities (Murakami et al. 2005). Jakarta and its surrounding region stands today as a patchwork of exclusive development interspersed with towns, villages, and farms that hold tenuously to their threatened land claims. It is a region in which spatial inequality has emerged as a fundamental organizing principle of urban development patterns, as state policy focuses on enabling corporate land speculation and on the development of self-contained elite enclaves.

The Institutional and Cultural Roots of Jakarta Circa 1997

Jakarta's explosion of master-planned new towns has drawn particular attention from sociologists, planners, and architectural historians in large part due to the tendency of these developments to adopt Western models of architecture and design, often with a flair of audacious kitsch. Scholars

have focused their attention on the sociological meaning of towns modeled on Japanese and European styles, and of statues of the Sphinx of Giza
and of cowboys from the American West that adorn some projects. They
have frequently viewed these Disneyesque manifestations as evidence of
a consumer class desire for escape from the perceived dangers, annoy-
ances, and aesthetic turpitude of Jakarta's urban space (Dick and Rimmer 1998; Cowherd and Heikkila 2002). In an intriguing twist on this
line of argumentation, Kusno, Budianta and Farid (2011) have proposed
that this desire to escape Jakarta's existing conditions has deep roots. It
amounts, they argue, to a cultural tendency toward the creation of new
urban spaces as a mechanism of escape—what they term "runaway urbanism"—extending far beyond the recent development of suburban new
towns, much deeper into Indonesia's colonial and postcolonial past.

> First, Jakarta has long been a 'runaway city'. In the 19th century, the capital
> (with its administrative and military center) was moved inland (to the area
> of Weltevreden) away from the ills that engulfed coastal Batavia, and, in
> postcolonial times, the symbolic centers of the capital continued to expand
> inland with the construction of Senayan complex in the time of Sukarno
> and the Beautiful Indonesia theme park during the Suharto era. Other mega-
> projects such as the new towns, shopping malls and the recent superblocks
> have the quality of fleeing from the distress of the urban environment. They
> tend to avoid, to abandon or refuse to become involved in the problem of
> urbanization they have helped create. In post-Suharto Jakarta, the quality
> of the built environment has left an impression that the city is getting out of
> control, or even is beyond control. (Kusno, Budianta, and Farid 2011, 473)

The most recent iterations of this history, they argue, play out "in a context where Jakarta has become increasingly the site for the circulation of
global capital and the battleground of extreme morality claims" (Kusno,
Budianta, and Farid 2011, 480). The newest forms of enclave urbanism,
therefore, mark the ascendance, as the market emerges as the pre-eminent
criterion in the allocation of rights to urban space, of wealth as a marker
of virtue.

In this chapter I argue that such cultural arguments provide only a partial explanation of the foundations of "runaway urbanism." The politics
of this restless quest to create new urban spaces was at least partially motivated by the presence of an available mechanism in the land dualism. The

cultural premises of these projects—the rejection of the *kampung*, vendors, and *becaks* (cycle rickshaws) as nonmodern others—also supported a coalescence of state and corporate interests in the potential for capital accumulation to be realized through their spatial exclusion. As capital and its state allies sought during the boom years of the 1980s and 1990s to realize new opportunities for land-based accumulation, the land-permitting system allowed the state to avoid politically unpalatable alternatives for acquiring land. The Sukarno-era eviction of eight thousand families from land acquired for the Senayan Sports Complex, developed in preparation for the 1962 Asian Games, demonstrated the damage that an agenda of heavy-handed compulsory acquisition could do to the state's political legitimacy (Silver 2007). When married to the idea of master-planned megaproject development, the permitting of unregistered land provides an incremental, distributed, and quasi-market mechanism for driving an urban development agenda that incentivizes action from powerful private-sector actors while also providing opportunities for state patronage.

The contemporary Jakarta Metropolitan Region (JMR) is a sprawling megalopolis consisting of the city of Jakarta proper, along with urbanizing municipalities and district governments in its surrounding region. This larger region is referred to in official planning documents as Jabodetabek, for Jakarta and the surrounding urbanizing districts of Bogor, Depok, Tangerang, and Bekasi.[1] The population of the city proper stood at about 9.6 million in 2010, while that of the entire JMR stood at close to 28 million. The metropolitan region has historically expanded through the development of large, master-planned urban initiatives, developed within a centrally conceived spatial planning framework, and the urbanization of villages at the fringe. Early on, under the Sukarno government, the government of postindependence Indonesia focused much of its planning efforts on new towns—two particularly notable examples being Kebayoran Baru in south Jakarta and Pulo Mas in the northeast of Jakarta—and implemented their plans by acquiring land from farmers and urban communities and then selling it to construction companies (Santoso 2009). Yet another thrust of Sukarno-era planning was the southward expansion of the central business district through road expansion and the development of high-profile public projects along the Thamrin-Sudirman Boulevard axis to the south of Jakarta, including the development of the Hotel Indonesia complex and the Senayan Sports Complex, developed in preparation for the 1962 Asian Games. It was under Suharto that the urban development industry experienced a fundamental transformation marked by the leapfrogging of planned development into the surrounding areas of Tangerang to the west of Jakarta and Bekasi to the east. This period also saw a qualitative shift toward privatizing the planning, construction, and management of urban space, toward corporate speculation in urban land, and toward the marriage of political and economic interests in land development.

The dualism of the land-tenure regime between registered and unregistered land is rooted in the country's colonial experience (Leaf 1992). Under Dutch colonial rule, all land in Indonesia was placed into two categories: *domein* lands, owned by the state; and *eigendom* lands, which were held under a form of freehold ownership limited to Europeans, foreign Asians, and a small number of elite Indonesians. Within this framework many Indonesians who had historically claimed and worked lands under precolonial *adat* or customary tenure were dispossessed of these claims but were accorded legal rights of exploitation and commercial use of land in exchange for tax (in the case of *domein* lands) and tribute (in the case of *eigendom*). These claims continue to exist today as *hak girik*, or formerly *domein* land upon which residents pay tax to the state, and *hak garapan* rights of use on formerly *eigendom* land.[2] Today, *hak girik* is generally held to provide a stronger land claim than *hak garapan* because there is a tax receipt, which provides stronger proof of long-term occupancy. Because of these legally recognized but subordinate land claims, relatively few low-income Jakartans live in what can be characterized as "informal" or "squatter" settlements; estimates generally hold that residents of illegally occupied lands represent a small percentage of Jakarta's population, perhaps 4 or 5 percent (Argo and Laquian 2004). Rather, a majority live legally in *kampung* settlements, which have developed incrementally as low-rise, densely built urban neighborhoods that continue to shape much of the urban fabric. According to Leaf's (1993) estimate, in 1988, near the beginning of the period described in this chapter, only 9 percent of households in Jakarta lived in "formally developed" housing, built by professional developers according to plan on registered land. In total, 31 percent lived on registered land and the remainder on unregistered land or as informal settlers. These unregistered land claims exist largely apart from the commercial property market, and during the Suharto era such claimants

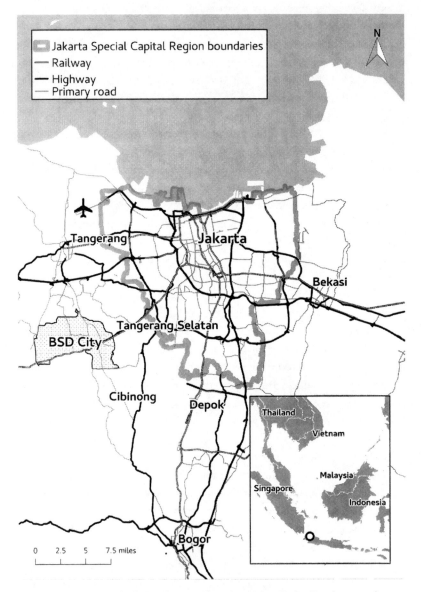

Figure 3.2. Map of Jakarta. Sources: OpenStreetMap, Badan Penghargaan dan Sayembara, 2014. Map developed by Antonio Vazquez Brust. Map data copyrighted OpenStreetMap contributors and available from http://www.openstreetmap.org.

were unable to access the mortgage market or to get building permits for commercial property development (Bertaud 1989). Such restrictions had the obvious impact of suppressing the escalation of property values.

The persistence of the land dualism to the present era contradicts the stated aims of postcolonial Indonesian land law, which positions the state as arbiter of a process of modernization of Indonesia's land-management system. The foundational legislation concerning land in the postcolonial period is the Basic Agrarian Law of 1960 (BAL), which ostensibly seeks to eliminate the land dualism by establishing systems for the registration of unregistered lands. The law attempts a "uniquely Indonesian framework for managing land and natural resources," one that posits the state as the arbiter of a distinctly Indonesian approach to property relations that, in contrast to Western capitalist property relations, is premised on social welfare (Thorburn 2004, 33):

> The law is based on Article 33 of the constitution, which states that land in Indonesia has a "social function" and that the earth, water, air and natural riches are controlled by the State of Indonesia as the representative authority of the people of Indonesia. Land is seen as the fundamental provider of food, shelter and clothing—rights that are guaranteed in the constitution and national philosophy Pancasila. (Thorburn 2004, 33)[3]

The BAL establishes categories of land rights—including rights of ownership, use, exploitation, and development—while establishing the state as the ultimate arbiter in questions of land use, disposition, and conservation (Struyk, Hoffman, and Katsura 1990). It also establishes the objective of registering all unregistered land, a task that initially fell to a Directorate under the Ministry of the Interior but since 1988 has been tasked to the Badan Pertanahan Nasional (BPN), or National Land Agency.

Despite the stated intentions of the BAL and various other policy pronouncements with respect to land registration, the reality is that the administration of land registration has foundered on the political economy of land. Registration has consequently occurred slowly and in a way that has favored the wealthy and well-connected. One study focused on the late Suharto and early post-Suharto era found that the documentation requirements for landholders applying for title—including documentation concerning their colonial land tax payments and of historical property rights sales tracing their claim back to the colonial era—are often nearly impossible to fulfill (Reerink 2011). There are also substantial formal and informal fees associated with registration that may exceed the market price of the land itself (Thorburn 2004). Even where landholders do pay these fees, "victims and observers tell tales of multiple certificates for single parcels of land, certificates being issued to the wrong people, and of land being expropriated without proper confiscation even after certificates had been issued" (Thorburn 2004, 34). A survey by Reerink (2011) found that 92 percent of respondents cite the high cost and administrative difficulties as their primary reason for not registering their land, while only 3.2 percent say they have not proceeded because they see registration as unnecessary. In all, the opacity and corruption that characterizes the land-registration system renders it impenetrable to most. The result is a system that favors the wealthy and well-connected, particularly large developers who can hire "full time 'file pushers' " tasked with navigating the bureaucratic maze (Bertaud 1989, 7).

Such obstacles help to explain the continuing predominance of unregistered land as the predominant site of housing production. Estimates have found that midway through the first decade of the twenty-first century, about 30 percent of nonforest land in Indonesia was registered and titled (as compared to 90 percent in Thailand and 80 percent in the Philippines), and the rate of registration indicates that it will take at least several more decades before the goal of full registration is met, if it ever is (Thorburn 2004).

During the middle to late 1980s, the system of land registration took a distinct turn toward what Rachman (2011) has referred to as a "land for development policy regime." This shift was marked by the ascendance of the *ijin lokasi*, or location permit, as a critical mechanism for spatial planning and urban development. While this tool had been used previously, the period coinciding with the formation of the BPN and with the rapid escalation of land values in the JMR saw the increasing use of this mechanism to transfer development control of very large parcels to private developers. While land dualism has generally been viewed within the bureaucracy and among academics as a paradox to be resolved by a modernizing state, at this important juncture the *ijin lokasi* came to provide a mechanism the state could use to exploit this dualism to guide urban development by acting as an intermediary in the real estate market. The land-registration system developed under the BPN became wedded to the country's spatial planning framework, which in turn gave birth to Indonesia's corporate real estate industry, a child that over time came to rule the roost.

The system described here, which prevailed during the late Suharto period, has changed little in terms of administrative detail since Suharto's fall, although the politics of the process has shifted in the postauthoritarian context of democratization and decentralization (Thorburn 2004; Hudalah and Woltjer 2007; Monkkonen 2013). Guiding the land-conversion system is a hierarchy of plans: a national medium-term spatial plan developed every five years by the National Development Planning Agency (BAPPENAS), a provincial spatial plan, and a municipal spatial plan.[4] While the latter must be broadly consistent with the national and provincial plans, it is much more detailed and includes regulations regarding land uses, building codes, and floor area ratios that guide development. Within the guidelines set by that plan, developers seeking to develop planned projects of fifteen hectares or more apply to the provincial authorities for the *ijin lokasi*, usually on state-owned land or on land upon which current users hold *hak girik*. The permit indicates that the planned development is consistent with government plans for the urbanization of the area (Struyk, Hoffman, and Katsura 1990; Winarso 2000). Once the location permit is issued, the developer gains exclusive rights to purchase the property from unregistered users or the state, to register the property, to apply for additional permissions such as the building permit, and finally to develop the property. Technically, therefore, the land-permitting process provides a means for the government to enforce its spatial plans, and it acts as a lever for the state to require elements like affordable housing in new development. Indeed, in 1974 the National Housing Authority (NHA) issued a regulation requiring developers to build at least six smaller houses and three medium-sized houses for every one larger, luxury house, a measure obviously intended to provide more affordable housing (Winarso 2000). This regulation was strengthened in 1992, near the height of the land-permitting boom, when the NHA further stipulated that developers had to provide the 6:3:1 ratio on site when developing properties of more than two hundred hectares. These regulations were largely ineffective because they were poorly implemented, as will be discussed at greater length later in this chapter.

Technocratic rationales aside, as "the primary mechanism for transferring lands from the informal popular sector to the formal private sector," the land-permitting system also creates opportunities to exploit the
planning system to capture windfall profits (Leaf 1992, 127–128). While
permit holders still need to purchase land from existing users in order to
proceed with development, the permits provide developers what economists refer to as *monopsony* rights, or exclusive rights to purchase. Unlike
in a monopoly, in which the seller can largely dictate the price and terms
of sale, in a monopsony situation the buyer enjoys this privilege. This issue
was formally recognized in the formation of a Land Release Committee,
a body consisting of local, national, and provincial officials tasked with
setting a suggested price for the sale of permitted land. Yet studies have indicated that these suggested prices have consistently fallen orders of mag-
nitude short of land values eventually realized in the development (see for
example Akosoro 1994). In practice, there has often been a broad recognition among landholders that land prices offered by middlemen (*calo
tanah*, discussed below) employed by developers are likely to be higher
than those offered by the committee. The capacity of developers to dictate
real estate prices was accentuated all the more when they were backed by
powerful local authorities who sometimes used real or threatened violence
to intimidate local landowners. During the height of the real estate boom,
stories circulated of small landholders being coerced to sell or evicted by
police, soldiers, and hired gangs (Harsono 1999).

The land-permitting process also created possibilities for large-scale
rent seeking by opening up the possibility of developers gaining control
of vast land banks by acquiring permit rights to large tracts of land. Such
an outcome runs contrary to the central stated intention of the *ijin lokasi*
system, which is intended to guide land development. As illustrated by
the Bukit Jonggol Asri plan and other large developments, however, it is
clear that interests associated with the real estate industry came to play a
powerful role in the direction of urban spatial planning. Administrative
mechanisms to thwart speculative land banking, such as a permit limit of
one year on land that remains undeveloped, have been ineffective, and
to date many developers hold permits to vacant land decades after the
permits were issued.

As land values escalated dramatically during the middle to late 1980s,
the rent gaps created by rapid urbanization and real estate investment created the potential for windfall profits through the use of the *ijin lokasi* to

commodify land. Visions of modernist urban transformation through new town development were deployed to rationalize increasingly unrealistic schemes that were clearly covers for speculative exercises in land banking. By late 1996, according to an analysis by Haryo Winarso (2000), developers held permits in the Jakarta Metropolitan Region to 121,631 hectares, with the bulk of these permits going to just fifteen developers with permits exceeding one thousand hectares. Of this total less than 14 percent had been developed. Winarso goes on to estimate that this land when developed could accommodate some twenty-six million people and projects that demand for such a supply would take two hundred years to develop at the current rate of the expansion of Jakarta's developer-built housing market.

Within areas held under location permit, the progress of development has tended to follow the path of least resistance for developer land acquisition rather than the logic of spatial planning or infrastructural connectivity. Plantations inherited by the postcolonial state from the Dutch occupy a significant portion of the Jakarta's periurban periphery, and developers have tended to focus on acquiring these lands first, as the executives of state-owned enterprises that administer these lands tend to be readily amenable to their sale.[5] Another prevalent practice in land acquisition is the employment of *calo tanah*, or land brokers, a practice that violates regulations stating that developers must negotiate directly with landowners but that according to Akosoro (1994) is nearly universal among developers. As discussed in Leaf (1992), *calo tanah* use their superior knowledge of master plans and proposed infrastructure investments to identify lands likely to be targeted for development and then convince (and sometimes coerce) landowners to give them power of attorney to negotiate with large real estate development companies. The frequent cooptation of local officials and coercion of landowners in these negotiations has led many to view the *calo tanah* as akin to a land mafia, yet as prices of land rose in the late 1980s and 1990s the propensity of landowners to resist their machinations rose as well (Leaf 1992, 157). In sum, the variable geography of land availability, as dictated by the patchwork pattern of accommodation, cooptation, coercion, and resistance, has assured that land development within the new towns has followed a patchwork pattern.

Despite the inherent inequities and irrationalities of the political and economic institutions in which the land-registration system evolved, however, it was not a foregone conclusion that the system would eventually result in the wholesale hijacking of Jakarta's urban spatial planning system. That this did come to pass was a consequence of two features of Jakarta's political economy in the late New Order. The first was an emergent crisis in the oil sector, which fed the increasing centrality of urban land speculation as a source of state patronage. The second was the appearance at this important juncture of an appropriate model of large-scale land commodification, that of the privately built master-planned new town. This model was Bumi Serpong Damai, or BSD City, the six-thousand-hectare permit for which was issued in 1984 following intense lobbying by a consortium of developers who included some of the most well-connected of New Order oligarchs. Permitting of such a vast tract of land had never occurred before, and as one Jakarta developer who was active during the mid-1980s stated, Bumi Serpong Damai opened a "Pandora's box" of possible massive profits from land speculation for major potential investors. The following sections explore these factors, first discussing the political economic context of the mutation of the *ijin lokasi* system, and then examining BSD City's role both as a prototype for new town development and as a case study in the spatial implications of the development that ensued.

Runaway Speculation: The Land-Permitting System Captured

While the dualism of the land-tenure structure clarifies the mechanism the Suharto-era state used to seize value through large-scale property permitting, it does not explain why this particular outcome came to be. Under different social and political circumstances, the existence of legal but subordinate claims might have led to a very different outcome. Even with bureaucratic obstacles in place, holders of unregistered claims elsewhere (for example in India) often become politically entrenched, placing pressure on buyers to offer something closer to the market price for land. Alternatively, in a more decentralized political system, decisions regarding land permitting might have been made more by local governments, resulting in a local politics of land rather than the centrally mediated, large-scale permitting that came to pass. Instead, however, the massive handout of land that occurred reflected the particular circumstances of late New Order Indonesia: the existence of an authoritarian regime based on patronage that, at the particular juncture of events that occurred in the late 1980s, fixed its sights on periurban land as a central element of its patronage regime.

Three features of New Order Indonesia help to understand the politics behind the regional and national-scale land grab that emerged as so central to the country's urban development. First, political scientists often refer to the New Order regime as an oligarchy, a system marked by the political dominance of a small minority that uses its hegemony as a means to control access to economic opportunity and wealth creation (Robison 1986; Winters 1996; Robison and Hadiz 2004). Winters (2011) has more specifically characterized New Order Indonesia as a "sultanistic oligarchy," marked by the dominance of one individual who maintains a highly centralized system of political control by using the state's economic power to cultivate and maintain a small oligarchic elite. This economic power is exercised, according to Winters (2011, 141), through a "muscular process of taking, skimming, and outright stealing of the country's natural resource wealth and its public treasure."

Early in the New Order era, Suharto built this oligarchic power structure through the use of "[p]olitical patronage and state protection [to provide] privileged access to state bank credit, forestry concessions, trade and manufacturing monopolies, official distributorships of basic foodstuffs, and state contracts for supply and construction" (Robison 1988, 62). In the early postcolonial period, the military, forced to self-finance by a resource-strapped state, maneuvered into positions of dominance in key economic sectors. Individual military leaders accomplished this in large part by forming alliances with business figures, usually of Chinese ethnic origin. A classic example of this is Liem Sioe Liong, also known as Sudono Salim, who as we will see played a prominent role in the story of BSD City's development. A Chinese migrant who started in trade and expanded (initially modestly) into manufacturing, Liem developed a business relationship with Suharto himself when Suharto was a regional commander in the military (Dieleman and Sachs 2008). When Suharto came to power as president, this relationship provided access to key military business partnerships and monopolies in such areas as cement production and flour milling. By the end of Suharto's rule, the business empire that Salim had been able to build through his association with the president had made him, according to many accounts, the wealthiest person in Indonesia (Landler 1999).

In 1973, however, a dramatic increase in oil prices led to a shift in state patronage toward the distribution of oil rents to state enterprises (Robison and Hadiz 2004). During a three-month period in 1973, the price of oil on the global market rose from US$3 to US$12 per barrel (Winters 1996). This oil boom created massive new sources of revenue for the state, enabling it to foster new developmental agendas independent of a reliance on private capital. The state used its newfound autonomy to create "opportunities for officials to replace market forms of regulation with their own patrimonial discretion," thereby strengthening the relationship between state and military functionaries and powerful corporate groups (Winters 1996, 110). During the early to mid-1980s, US$60 billion of state funds, derived largely from oil and other natural resources, was distributed to various private enterprises through state investment and public procurement, an amount "almost four times the total realized domestic private investment during the same period" (Winters 2011, 164). The float of oil revenue also provided the Indonesian state with the autonomy to enact protectionist measures in support of domestic business interests (Winters 1996).

The New Order oligarchy during the period of this study, therefore, was distinctly *not* characterized by a "capture of the state" by corporate interests, as was arguably the case in Thailand in the late 1980s and in the Philippines after the fall of Marcos during this same juncture. Indeed, Robison and Hadiz (2004, 42) have argued to the contrary that this was a system in which "office holders are the main beneficiaries of rent extraction from a disorganized business class." The late New Order state continued to hold key economic cards through its control over licenses for natural resources, its substantial resource-based revenue, and its cultivation of a corporate sector dependent on its regulatory largesse. The result was a fusion of state and corporate interests, embodied in the emergence of a "broad and complex political class of officials and their families, political and business associates, clients and agents who fused political power with bureaucratic authority, public office with private interest" (Robison and Hadiz 2004, 53). Within this system, rent extraction became a primary function of government bureaucracies. Based as it was on favoritism and the extraction of rents from natural resources and the production of basic commodities, the impacts of this system, according to Winters (2011), were extremely regressive, as the rents paid by corporate actors were inevitably passed on to mostly poor consumers of primary goods. He further argues that the suppression of competition stifled the country's economic dynamism.

Early in the New Order the Suharto regime was able to sustain its pre-eminent authority through the same violent suppression of political dissent that led to his ascension to the presidency.[6] As Indonesia's economy and society grew more diverse and complex, however, the continued legitimacy and control of Golkar, the ruling party of the New Order, required the articulation of a broadly defined project of development. The 1970s and 1980s marked the ascendance of a large developmental bureaucracy, supported through investment and technical support from the World Bank and other bilateral and multilateral aid organizations. It also saw the state cultivation of civic and religious groups that were carefully controlled by the state, simultaneous with state repression of independent civil society organizations (Robison and Hadiz 2004).

Many analysts have identified the period of focus of this chapter—the mid-1980s until Suharto's resignation in May of 1998—as a period of unraveling of the New Order regime. Two important factors—both central to the story of land-based rent seeking that is the focus of this chapter—helped to precipitate this decline. The first was the decline in oil prices. From US$38 a barrel in the beginning of 1982, oil fell to US$12 a barrel in 1986, which deprived Golkar of an important mechanism of patronage. This decline lent a greater sense of autonomy to business interests, who became increasingly vocal in their calls for economic reforms to encourage foreign direct investment (Winters 1996). In response, the New Order state undertook a series of reforms for economic liberalization and deregulation aimed at rekindling economic growth and revenue generation on the basis of foreign direct investment. The depreciation of the rupiah relative to the dollar and yen further exacerbated a looming debt crisis. It also led Golkar to scramble to cultivate new state-controlled resources that could be exploited as a source of patronage. As will be detailed later in this chapter, land was to become one of these resources.

A second important factor in the unraveling of the New Order regime was the coming of what Winters (2011) has termed the "family stage" of Suharto's rule with the coming of age of Suharto's children, who sought to maneuver their way to ultra-oligarchic status by exploiting their proximity to the central font of power. Their increasing rapacity (evidenced in the story of the Bukit Jonggol Asri plan) began to undermine the balance within the oligarchic elite and to tarnish the carefully cultivated veneer of state developmentalism that had been central to Suharto's maintenance of power. These factors encouraged opposition to the regime from a number of quarters: from an increasingly restless middle class and indeed from within the business oligarchy itself.

These shifts in the political economy of the Suharto regime help to frame the context of reforms in land acquisition and titling. As land values rose—increases in Jakarta were six- to eight-fold between 1988 and 1992 according to one analysis—land development was an increasingly important source of rents for the state (Akosoro 1994; Arai 2001). At the same time, speculative inflows of investment from international markets opened up opportunities to build large new developments. Simultaneous reforms in the land-permitting system and in the banking sector enabled oligarchs to engage in large-scale land speculation, as property became a mechanism to tap into the massive amounts of equity flowing into Asian markets. In Indonesia prior to 1988, the banking sector had consisted of five government-controlled banks, but in that year deregulation opened the sector to private investment and created a relatively loose licensing system (Fischer 2000). The result was an explosion in the number of banks and bank branches and a rapid influx of equity into Indonesia, with much of this equity going into the real estate market (Winarso and Firman 2002). The immediate aftermath saw many of the families who were part of Suharto's network of oligarchs branch significantly into land development while simultaneously expanding into finance and becoming major financiers of real estate development projects. One result was what Fischer (2000) has referred to as "turpi-financing," in which bankers and developers, sometimes linked closely through kinship or close business ties, engaged in collusive transactions, channeling freely available capital into ever more speculative real estate investments.

As Winarso (2000) has documented extensively, access to *ijin lokasi* for huge tracts of land was highly correlated with access to the highest levels of power within the Suharto government. While several hundred developers received permits, as noted earlier the bulk of permits were held by a small number of large developers. The largest beneficiaries constitute a who's who list of New Order oligarchs, most of whom had not previously been major real estate players. Sudono Salim's Salim Group, the largest conglomerate in the country for much of the 1980s and 1990s, emerged as a key player in periurban land markets during this period, both through its own ventures and through partnerships with Ciputra, a prominent developer. According to Winarso (2000), the Salim Group held permits to about 19,500 hectares of land by 1994, although about half of this was in joint venture projects with other groups. Its Bank Central Asia, the largest bank in the country, was also heavily invested in property projects. Another key actor was Mochtar Riady, whose fortune was based in large part on banking but whose Lippo Group initiated an aggressive move into the property sector in the late 1980s with the initiation of the 5,500-hectare Lippo Cikarang project in 1989 (Arai 2001). By the late 1990s, the Lippo Group had pushed more than ten thousand hectares of projects through the approval process. Other major actors who emerged as players in periurban land markets beginning in the late 1980s were Eka Tiptja Widjaya's Sinarmas Group and the Ning King's Argo Manung-gal Group. Of course one of the later and certainly most aggressive mov-ers was Bambang Trihatmojo's Bimantara Group, with the Bukit Jonggol Asri plan.

The context described in the preceding pages has important implica-tions for how we interpret the spatial development of the JMR. In a sys-tem in which the interests of the state and capital are utterly blurred, and in which the state has such a direct, personal stake in capital accu-mulation, urban planning came to be subordinated to an unusual degree to oligarchic interests in land commodification. A state that is captive to corporate interests may still resist the terms of its captivity, or at least it may attempt to negotiate these terms on behalf of other bases of political power. In a pluralist political system in which corporate interests predomi-nate, state actors may still feel compelled by pressures from the electorate or organizations of civil society to exercise some restraint on corporate actors through regulation and planning. In the case of New Order Indone-sia, where constraints of electoral politics and civil society barely existed and where oligarchs had close and sometimes familial relationships with Suharto himself, regulation and planning were instead deployed to legiti-mize state strategies of urban development and to enable a land rush that resulted from the focus of land policy on appropriating rents.

This political arrangement shaped urban development in two main ways. First, it encouraged a frantic process of urban expansion. From the very beginning of the formulation of new towns, permits were issued for projects that violated the letter and the spirit of government plans and contributed to the metropolitan region's sprawl and fragmentation. Second, the coalescence of state and corporate interests ensured that planning at the scale of neighborhoods and urban districts was driven primarily, if not exclusively, by interests of profit. In an administrative structure where decisions about granting permits were made at the level of the national government, specifically the BPN with input from the very highest levels of the Indonesian state, provincial and town regulators who conducted spatial planning at a local level saw their task as one of enabling corporate actors to realize their objectives. This dynamic is captured in the account of one real estate professional who was involved in developing the master plan for Bumi Serpong Damai. In his telling, the West Java government, responsible for the regulation of the project as it emerged in the mid-1980s, evinced a lack of interest in the details of the project and a marked deference to the developer.

> They essentially said "you tell us what you want to do". You plan it, build it, run it. There was no strong planning authority to which you could look to for direction.

As the story of Bumi Serpong Damai will show, the early stages in the development of new towns as models for the planned expansion of Jakarta were marked by the ascendance of visionary individuals and gestures toward inclusivity and sustainability. Yet the deployment of permitting as a tool for land monetization led to an inexorable shift upmarket as developers sought to maximize profits by building for a narrow sliver of the wealthiest consumers.

The Bumi Serpong Damai Precedent

This section will explore the consequences of the *ijin lokasi* system for the spatial development of the Jakarta Metropolitan Region through an examination of one project, BSD City. BSD was the first project of its scale, and as we shall see it explicitly contravened government plans for the spatial expansion of the metropolis. It therefore encountered some initial resistance from government bureaucracies, and its eventual realization required a substantial investment of time and the articulation of a rationale and planning framework for the project. Early in its development, project planners and designers exhibited some ingenuity in shaping the project both to the regulatory requirements and to the social and environmental context of the site. It was only later that the project would emerge as a stalking horse for more speculative, socially regressive, and environmentally destructive projects such as the Bukit Jonggol Asri plan. And indeed BSD itself came to be drawn by the gravitational lure of the imperatives of profit maximization and speculation. Beginning as it did as a prototype for a different model of master-planned urbanism, BSD therefore represents not a typical but rather an exceptional case of late New Order urban real estate megaproject development. Yet it is an exception that helps illustrate the key argument of this chapter: that the context of oligarchic exploitation of emergent opportunities presented by rent gaps drove Indonesia's planning system in the direction of a massive speculative and socially and ecologically disruptive agenda of wholesale land monetization.

Bumi Serpong Damai, which translates from Bahasa Indonesia as "peaceful world of Serpong," is a six-thousand-hectare urban real estate megaproject in the Serpong subdistrict of the City of South Tangerang in the southwest suburbs some twenty-two kilometers from central Jakarta. The master plan for the project calls for a population of 800,000 and more than 140,000 jobs when fully built, a goal that was to be met by 2015 (Gotsch 2009). To date, however, only the first phase of the project, totaling about 1,300 hectares, is near completion, and the current developer, Sinar Mas Land, estimates the current population to be 160,000 (Gotsch 2009). While it has fallen dramatically short of its stated objectives, this track record nonetheless makes it perhaps the largest and most commercially successful new town in Indonesia.

The story of BSD City's development begins with the figure of Ciputra, a shopkeeper's son of ethnic Chinese origin who trained as an architect and emerged in the 1970s and 1980s as the most visionary and influential individual in the transformation of the Jakarta Metropolitan Region (Leaf 2015). Ciputra's rise to prominence was bankrolled in large part by Sudono Salim, with whom he had first partnered in 1972 and who financed Ciputra's projects as he sought to move into the property sector from the late 1970s on (Sato 1993). Ciputra was eventually able to build an independent business and property empire, and he remains one of the largest developers in Indonesia. More recently, he has expanded internationally, with major new town developments in Hanoi, Phnom Penh, and Kolkata. Ciputra was, more than any other figure, the key agent in the modernization of the Indonesian real estate industry. In 1972 he founded Real Estate Indonesia (REI), which remains the most important developer association in the country, and later became the president of the international real estate organization Federation Internationale des Administrateurs de Biens Conseils et Agents Immobiliers (FIABCI) (Leaf 2013).

As is true of many other iconic and revolutionary urban real estate megaprojects, BSD City has a fantastical origin story.

> According to Ciputra's version of the story, Eka Tjipta Widjaya, who headed the powerful Sinar Mas Group, asked the developer/architect to view some land he was assembling. Accompanying Ciputra and Widjaya was [Sudono] Salim's son, Anthony, who had become involved with suburban real estate development through property acquisition activities for Ciputra in Pondok Indah. On this noon time excursion, Ciputra claimed to have fallen into a deep sleep (allegedly triggered by a solar eclipse) and dreamed of a new city within the Jakarta suburbs but completely self-sufficient. Shortly afterwards, plans for the new city of Bumi Serpong Damai (BSD) were announced, supported by ten corporations but controlled by the three who had made that fateful noon visit. It is notable that the consortium of investors in BSD appointed as its Chief Executive Advisor Sudwikatmono, cousin of President Suharto. (Silver 2007, 169)

What stands out about this story is the way it marries an architectural and urban vision with the realpolitik of urban development in New Order Indonesia. The focus of the tale is cosmically derived inspiration, yet it also brings together three individuals who embody the nexus of state and corporate power upon which the New Order regime rested: Salim, Sudwikatmono, and Widjaya, who built a business empire on the basis of forestry concessions granted to his Asia Pulp and Paper company. The realization of the project would depend heavily on the influence of these three individuals.

While the subsequent explosion of new town proposals has made such projects appear to be the norm, at the time of its formulation the proposal for Bumi Serpong Damai represented a significant departure from planning practice. The Jabotabek Metropolitan Development Plan (JMDP) of 1981 had deployed environmental criteria to identify priority areas for future urban development in Jabotabek (Douglass 1989; Hasan 2003). This plan proscribed development in low-lying coastal areas, flood-prone and agriculturally intensive zones, and steep-slope and upland forest areas, and it focused development attention on a band of land stretching east and west of Jakarta that was at a suitable elevation and slope. It specifically recommended Tangerang City, immediately west of Jakarta along major transport lines and close to a new international airport that was soon to open, as a focus for westward expansion of industrialization and the development of new residential areas. This development was to be encouraged through an approach of "Guided Land Development" that involved state provision of low-cost serviced land to private developers. Yet both the JMDP and the West Jakarta Urban Development Project (WJUDP), undertaken in 1985, specifically proscribed the development of a large-scale new town in the Serpong subdistrict. As Douglass (1989) notes, while Serpong was within the area slated for urbanization in the JMDP, the WJUDP argued that its potential was as a dormitory suburb. Responding to the plans for BSD the report "went as far as to declare that new town or satellite city development [in Serpong] was not to be pursued because it would divert investments away from the five targeted urban centers" identified elsewhere in the plan (Douglass 1989, 226). The continuation of the Bumi Serpong Damai plan hence represented a "sweeping challenge to all of the *Jabotabek* plans" (Douglass 1989, 227).

The challenge was successful. The Metropolitan Group, representing the ten consortium partners, employed Pacific Consultants International, a Japanese firm, to conduct a prestudy for the project (P. T. Bumi Serpong Damai 1985). The publication of this plan, issued in 1985 around the time of the publication of the WJUDP, goes to some length to rationalize the development of the project within the existing framework of plans for the metropolitan area. It also documents the existence of some fifty-five thousand residents of the site to be developed. The plan calls for a four-phase process of plan development, proceeding from infrastructure development to the development of CBD functions as a means to create an economic center in the region, to residential development and the push toward a "maturity phase" beginning in 2006. The process of lobbying for the location permit for the proposed project unfolded over two years and involved negotiations between project backers and high-level representatives of the Ministries of Public Works, Human Settlements, and Planning (BAPPENAS) (Hasan 2003). During this period, environmental impact studies were carried out. In addition, according to Winarso (2000, 113), the structure plans for Kabupaten Tangerang were prepared by a group of consultants owned by Ciputra, and not surprisingly they allowed for the possibility of a new town development in the Serpong area. These plans were later approved by BAPPENAS.

Even as it violated specific government plans and regulations, the Bumi Serpong Damai scheme undoubtedly gained some traction from the plans put forth by the consortium. These called for a comprehensively planned, self-contained settlement that fit broadly within stated government goals of ecologically sensitive and socially sustainable urban development. The plans also drew on the prestige of well-known international consultants to lend credibility to the project. In addition to the Pacific Consultants plan, a more detailed plan for the project was developed in the mid-1990s by a team of internationally renowned architects, including Doxiadis and Associates and John Portman and Associates (Doxiadis et al. 1995).

The BSD project area spreads over six thousand hectares lying south of the Jakarta-Merak toll road, the major artery connecting Jakarta to the periurban areas to its west. The plot is roughly bisected by the north-flowing Cisadane River, which played a strong role in site selection as an amenity as well as a source of fresh water and for drainage. The master plan calls for development to proceed in three phases, which were originally planned to be completed in 2005. The first phase, on approximately 1,500 hectares of land to the east of the river, has largely been completed. Several elements of phase two, an area of 2,000 hectares in the central portion of the site that straddles the river, have commenced, while the remaining 2,500 hectares constituting phase three remain largely untouched by development.

The process of building the project has been largely dictated by the capacity of the developers to acquire land. Approximately a thousand hectares of the site was government-owned plantation land, and this was the first land acquired.[7] Early in the development of the project, before the early successes of the scheme sent land prices skyrocketing, planners of the project recall open-air meetings with locals to discuss land prices extending late into the evenings, and transactions in stacks of rupiah notes conducted under the shade of village trees.[8] Today, Sinar Mas Land continues to operate an active land-acquisition office, but in the postauthoritarian context further land acquisition has progressed more gradually. In interviews for this research, representatives of BSD City Ltd. stated that five thousand hectares of the original six thousand has been purchased, a much higher rate than most other new town developments. Nevertheless, of the remaining thousand hectares, substantial portions lie in heavily populated areas that are likely never to be acquired, and much of the remaining land is scattered in small parcels across the site, which creates obstacles to the consolidation of large parcels.[9]

As land values have risen and local residents have become more aware of the potential value of their land, and as Indonesia's political climate has changed, the company has deployed both carrots and sticks, launching a "corporate social responsibility" agenda as a public relations tool while also sticking hard in bargaining to their established prices for land. But the company has also been criticized for deploying the widely used strategy of walling off recalcitrant *kampungs* as a way to insulate them from the benefits of the project and presumably to persuade them to sell rather than endure the hardships that walling imposes (figure 3.3). Walled-in

Figure 3.3. Walled-in *kampung*, BSD City. Walling in *kampung* settlements on permitted land is a common strategy of real estate developers who seek to isolate settlements from the benefits of new town development and to strengthen their incentives to sell. Source: Author

kampungs face deteriorating environmental conditions and increased difficulty of accessing and leaving the village (Winarti 2007). This effort has become an increasingly high-stakes game as land values have continued to rise. One indication of this rise in value was the sale in 2013 of a plot reported to be between seventy-five and ninety-five hectares to Hong Kong Land for US$208 million (Jakarta Globe 2013).

In developing a planning and design concept for BSD City, Ciputra tasked the architects and planners with conducting a broad global survey of new town typologies. Project personnel took government officials on a whirlwind international tour of Japan, Finland, England, France, and the United States to establish a broad typology and to identify models that might be suitable to the context of Serpong.[10] The model that largely prevailed in the discussions that followed was Irvine Ranch, the master-planned suburban area spreading south of Los Angeles, which had been initiated in the 1960s.

While the influence of Irvine Ranch is apparent on paper, parts of the first phase of the development have come to evolve into their own distinctive model of urbanism. This first phase is laid out along a major artery, Jalan Pahlawan Seribu, that cuts south from the Jakarta-Merak toll road and forms the commercial and office core of this part of Bumi Serpong Damai. The plan for the town is organized into seventeen sectors to the east and west of this artery, each of which contains eighty neighborhoods. Each neighborhood is secluded from large roads and commercial centers in residential enclaves that are laid out along cul-de-sacs and quiet one-lane streets. The phase also includes Taman (Garden) Tekno, a two-hundred-hectare technology park with almost six hundred hectares allotted to a central business district and a number of amenities and services including a golf course, university, and hospital (Hasan 2003).

While this layout is broadly consistent with a Southern California model, the early portions of the development depart from this model in the typology of housing units and commercial structures. Commercial structures along Jalan Pahlawan Seribu, which are a mix of low-end malls and shophouses, contrast starkly with the opulent malls anchored by Japanese department store chains and dominated by global brands that characterize most later new town developments and more recently the superblock developments that have begun to reshape the geography of

Jakarta proper. Today, the main artery itself buzzes with a mix of cars, buses, minibuses, and motorcycles that is typical of much of the metropolitan area. Indeed, its character, while more ordered and more fully developed, is not substantially different in mixes of transport and land use from other periurban parts of Jakarta.

Housing typologies at this stage also adhered much more closely than later new town projects to the government's 6:3:1 policy, discussed earlier, which dictated a predominance of smaller housing units. This regulation shifted over the years and was unevenly implemented (Silver 2007). According to at least one member of the planning team for BSD City, the 6:3:1 formula was viewed more as a "gentleman's agreement" than as a legally binding regulation.[11] It was nonetheless taken more seriously in the implementation of BSD City than in later urban real estate megaproject developments, as is seen by the presence of dense, moderate-income settlements that characterize some early portions of the project (figure 3.4). This was a consequence of a variety of factors: the realities of the Indonesian real estate market at this early stage in its development, the greater

Figure 3.4. Residential street, BSD City phase one. Early phases of Bumi Serpong Damai contained a mix of housing and business types, including smaller houses and shops catering to moderate-income families. Source: Author

government oversight of the project, and the influence of key BSD City planning personnel. Jo Santoso, lead planner of the project in its early years, focused significant attention on developing settlements of predominantly smaller and medium-sized households. His neighborhood designs included facilities such as wet markets and bus and minibus depots, features entirely absent in the later development of the town.[12] According to Hasan (2003), of the housing units completed by 1998, 64.6 percent were of the smallest typology, mostly 21-square-meter rowhouses packed tightly onto 60-square-meter lots set along narrow roads, and a further 27.1 percent were between 22 and 70 square meters. Only 8.3 percent were larger suburban homes sprawling over lots of 250 square meters or more, that more closely resemble the densities and building massing of a Southern California suburb.

These notable efforts were not enough, however, to ensure that the units would remain affordable. Winarso (2000) finds that the smallest 21-square-meter units, which initially sold in 1990 for about US$2,000, rose in price between four- and seven-fold by 1996, so that even these most modestly priced houses were soon too expensive for most of Jakarta's residents. In one analysis of data on demographics of BSD residents, Hasan (2003) found that middle- and upper-income earners dominated buyers of properties in the development. More remarkably, the study cites data indicating that only 22 percent of residents are Muslim, with high concentrations of Christians and Buddhists (57 and 17 percent respectively). This in part seems to indicate a highly disproportionate concentration of ethnic Chinese Indonesians among the buyers of property in the city.

Later in the development of phase one, and more markedly as the project has expanded westward with phase two of the project, Sinarmas Land (which bought out other partners in the development in the aftermath of the Asian financial crisis) has given in to what one former planner involved in the project described as the "irresistible urge to go up-market."[13] The physical character of phase two consequently contrasts dramatically with that of phase one. The gateway development of this second phase is Green Office Park, a high-end office complex that includes the Sinarmas Land marketing office and that has won several awards for environmentally sustainable architecture and urban design. Its commercial component, the Breeze, is a 13.5-hectare open-air "lifestyle mall" that features high-end dining and an eclectic mix of shops and services set in a context

Figure 3.5. The Green, phase 2, BSD City. This elite gated residential subdivision is an example of the high-end residential enclaves that predominate in Bumi Serpong Damai's later developments. Source: Author

of low-rise modernist buildings and plazas featuring fountains and public art. Residential districts in phase two consist largely of gated and secluded subdivisions containing villas and mansions set on expansive lots, marked by meticulously maintained landscaping. These projects are themed and marketed as "lifestyle" communities that emphasize the exclusivity of the developments and their remoteness from the worries of urban life. These include Greenwich Park, a "quality vacation resort" development; the Eminent, fashioned as a modern style of life that is "like the big cities in the world"; and de Park, which fashions itself an "aristocratic estate" (BSD City 2015). The advertisements for these developments emphasize their amenities: jogging tracks, nature trails, swimming pools, and access to nearby golf courses.

This shift is consistent with the broader trend in the development of new towns in Indonesia. Perhaps most notable in this regard is Lippo Karawaci, developed by the Lippo Group, one of the most prominent new town developers in Indonesia. Lippo has taken the branding of its developments a step beyond that of BSD City, using playful names and building styles, such as Taman (Garden) Britania for British style, Taman

Pattaya for Thai style, and Taman Osaka for Japanese style to showcase the "international" and "prestige" orientation of their development. This upmarket strategy is reflected in the demographics of their residents. In a survey in eight Lippo Karawaci communities, Leisch (2002) found that four contained less than 11 percent Muslims and the highest proportion of Muslims in any of the communities was 34 percent.

In sum, despite its status as a "showcase" development that was intended to introduce a new model of integrated urban development to Indonesia, BSD City has, despite the good intentions of some of its planners, reproduced many of Jakarta's social and spatial ills and has exacerbated its ongoing regional ecological crisis. While agendas of regional economic development and inclusive urbanism influenced its early stages, it is not surprising that principles of "highest and best use" would, in the absence of sustained bureaucratic interest in the maintenance of broader social goals, persuade the developer to largely abandon these principles. The socioeconomic mix of BSD City has come to reinforce social inequality, as access to property has largely remained the purview of a relatively wealthy minority and local *kampungs* are relegated to a state of insecurity and infrastructural subordination. The contrast between phases one and two, moreover, reflects a broader trend in the JMR toward the enclavization of the wealthy, as developers pursue a strategy of maximizing property values through the production and marketing of exclusive urban environments.

BSD City's more enduring legacy, however, is in the extent to which the state's planning agenda came to be framed around the opportunities for profit for large corporate developers. The continued existence of the late New Order permits has ensured that this dynamic has continued to date, albeit under quite different political conditions. The nature of this shift is evident in the comments of one real estate professional who has worked for a number of developers in both the pre- and post-Suharto eras. Over coffee at one of Jakarta's upscale shopping malls, he bemoaned the crassness of local governments, newly empowered in the era of decentralized democracy, who were mostly interested in the rewards of petty corruption and in cultivating vote banks. He looked back wistfully on the Suharto era, when the provincial and national public officials he dealt with were more competent and were interested in big planning ideas. Under Suharto, he said, developers could engage the state in conceiving of larger urban and regional models for Jakarta's transformation.

His nostalgia was layered in ironies. The schemes that his Suharto-era employer had launched were rooted firmly in speculation and large-scale commodification of space at a regional level, and their very logic was inimical to stated regulatory and planning goals. Yet the corporate head in whose employ he sought out planning and policy officials had access to a far higher level of the state than the officials he was dealing with. Both in fact functioned largely as proxies for much higher authorities. It was not that the corporate head who employed him was above the law, or even that he controlled the state; rather, he was a product of the law and of the state itself. The meeting of minds of developer and state representative was a logical extension of the political economy of oligarchy. The developer must deal with a more diffuse arrangement of political power today. Yet the legacies of that era—the concentration of economic power and the monopoly on development rights provided by development permits—mean that this shared state and developer interest in perpetuating a fragmented and segregated model of development continue to define the metropolitan region. Bureaucrats and local officials today certainly enjoy more leverage and autonomy, and the oligarchy has diminished in importance, but an unusual degree of concentration of corporate power over urban space remains.

The spatial forms that large developers have pursued have changed since the end of the Suharto era, but the confluence of incentives presented by the land-permitting system and the cultural preferences of Jakarta's elite continue to shape developer preferences for large, enclave developments. During the 1990s the metropolitan region saw a shift away from emphasis on the peripheral new towns, many of which experienced a housing glut. A study conducted in 2010 found that most of the new towns proposed between 1985 and 1995 had seen modest to no progress, and in ten of these projects developers were still sitting on land banks in excess of a thousand hectares (Herlambang 2013). While the new towns have continued to experience fits and starts of development in the new millennium, developers have also turned to the model of the superblock: hyper-dense, mixed-use complexes built in pockets of developed urban areas. These projects, which are in many respects a response to the intense traffic congestion imposed by Jakarta's sprawled pattern of development, continue to be developed through the mechanisms of the development permit. A representative example is St. Moritz Puri Indah, a twelve-hectare development containing seventeen high-rise buildings in-cluding a shopping mall, high-rise luxury apartment buildings, and office towers, including one sixty-five-story structure (Lippo Group 2015). Con-sistent with other superblock developments, the project was built by one of a handful of large developers who had previously focused on new town development. With a floor-to-area ratio greater than eight, the project is to contain a million square feet of built floor space. A study conducted in 2009 argued that many such superblocks exceeded the density regulations of Jakarta's spatial plans and threatened to exacerbate problems of traffic, land subsidence, and infrastructural overload (Winarti 2009).

The extent to which state actors have hitched the development agenda of the JMR to the interests of large developers is evident in recent plan-ning initiatives. One significant example is the National Capital Integrated Coastal Development Plan (NCICD), a major planning initiative to ad-dress the chronic flooding that Jakarta is already experiencing (Ministry for Economic Affairs 2014). The plan focuses on the development of a sea wall to protect against sea level rise and storm surge, even though analy-ses have shown that the drivers of increased flooding are varied and are primarily unrelated to the threat from the sea. Rather, they have more to do with the fragmented nature of the land development and infrastructure delivery. Significant causes include land subsidence due to urbanization and groundwater extraction that can reach several centimeters a year in parts of the city, intensified rainfall due to climate change, and increase in impervious surface and loss of vegetation due to the sprawled pattern of urbanization (Marfai, Sekaranom, and Ward 2015). The NCICD plan, however, chooses to focus on a real-estate-driven approach to resolving the flooding issue that largely ignores these causes. The proposal calls for the construction of a massive sea wall along Jakarta's coastline, to be financed in large part through the leasing of land created along this sea wall to a consortium of developers. The reclaimed land is to be symboli-cally shaped in the powerful form of the Garuda, the mythical bird of the Hindu religion, and is to accommodate new urban settlements accommo-dating 1.5 million people. It is unclear from the scheme where the market for this development will come from in a metropolitan region where de-velopers continue to sit on massive land banks that are already connected via infrastructure.

The corporate focus of urban policy is also evident in the area of af-fordable housing. In 2006 the government of Indonesia launched the one thousand towers initiative, a heavily subsidized program that was intended to shift urban dwellers from "slum-like" conditions to modern high-rise apartments. Yet in Kusno's (2012a, 47) analysis, this program functioned as "a vehicle for private developers to acquire the remaining 'unused' or informally registered state land in the city." Prominent participants in the program included holders of the largest land banks, developers like Bakrieland, Modernland, and Agung Podomoro. What began as a major affordable housing initiative morphed into an opportunity for large developers to form partnerships with government agencies to develop what often ended up being middle- and upper-income housing on scarce central city land.

Conclusion

New Order Jakarta stands as a remarkable case of state success in land monetization, albeit one with consequences of social inequality and ecological degradation. The Suharto regime was able to harness the explosion of real estate development during from the mid-1980s to the late 1990s to help reinforce the crumbling foundation of its oligarchic rule. The regulatory subordination of existing usership rights to the real estate market through the exploitation of the dualist nature of land tenure relations allowed the state to overcome potential sources of opposition to its agenda of corporate land acquisition. The state was further able to frame the real estate push in terms of developmentalism and modernization as a means to silence opposition. To the extent that state and corporate actors refrained from using excessive violence in evicting existing residents, it was arguably because legal and regulatory mechanisms and the pervasive threat of violence and systematic dismemberment of organized opposition often rendered actual violence unnecessary. Indeed, the only major obstacle that corporate and state actors experienced in their agenda of land monetization was from the market itself. In the absence of market constraints on land, and with the existence of perverse incentives to engage in collusive transactions, the stage was set for the real estate market collapse of 1998 and the resulting financial crisis.

What does this analysis of the Jakarta case tell us about processes of neoliberalization? The account in this chapter highlights the ways that introducing market mechanisms to the production of urban form often plays out not as an arm's-length state effort drawn from an abstract neo-liberal playbook. Rather, it emerges in some contexts as a deliberate production of certain types of markets, and market constraints, that suit key interest groups. Here the creation of a system granting monopsony rights to key state allies helped form the distributional and spatial outcomes of the reforms. The account here also highlights manifestations of what I referred to in the introduction as land monetization both as a strategy of accumulation and, for some state actors, as a tactic of rent seeking.

There are parallels to other authoritarian states in Asia and elsewhere. The case of Cambodia, discussed briefly in chapter 1, is one notable example. Interestingly, the Cambodian People's Party has, like the New Order state, harked back to colonial-era mechanisms of urban expansion to realize its ambitions for land monetization. Specifically, it has used its exclusive rights to allow the reclamation of land as a means to distribute land-based patronage. Similarly, as Myanmar has opened to investment and trade with political liberalization, Yangon's property market has become increasingly speculative, with state-owned land emerging as focal points for real estate investment and with the country's military rulers emerging as central players in this process of land commodification. As the Jakarta case illustrates, the spatial implications of these moments are potentially dramatic and far-reaching. The question of how states seek to seize control of land markets—the regulatory and planning tools they use—is therefore significant both to the urban future and to the political future of these metropolitan regions.

4

EXPERIMENTS IN POWER

Urban Politics in Postliberalization Kolkata

India's frenetic and contested urban landscape seems to present itself to urban theorists as a Rorschach test. Scholars have produced myriad and often conflicting theories, often reflecting their own theoretical proclivities as much as the data themselves, to explain the dynamics at play in shaping urban form. For some, the persistence of extralegal and "unplanned" claims to urban space—for shelter, trading, religious observance, small manufacture, and myriad other uses—reflects the tenacity of culturally rooted spatial sensibilities, of an organic and improvised form of urbanism, in the face of abstract logics of the plan and the market (Benjamin 2008; Schindler 2014). Solomon Benjamin's (2008, 719) concept of "occupancy urbanism" is perhaps the definitive framing of this strand of thought. He argues that efforts to plan Indian cities are serially undermined by rights of occupancy born of "vote bank" politics and "multiple de-facto tenures deeply embedded in lower bureaucracy." Marxist political economists, on the other hand, frame India as yet another variant of what Harvey (2003) has termed accumulation by dispossession, in which policy and planning are successfully used as tools to systematically dispossess the poor and pursue capital accumulation. Levien (2012, 2013a), for example, has drawn attention to the massive push for land acquisition and eviction accompanying the explosion of export processing zones (EPZs) in the late 1990s and early 2000s. Yet others point to cases of "win-win" scenarios, in which accumulation-driven urban development seems to have led not to marginalization but to benefits for poor communities and farmers at the periurban fringe (Balakrishnan 2013; Sami 2013; Peterson 2013). Sami (2013) cites as one notable example in the case of Magarpatta, discussed at the beginning of chapter 2, where farmers near Pune pooled their land and formed a corporation to develop a new town, the profits from which have benefited them as shareholders.

How do we make sense of these diffuse representations of India's urbanization and the empirical evidence deployed to support them? It may be tempting to debate whether one of the above perspectives is somehow more representative of broader trends in India's urbanization, but this chapter will argue that such a debate is fruitless. The analysis that follows is framed around a different question: What do these very different perspectives, and the cases mobilized to support them, tell us about the contests for power that are shaping processes of urban development, land monetization, and displacement in India's process of economic and political transition? The postliberalization era, initiated in earnest in 1991, has introduced new economies, new interests, and new actors (as well as established actors who are newly empowered) to the urban stage. The potential for profit from urban land-based accumulation and the potential for attracting investment through the creation of new urban spaces have encouraged new formations of collective action of economic and political elites that span levels of governance. These collectivities confront a context where political power is deeply diffused through electoral mechanisms and where land ownership is highly fragmented. The questions of interest in the Indian case are: How are these emergent political coalitions of real estate developers, corporate heads, middle-class associations, land sharks, and local politicians strategizing their push to seize control of urban space? How are communities facing displacement responding, and what sources of political influence are they able to draw on? And how are the political and institutional contexts of urban places shaping the outcomes of these engagements?

Hence the India case represents a different set of insights into the dynamics of neoliberalization than the case of Jakarta discussed in the previous chapter. The Jakarta case highlights the dynamics of urban spatial development under a national state that successfully shaped markets to channel opportunities for land commodification to allied business interests. In India, while national and state-level government actors have made moves in the direction of playing a stronger role, much of the action in spatial change and land monetization has taken the form of discrete and strategic acts of collective action by both state and nonstate local actors.

The chapter will further argue that the fragmented and contested nature of the neoliberalization of urban politics in India is in part due to an ambiguity in the country's political, legal, and institutional structures of governance. This ambiguity lends urban political struggles their notably open-ended and indeterminate character and has allowed for divergent outcomes. Indeed, the postindependence Indian state has yet to put forth a coherent model of urban politics. This is not to say that there are no urban politics in India; political economists have long argued that cities represent spatial accretions of interests that inherently form through political conflict and contestation. The argument is instead that the systematic lack of institutional spaces for the adjudication of urban claims, a phenomenon rooted in an antiurban and antilocalist tendency in India's postindependence legal and political institutions, has left the issue of urban spatial relations to be defined less through the guidance of policy and planning and more through collective action and ad hoc assertions of power. It has also left Indian cities largely lacking in political forums for the formation of strong coalitions able to shape and implement a shared vision of urban development at the metropolitan or regional scale.

Liberalization has brought two forces to bear on this context of urban political ambiguity. First, the opportunities opened up by new economic sectors and the explosion of property markets have restructured the basis of political power in cities, shifting power from those with connections to the state-run economy to those with links to global economic and financial interests. A new generation of titans of industry, real estate players, and an emergent "middle class" have emerged as centers of political influence (Fernandes 2004). Second, liberalization has placed cities and their hinterlands at the spatial center of a new geography of power. The perception of urban dysfunction among powerful state and corporate actors has given rise to aspirations and anxieties about the need for a transformation of the aesthetic and functional order of urban spaces and about the potential profits to be realized from such a transformation (Ghertner 2011a). The result has been mobilizations of collective action and public policy aimed, on the one hand, at forging power and profit out of political ambiguity and, on the other, at formulating an institutional structure that will decrease this ambiguity and give policy makers and planners greater control over processes of urban spatial change and land monetization. These power plays range from efforts to seize control of particular pieces of land, to political reforms to decrease the political power of the poor, to broad-ranging effort to formulate a new model of urban politics at the national level.

These varied mobilizations are the "experiments in power" referred to in the title of this chapter. They occur across levels of government, among elite interest groups, and in some cases among urban residents and (as in the case of Magarpatta City) in communities of farmers. Each experiment seeks to gain control of the spatial development of cities in the service of the economic and social aims of the actors involved, and each involves efforts to gain control of land in order to appropriate land values and shape development trajectories. These experiments vary widely and test very different "theories" of political economy. Are land-value increments better wrested from existing claimants to land through coercion or cooptation? Can the political empowerment of elites through the formation of new civic organizations break the power of "vote bank" politics? Can state rhetoric of globalization-driven development diffuse political opposition to dispossession? Is overwhelming violence effective in overcoming the will to resist displacement? Collectively, these experiments in power are gradually reshaping the political landscape of cities as the urban question becomes a basis for political cleavages.

As the analogy of "experiments" in power implies, these questions are subject to intense debate within the state and between the state and other actors in urban politics. Each of these mobilizations therefore has the potential to reshape the state itself by empowering some claims to urban space while disempowering others. There is ample evidence for the direct political impact of contestations over land. The 2006 effort by the government of West Bengal to take agricultural land from small farmers at Singur for an auto manufacturing plant and township played a major role in the fall of the ruling Communist Party of India-Marxist (CPI-M), which had ruled the state for more than thirty years. More recently, the election in 2014 of Narendra Modi as prime minister, seen by many as a transformative national leader, was based in large part on his promise to enable investment by, among other means, revolutionizing the process of land acquisition for urban development.

The examination in the pages that follow will reveal that while the precise direction of change wrought by urban development reforms is as yet undetermined, the tendency of many of the "experiments in power" that have gained traction among powerful political and economic actors is toward the tightening of state control over land through the destabilization or extralegal claims to space, and toward the creation of new political institutions that reorient the (national, state, and local) state toward the interests of capital. As the Indian land rush unfolds in stages, the predominant trends in both elite discourse and political reform are in the direction of enabling large-scale transfers of land to state and corporate actors and of stripping those communities who stand in the way of land commodification of their legal claims and political legitimacy. In India's context of pluralist democracy, while such moves are bound to be deeply polarizing, these trends point toward the possibility of protracted conflict and political division. The analysis that follows will attempt to unpack the context for the varied approaches to urban land management that are being proposed and to interpret why communities of the urban poor appear increasingly under threat.

The chapter will begin by exploring the historical forces that continue to shape the politics of land and urban development in India. It will then examine debates about the nature of political power in contemporary Indian cities before analyzing the illustrative case of Kolkata. Finally, it will examine a case study of Calcutta Riverside, an urban real estate megaproject that is currently being built in Kolkata, to understand how contestations over claims to urban space play out on the ground in this particular instance.

The Historical Roots of India's Ambiguous Urban Politics

Partha Chatterjee's influential 2004 book *The Politics of the Governed* argues a perspective on political theory that has had a significant influence on urban studies, particularly in India. Chatterjee argues that the universal norms of national citizenship that are taken as a central tenet of capitalist modernity in much political theory in fact have only a tenuous hold on everyday politics in India and much of the rest of the postcolonial world. Arguing from Indian examples but generalizing to other parts of the world, Chatterjee argues that norms rooted in ingrained forms of identity other than national citizenship—of family, religion, community, caste—continue to shape political identities despite the efforts of the postcolonial state to impose universal citizenship norms. This culturally ingrained identity politics constrains the reach of state planning and the formal economy and weakens adherence to norms of the law, of formal institutions, and of civil society. Chatterjee argues for a distinction between civil society and what he terms "political society," a space of state negotiation with population groups over their specific claims, often claims outside the law or formal citizenship rights. In the context of cities more specifically, Chatterjee argues that the proliferation of illegal claims to space and services that burgeoned in India during the 1970s and 1980s have led to the seemingly paradoxical integration of these illegalities into the fabric of public policy. Urban reality is defined less by state regulation and distinctions between public and private space and more by the "messy business of striking deals between municipal authorities, the police, property developers, criminal gangs, slum dwellers, and pavement hawkers" (Chatterjee 2004, 142).

Chatterjee's argument has been subject to extensive critique and debate, yet it has emerged as a fundamental reference point for scholars studying Indian cities, from studies of slum dwellers to street hawkers to small manufacturers (see for example Anjaria 2009; Arabindoo 2011; Bandyopadhyay 2011). The central thrust of urban scholarship on India has been to explore the implications of fragmented postcolonial sovereignty for questions of urban space. The theme of contestation in property rights and deeply contested governance is evident in the titles of studies in this genre, which have examined "why India cannot plan its cities" (Ananya Roy 2009), the perseverance of the "durable slum" (Weinstein 2014), and the previously mentioned "occupancy urbanism" (Benjamin 2008). Studies have also drawn attention to the ways that the subversion of property relations and state regulation has become endemic across class lines, as the wealthy are in some cases more likely to transgress the law than are the poor (Ghertner 2011b). Indeed, one influential critique of Chatterjee's framing of "political society" argues that the concept does not capture the contradictory position in which the poor find themselves as they struggle alternately to break the law as a means to create livelihoods and to call on its protection as they defend their claims to urban space in the face of elite transgressions of the law, which are protected by dynamics of class and economic privilege (Baviskar and Sundar 2008).

I will focus on a different critique of Chatterjee's framework here. This is that his explanation for the importance of political society does not allow that its centrality in India might be a consequence as much of the historically contingent nature of India's political institutions as it is of an inherent postcolonial condition. Indeed, throughout the literature on Indian cities, there has been relatively little attention paid to the institutional, political, and legal factors that make India, if not unique, then at least particularly skewed toward a more fragmented form of urban governance. The argument of this chapter is that these factors deserve some attention, as they are precisely the focus of the experiments in urban politics and the re-engineering of urban space that this chapter argues are the crux of current political contestation.

The fragmentation of India's urban politics can arguably be traced back to two contradictory and paradoxical aspects of the country's postcolonial framework of urban governance. The first is a tendency toward antiurbanism and antilocalism that was written into the country's governance framework, which has resulted in an urban governance system that is consciously designed to avoid the formation of a coherent politics at the metropolitan level. India's postcolonial political system reflected the viewpoint of the framers of the constitution that only higher levels of government, and particularly the national government, were suited to the role of guardians of the nation's development. Local decisions, in this view, were inherently tainted by nepotism and bigotry on the basis of class and caste. As Ren and Weinstein (2013, 116) note:

> Although Gandhi famously asserted that India "lives in her villages," most of the English-educated delegates to the Constitutional Assembly, including the first Prime Minister Jawaharlal Nehru, perceived India's villages to be backward, archaic, and inherently corrupt. They believed that local elites (in both villages and cities) organized power on the basis of communal sentiments, rather than on enlightened democratic principles. The less local the political system, the more democratic they believed it would be.

This antilocalism is inscribed in deliberate institutional ambiguity with respect to metropolitan governance that marks the country's political framework. The constitution adopted in 1949 made no mention of city or village governance and left most responsibilities for infrastructure, housing, land-use planning, economic development, and other aspects of urban governance in the hands of state governments. State governments in turn hewed to federal guidelines and five-year plans that set the agenda of physical planning and economic, urban, and infrastructure development (Weinstein 2014). In most Indian cities, even in the aftermath of the 1992 passage of the 74th Amendment formally mandating more power to local governments, mayors continue to enjoy little formal authority, as state governments jealously guard their powers with respect to urban management (Chatterji 2013). The most powerful executives in most cities are municipal commissioners, who are generally Indian Administrative Service (IAS) officers appointed by state governments. In a measure intended to reduce corruption by avoiding the development of close social connections between municipal commissioners and local elites, these figures are usually appointed for a fixed term.

The second central tendency shaping urban politics is the strongly statist agenda of development planning that has shaped the urban planning system. The National Planning Commission had in 1938 argued that India's postcolonial modernization should be strongly based on a technocratic, state-driven approach. Planning, it stated, "may be defined as the technical co-ordination by disinterested experts" of social and economic objectives (cited in Prakash 1999, 198). This technocratic approach was pursued through a number of mechanisms. As with other postcolonial societies that adopted socialist principles, urban agendas were written into national five-year plans. The national state also pursued its objectives through the establishment of a strong regulatory agenda focused on forwarding state goals of modernization and social equity (Weinstein, Sami, and Shatkin 2014). These included, importantly, regulations controlling rents and preventing large-scale urban land ownership. Technocratic ideals were also pursued through state sponsorship of key institutions such as the Institute of Town Planners and the School for Planning and Architecture in Delhi, and through high-profile projects like the modernist planned towns of Chandigarh and Bhubaneshwar, which were intended to model a new form of architecture and urbanism for India (Prakash 2002; Vidyarthi 2015).

The technocratic approach and modernist agenda that took hold in planning throughout much of the world during the middle portion of the twentieth century engendered social pushback everywhere, but in India it was also implemented in a context of a more-than-usual hollowness of political institutions. Within the antilocalist framework described above, there simply has been no administratively empowered authority with a direct interest in urban development to craft political coalitions around a shared urban agenda. Electoral mandates link the primary actors in urban development, the states, most closely to rural constituencies. The most powerful political actors acting at the municipal level, municipal commissioners, are beholden to state governments for their positions and are deliberately insulated from networks that might emerge as a constituency for elite or popular collective action around a municipal reform agenda. Hence, while the state developmentalist agenda clarifies the interests to be prioritized in development, the governance agenda provides no political space in which the diverse interests impacted by this agenda can define shared interests and hash out the terms of policy and planning. Hence, as Weinstein, Sami, and Shatkin (2014, 43) argue, while there are "multiple governing layers and administrative webs that touch the Indian city—including the central, regional state, and municipal governments, as well as the myriad special purpose bodies, para-statal agencies, and development authorities—the Indian city remains undergoverned even as it is subjected to extensive (albeit ineffectual) planning and regulation."

It was during the period of the 1970s and 1980s, which Chatterjee specifies as marking the rise of political society and Appadurai (2000) talks of the emergence of a "malignant city" of poverty, slums, and overwhelmed infrastructure systems, that the contradictions between the ambiguity of urban governance and the state-centered urban development agenda became a central issue in India's economic crisis. India's urban population doubled between 1970 and 1990 to 222 million, according to United Nations statistics (United Nations 2014). Combined with a slowing of economic growth, this population growth put growing pressures on infrastructure and housing development systems. Yet this growing urban crisis failed to elicit a coherent response either from government or from capital. The strong hand of the regulatory state continued to constrain the ability of capital to reorganize urban space. At the same time, the hollowness of urban governance institutions inhibited the ability of local state actors to seize control of an urban development agenda or to organize capital or galvanize national or state-level government to pursue shared urban development aims. This period saw two significant trends in urban governance. The first was the increasing centrality of ward-level politics to urban governance. As the ward was the primary space of interaction between the populace and the state, it was here that many of the specific questions of urban development and access to state resources were decided or were translated into struggles for influence over the state. The second was the growing importance of development authorities like the Delhi Development Authority (DDA) and the Calcutta (later Kolkata) Metropolitan Development Authority (CMDA or KMDA). Development authorities emerged as central agents in urban planning and development in the 1970s and were empowered to acquire land and develop urban settlements in an effort to reassert the role of planning in shaping urban spaces.

Hence, while the state did undertake extensive efforts at urban planning and land management in the preliberalization period, these efforts were guided by a fragmented set of bureaucratic and political interests. Specifically, in the preliberalization era urban planning and development occurred through four main modes of operation. As will be argued in greater detail in the next section, these modes of state action in the urban arena tended to create obstacles to the realization of elite interests in urban economic development and the commodification of land. Each has therefore been subject to reform efforts seeking to reassert state and corporate power over urban space by superimposing market criteria in ways that had not previously existed.

The first preliberalization mode of urban planning and development was through modernist master planning. This was manifest most visibly in the national and state government development of new towns such as the new state capitals of Chandigarh and Bhubaneshwar, new urban districts like Bidhannagar (Salt Lake City) in Kolkata and Navi Mumbai, and in industrial towns like Jamshedpur. Less widely analyzed, though of perhaps greater import, was the importation of ideas of master planning such as Clarence Perry's neighborhood unit concept. Perry's formulation of pedestrian-oriented planned neighborhood settlements centered on parks and public facilities, informed by the reality of early twentieth-century American and European cities, was adopted by the Indian government as a foundational principle of postindependence master planning in major Indian cities, and indeed it was a central element in plans for the new towns mentioned above (Vidyarthi 2015).

The central theme that runs across the literature on master-planned urbanism is the serial subversion of master-planned spaces. In his study of the history of the neighborhood unit concept in India, Vidyarthi (2015) aptly captures this dynamic in his analysis of the ways that "acts of appropriation" by users of these spaces—the violation of building codes and the occupation of urban public space for seemingly private purposes like temples and private health clinics—subvert the central objectives of the neighborhood unit. In the postliberalization era, the agenda of master planning has taken a very different form: a proliferation of plans for very-large-scale privately built urban spaces. This shift, I will argue later, is intended both to generate new sources of revenue for corporations and the state, but also to assert new forms of market-oriented control over urban space.

Second, state governments have engaged in limited intervention in the development of housing and other public facilities. Through the creation of public-sector entities and special purpose agencies like the West Bengal Housing Board and the Delhi Development Authority, national state governments sought, particularly during the 1970s and 1980s, to gain some semblance of control over urbanization through the construction of public housing and planned urban communities. Many of these agencies have since shifted toward marketized forms of development, aggregating land to be auctioned to private developers for commodified developments (Sengupta 2006).

Third, national and state-level governments operated through a regulatory mode, primarily with the objective of ensuring social equity in urban development. Notable here is the Urban Land Ceiling and Regulation Act, enacted by the government of India in 1976. The act places ceilings on individual land ownership in urban areas and enables state governments to acquire land above the ceiling through compulsory acquisition (Acharya 1989). State governments have also launched bureaucracies to regulate various aspects of urban development, including land use, building codes, and regional integration. Scholars have argued compellingly that the regulatory state, by creating layers of bureaucratic and regulatory barriers to any form of urban development, has been complicit in the proliferation of informalities that defines urban development in India (see for example Roy 2003; Sengupta 2006). A great deal of postliberalization urban governance reform has focused on reducing regulation and bureaucracy in land development, ostensibly to clarify property claims and enable land markets to function. Nevertheless, the modes of operation and objectives of this regulatory state continue to shape the ways state and local government actors interact with development, as is evident from the reflections of one developer interviewed for this research on regulatory interventions in contemporary new towns.

> None of the developments are large enough to have that kind of integrated sense. Government doesn't want to create space they cannot control. Say a developer wants a million square meters—first thing the government will say is "cut it up so I can go across it"—they are not going to let developers create an enclave.[1]

Hence the regulatory state continues to shape urban development in India, even as reforms have attempted to reduce constraints on private-sector land acquisition and development.

The final way that the Indian state has shaped urban development is through the management of illegalities, the negotiations over recognition, legitimacy, and providing services to the substantial majority of urban populations who rely on shelter and livelihoods that are in various ways illegal or unregistered. The state's relationship to these illegalities has, of course, been the subject of a great deal of analysis, for example in Chatterjee's (2004) work on "political society," Benjamin's (2008) work on "occupancy urbanism," and Roy's (2005) work on informality as a mode of governance. What I would like to draw attention to here, however, is the ways that regimes of informality change in response to changes in regulatory regimes and planning agendas. While it is often presented as a stable and universal condition of Indian urban politics, what Benjamin has termed "occupancy urbanism" is perhaps better understood as a process of interaction between the state and informal economies that is subject to changing conditions of political economy. Regulations always produce opportunities for rent seeking and patronage, and therefore for the production of illegalities that can be managed and manipulated for political gain. Likewise, regimes of master planning produce structural conditions—displacements, exclusions, market failures—that produce illegalities that can likewise can be managed through political processes. Yet the goals of the state regarding the managing of illegalities may shift in response to changing objectives in the management of urban space. The fundamental change in India over the past two decades or more has been from a system in which land has been deployed as a tool to manage processes of urbanization and modernization to one in which land has become a tool of capital accumulation and state legitimation through a model of economic growth based on a liberalized, globally connected economy. The question is: How have the varied fragments of the Indian state attempted to shift their strategies of managing illegalities to overcome obstacles to capital accumulation created by the preliberalization regime?

Debates over the management of illegalities are central to postliberalization urban politics. These debates play out against a backdrop in which these illegalities are deeply embedded in politics and policy. This embeddedness arises in part from the political hollowness of governance institutions at the urban level, which has has meant that local state actors tend to have neither the power to seize control of urban development agendas nor the incentives to invest substantial political capital to do so. As argued previously, the lack of direct electoral accountability of municipal leaders has meant that electoral bargaining has played out instead at the ward level, which has arguably given ward-level political leaders strong incentives to enable their constituents to subvert laws and regulations that create obstacles to their quest for shelter and livelihood.

The political embeddedness of illegalities has also arguably been facilitated by the structure of incentives of state governments with respect to urban management. With their electoral bases for the most part solidly in rural and to a lesser degree urban poor settlements, and with little financial incentive for them to pursue urban economic development as a central focus of policy, state leaders in the preliberalization era had little incentive to regularize land tenure and pursue a concerted agenda of urban redevelopment. Indeed, their efforts at urban spatial control have often focused on the management and manipulation of illegalities rather than on their eradication. In Kolkata, Roy describes the resulting dynamic as an "unmapping" of Kolkata that occurred as the CPI-M rewrote the rules with regards to the ownership and use of land through a systematic process of land grabs, politically sanctioned land invasions by the poor, and "vesting" of land, largely through the use of agricultural and urban land ceiling acts, among other means. These maneuvers, she argues, have deliberately created ambiguity with respect to land claims as a tool of spatial control. In Delhi, Bhan (2009) describes the proliferation of categories of the "unplanned" and "informal" settlements that make up more than three-quarters of the city's population. These categories differentiate settlements based not only on technical and legal criterion (rural versus urban land-use designation, planned or unplanned for development), but also on political prerogatives, as informal settlements have gone through waves of "regularization" at the discretion of the Delhi Development Authority. In both cases, politically mediated processes of legitimation and regularization helped position state-level bureaucrats as arbiters of the stability of claims to land. They also provided state- and municipal-level authorities with ways to bargain with ward-level officials and communities and therefore exercise some control over "occupancy urbanism."

The postliberalization period has placed tremendous pressure on all aspects of this preliberalization urban management system. Initiated in earnest in 1991 in response to a mounting fiscal crisis, the liberalization agenda led to a fundamental restructuring of the Indian economy. The list of industries reserved for public-sector participation, which had formerly covered a range of manufactured goods, basic materials, and services, was scaled back to those related to defense, atomic power, and railways (Ahluwalia 2007). A variety of regulations on business practices were scaled back, tariffs and import restrictions were reduced, and the ban on the import of manufactured consumer goods was lifted, as was import licensing for capital goods. A flexible exchange rate regime was instituted, and 100 percent foreign ownership was allowed in some industries. As a result of these changes, exports rose from less than US$18 billion in 1991–1992 to US$163 billion in 2008–2009 (Reserve Bank of India 2008–2009). Growth was particularly rapid in the information technology sector, where exports grew from a mere US$194 million at the beginning of reform to more than US$50 billion in the 2008–2009 fiscal year, with more than 70 percent of this growth occurring in software exports (Heeks 2010). With these changes also came growth in real estate investment and a rapid climb in land values.

These changes transformed the land-management regime in two ways. First, they led to demands from investors for access to land and for increased legibility of land markets. Second, they fostered a spike in land values that has placed land-based revenue, and therefore control of land markets, at the center of the political economic agenda. The occupation of urban space by informal economies of the urban poor has therefore come to be increasingly intolerable to those with an interest in land commodification, while the cost of land has hobbled state and municipal governments' ability to move the poor from place to place. In many parts of contemporary urban India, the strong but somnambulant hand of the regulatory state (particularly at the state level) continues to exercise control over the production of urban space in important ways. To the degree that state regulation of land has come to constrain the ability of capital to reorganize urban space, however, it has come to be seen as an obstacle to the realization of goals of capital accumulation by an increasingly influential corporate, social, and political elite.

As these constraints have become clear, political coalitions have emerged around the need for a new agenda for managing land. These coalitions have argued for new mechanisms of state control over land, which alternately could involve the destabilization of existing informal claims to land and the state sanctions that recognize them, or the development of a new social contract around access to land for the poor. The emergence of these coalitions has also attended a call for state or municipal governments to overcome the power of ward-level political officials and create new political forums for the empowerment of capital and a growing urban consumer class.

It is this new set of political imperatives that has given rise to the "experiments in power" referred to in the introduction, and it is to these experiments that this chapter now turns. As the following review of these reforms will reveal, these experiments respond at various scales and in various ways to the obstacles to capital accumulation inherent in the preliberalization urban management framework. In doing so, however, each upsets existing political interests in a context where power is highly diffuse and where different factions of the state may have competing interests in land commodification. These are also contexts where no single actor exists to enforce a new regime. Each of these experiments is thus potentially contentious and destabilizing. In pursuing redevelopment, state actors risk fomenting conflict and possibly delegitimizing the state by undermining some of its core legitimizing ideologies.

Theories of Political Economy, Experiments in Power

It is well beyond the scope of this brief chapter to engage in a comprehensive review of the urban reform agenda that has unfolded in postliberalization India. Perhaps the most concise way to summarize these reforms is with reference to three dimensions through which they play out. The first dimension is time; the reform agenda has unfolded in distinct and identifiable phases. The second is levels of governance. Reform experiments have emerged at the national, state, and local levels, and also across these levels. The final dimension is the substance of the reforms themselves. Reform experiments have attempted to reshape the state's legal, regulatory, and administrative apparatus for managing urban land, and to transform governance agendas more broadly. The objective of these reforms has often been to increase the power of corporate and real estate elites and middle-class civic groups in political processes and to destabilize informal claims to land and to formalize tenure. The following discussion will attempt a broad review organized according to phases of reform and touching on shifts across levels of government and sectors.

The first phase of the reforms spanned from the initial push to liberalize the Indian economy in 1991 to the beginning of the spike in foreign direct investment in the early 2000s. This was a period when the development of infrastructure and space to accommodate globally oriented growth began to be seen as an imperative. In the national government this period witnessed important reforms that were to lay the groundwork for further change in the new millennium. One of the most significant reforms is the 74th Amendment of 1992. While its passage appears to have had little to do with any conscious effort to reform urban governance for an era of liberalization, the amendment defines urban local bodies (ULBs) for the first time, provides them with important powers and sources of revenue, and creates a democratic and decentralized governance framework in which they should operate (Weinstein 2014). Critics have argued, however, that the lack of penalties against states for noncompliance has led many state governments to guard their powers over urban governance by dragging their feet in implementing key provisions of the amendment (Dupont 2007). This period also saw the publication in 1996 of the India Infrastructure Report, better known as the Mohan report, for Rakesh Mohan, the chair of the Expert Group on Commercialization of Infrastructure Projects, which had been assembled by the Ministry of Finance. The report called for the widespread commercialization of infrastructure through public-private partnerships (PPPs) and also called for responsibility for urban infrastructure provision and for constituting PPPs to be passed from central ministries to urban local bodies (Expert Group on the Commercialization of Infrastructure Projects 1996).

During the same period, state governments were also emerging as active agents in the acquisition of land for infrastructure and urban megaprojects. In his study of the development of special economic zones in India, for example, Levien (2013b) finds that land acquisition by the Rajasthan State Industrial Development & Investment Corporation Limited doubled between the 1980s and 1990s. Private-sector actors also began to mobilize at this early phase, and there were scattered efforts to create new urban landscapes through property development. Most important here was DLF City, which emerged less as a master-planned "city" than as a scatter clustered of residential and commercial property developments that began to sprout just across the border from Delhi in the city of Gurgaon in the neighboring state of Haryana. This development capitalized simultaneously on the emergent demand from foreign and domestic private capital for urban space, and on the presence of a lightly regulated state just across the border from Delhi, where the highly regulated environment created by the Delhi Development Authority continued to constrain real estate development (Chatterji 2013).

The second phase of reform was touched off in the early 2000s by the explosive growth of FDI in India and increasing investment in the real estate sector. It was during this time that the ideal of the master-planned new township took hold in India. Reliable figures on the number and scale of these planned projects are hard to come by, but during this period press reports related a string of stories about audacious plans. A new hill resort near Pune called Lavasa, one of the notable projects that had already broken ground by the mid-2000s, was being built on ten thousand hectares. Its economy was based largely on tourism and hospitality, with some investment as well in education, information technology, and the pharmaceutical industry. In 2007 the Delhi Development Authority unveiled a plan to engage private developers in developing five new towns around the city to accommodate 7.3 million people (Das Gupta 2008). Under a separate plan, the Haryana state government unveiled a scheme to develop a

Global Corridor on sixty-two thousand hectares of land along the KMP Expressway, which circumnavigates New Delhi. The plan involves the development of themed cities, including Education City, World Trade Financial City, Biotech City, and Fashion City, to name a few (Ahuja 2008). The Bangalore Metropolitan Regional Development Authority unveiled plans for the development of five satellite towns of twenty-four thousand hectares. In all, one newspaper commentator counted two hundred integrated townships that were in various stages of planning and development, and DLF alone, according to one report, had plans under way to build seventy townships of 120 to 200 hectares each in fifty cities (Singh 2008).

National economic reform encouraged this push toward large-scale land commodification. Guidelines developed by the Ministry of Commerce and Industry in 2002 extended liberalization to the real estate sector, allowing up to 100 percent FDI investment in integrated townships (Ministry of Commerce and Industry 2002). The guidelines specify that integrated townships must be of a minimum forty hectares and two thousand dwelling units for about ten thousand residents and that they must contain schools, a shopping complex, community centers, and a hospital/dispensary. The Special Economic Zone Act, passed in 2005, allowed the creation of tax-free zones for inward investment in industry, but also allowed significant portions of the acquired land to be developed for housing and other commercial purposes (Levien 2013b). According to Levien's (2012) analysis, within sixteen months of the passage of the act 464 EPZs had been approved, slating more than 200,000 hectares of land for acquisition by state-owned industrial development corporations.

This new push toward the development of urban real estate megaprojects accompanied a shift in corporate and state focus toward land acquisition and real estate investment. According to Indian government statistics, FDI in real estate and construction skyrocketed from a sum so negligible it was not reported in 2004–2005 to US$2.84 billion in 2009–2010, at which point it was the second largest target for investment (Department of Industrial and Policy Promotion 2011). During the mid-2000s, many major developers like DLF, Unitech, Sahara Group and Emaar MGF aggressively amassed land banks around Indian cities in anticipation of further investment, escalation in land values, and demands for new urban space and infrastructure. For a period in the mid-2000s, with the real estate sector growing at more than 20 percent per year, Indian developers experienced massive increases in valuation, with these valuations being driven largely by landholdings (Karmali 2006). Real estate magnates became some of India's wealthiest individuals.

This period saw a significant shift in public opinion and in the way state actors conceived of their goals in urban development. It was during this period that government officials began framing their governance strategies in comparison with the "model" globalizing cities of Singapore and Shanghai, seeking to emulate what they viewed as exemplars of control, technocratic competence, and unity of action. This period also saw a rise in public interest litigations (PILs) by elite civic groups against encroachments of the poor (Bhan 2009). As Bhan (2009) and Ghertner (2011b) have documented, this legal push accompanied a shift in the way the Delhi High Court and other courts framed illegal occupations of the poor, away from a view that held them as worthy of state protection and toward one that saw them as criminals whose very claims to citizenship were questionable.

The mid-2000s also saw an explosion of initiatives in the areas of land management and urban governance focused on solidifying state control over the acquisition and transfer of land. At the state level, perhaps the most significant move was simply the increasingly aggressive use of the colonial-era Land Acquisition Act (LAA) of 1894, which allows the state to take land for projects deemed in the public interest. Under the LAA, compensation was set at the price of the land at the time of acquisition, which allowed the end user to capture any benefits from land use change and improvement (Chakravorty 2013). It was the intensified use of this tool, the increasing looseness with which the "public purpose" of projects was defined, and the gap between farmers' perceived value of their land and the compensation they received, that were to render the use of the LAA increasingly controversial into the late 2000s.

The mid-2000s also saw a proliferation of governance experiments at the state level focused explicitly on empowering elite and "middle-class" actors in ward and municipal politics. The Bhagidari program in Delhi, for example, was an initiative of the state government of Delhi that created forums in which members of resident welfare associations (RWAs) of property-owning constituents networked with public officials and bureaucrats in events staged to highlight the state government's agenda for urban development and "global city" formation. Ghertner (2011c) argues that this effort to empower elite associations was intended explicitly as a means to "gentrify the state" by countering the influence of street-level negotiations between urban poor "encroachers" and lower-level bureaucrats. By providing forums for elite RWA members and state representatives to network, and for RWA members to seek to inform and influence lower-level bureaucrats, the Bhagidari scheme explicitly seeks to reduce the influence of lower-income communities as a means to destabilize extralegal claims to urban space. Perhaps the most widely discussed local experiment in civil society participation in governance was the Bangalore Agenda Task Force (BATF), which emerged from the friendship of the chief minister of Karnataka and the well-known information technology executive Nandan Nilekani. Formed in 1999, the BATF was conceived as a "public-private partnership" in governance that brought leading corporate and civil society actors to the table with the heads of several major state-level authorities dealing with urban issues. This partnership resulted in several high-profile initiatives in e-governance, transportation, and urban beautification.

The national government also undertook significant efforts to reframe the country's urban governance framework during this period. Most significant was the Jawaharlal Nehru National Urban Renewal Mission (JNNURM), which was directly influenced by the governance experiments initiated by the BATF (Sivaramakrishnan 2011). Initiated in 2005, the JNNURM recognized that mandates for urban governance reform like the 74th Amendment had been frustrated by the politics of state-local government relations. The program instead sought to increase local government powers and capacity through incentives: US$20 billion in infrastructure grants and capacity-building funds. These grants were conditional on states undertaking reforms, including the modernization of accounting systems, improvements in property tax collection efficiency, increased cost recovery in infrastructure and service delivery, more effective implementation of the 74th Amendment, and the repeal of the Urban Land Ceiling and Regulation Act (ULCRA) (Mahadevia 2006).

The mid-2000s were also a period of dramatic local experimentation in models of urban development. These experiments tended to cobble together opportunistic coalitions composed of key state-level politicians and bureaucrats, high-profile economic actors, and representatives of civil society and the press. A particularly remarkable early example of this was the Magarpatta City development in Pune, introduced at the beginning of chapter 2. The town was developed through the effort of 120 farming families belonging to the Magar clan, who pooled their 160 hectares of land and incorporated as the Magarpatta Township Development and Construction Company. The Magarpatta case would have been impossible without the connections and political savvy of Satish Magar, a leading member of the community who owned much of the land and whose grandfather had been Pune's mayor. Magar carefully cultivated his networks among state and city politicians and prominent city businessmen to realize the necessary regulatory clearances and raise the capital for the venture (Sami 2013). Hence the Magarpatta case should not be construed as an example of the empowerment of downtrodden farmers, but rather as one of the shrewd deployment of power by a politically connected farming clan.

A more representative case of these local initiatives to mobilize coalitions for specific projects was the Dharavi Redevelopment Project in Mumbai, an initiative to redevelop a settlement of more than a half a million people, frequently described as Asia's largest slum, into a real estate megaproject that would accommodate the existing residents in high-rise housing at the periphery of the plan (Weinstein 2014). The concept was driven by the tenacity of a lone individual, Mukesh Mehta, who sought to bring a variety of actors—state elected officials and bureaucrats, parastatal entities, corporate financiers and consulting firms, and community groups—around the table to hash out the details of the scheme. In an interview with Weinstein (2014), Mehta succinctly describes the need for entrepreneurial individuals to "fill the void" left by the lack of a center of urban governance in Indian cities, to provide "the coordination function, to make people talk to each other and make deals." As was the case with many such efforts to cobble together power to realize ambitions of redevelopment, displacement, and land monetization, Mehta's scheme eventually failed.

The third phase in the development of India's postliberalization urban agenda began at the end of the first decade of the millennium. This phase was initiated both by a softening of the real estate industry, as India felt the effects of the global financial crisis of 2008–2009, and by the political backlash engendered by the displacement, protest, and political controversy created by land-acquisition efforts, as symbolized by the Singur case. This latest phase has been marked by competing reform proposals intended to overcome some of the obstacles to land acquisition that have arisen with widespread public protest. This agenda has included, in some proposals, efforts to develop a new social contract around land acquisition to overcome some of the criticisms of the use of the LAA. In 2008 the government of India issued a National Policy on Resettlement and Rehabilitation (NPRR), which introduced guidelines recommending a requirement for a social impact assessment in instances of displacement, among other measures. Many of the recommendations of the NPRR were later folded into the Land Acquisition Resettlement and Rehabilitation Bill of 2011, a version of which was passed in 2013. This law requires that 80 percent of potentially displaced families consent to land acquisition and that displaced families receive much more compensation for the land acquired than they previously had.[2] While ostensibly addressing many of the concerns with the land-acquisition process, this law has if anything amplified the controversy and debate over land acquisition. Key issues of contention include the continued lack of a clear definition of "public purpose" and shortcomings in the measurement of "market value" that some say will to lead to a continued lack of fairness in relocation and resettlement. Meanwhile, advocates for business interests argue that the provisions for consent by those displaced are unwieldy and render land acquisition onerous, which stymies development efforts and discourages investment. Indeed, in 2014 the newly elected Modi government sought to pass an ordinance overturning many aspects of the new bill, largely doing away with requirements for a social impact assessment and giving the government greater latitude to bank land for extended periods of time after acquisition (Ramanathan 2015).

While the debate over the land-acquisition law has unfolded, state actors have continued to seek new means to capitalize on the rent gaps that could be realized through regularization of tenure and urbanization of rural and state-owned land. This effort has increasingly been spearheaded at the national level. In 2010, the Indian government initiated an effort to establish a Public Sector Land Development Authority responsible for leasing to private developers lands currently occupied by ports, railways, and public-sector enterprises (Tiwari 2012). Shortly after taking power in 2014, the new Modi government announced a "smart city" initiative that, when paired with its proposed land-acquisition ordinance, seemed intended to ease state government efforts to take large parcels of land for the development of new towns through public-private partnerships. In June of 2015, the Modi government announced three new programs aimed at the creation of smart cities and the provision of housing and infrastructure that totaled four trillion rupees in investment, or about US$63 billion at exchange rates prevailing at the time (*Economic Times* 2015).

The debate about land acquisition and "smart city" development unfolds against a backdrop of farmer suicides, protests over the proposed land-acquisition ordinance, and accusations from academics and civil society groups about the potential for displacement and exclusion that appear inherent to the "smart cities" initiative (Datta 2015). This discontent reveals that questions of access to land and urban space lie at the heart of the social divisions that define politics in the current moment of globalization-driven neoliberalization and economic change. The following discussion of the Kolkata case will explore how these dynamics have played out in one city, and in one particular instance of urban real estate megaproject development.

The Kolkata Story

On May 25, 2006, the government of West Bengal did its part to light the fuse on the politically explosive issue of land acquisition for urban development. On that day, state officials accompanied executives of Tata Motors, one of India's pre-eminent industrial corporations, on a site visit in the district of Singur, about thirty kilometers outside of Kolkata (Banerjee 2006). The state soon made known its intention to acquire about four hundred hectares of agricultural land under the Land Acquisition Act of 1894 for development as a factory and associated township for the production of Tata's Nano car, a low-cost vehicle that Tata intended as a major new thrust of its automotive production. The proposal immediately met with strong opposition from some of the hundreds of households and farmers who stood to be displaced by the project. A constellation of NGO activists, academics, celebrities, and most importantly the powerful Trinamool Congress opposition leader Mamata Banerjee decried the project for its proposed forcible acquisition of farmers' land, for the questionable legality of the claim that forcible acquisition was warranted based on the public interest, and for its proposed conversion of prime agricultural land in the name of a project whose economic impact was uncertain. The controversy dragged on for more than two years, with repeated protests and allegations of government coercion of farmers and threats of violence from armed henchmen. Tata eventually decided to pull out of the project, relocating the factory site to the more favorable climate of Ahmedabad in the state of Gujarat, where chief minister and future prime minister Modi had developed a reputation for clearing hurdles to land acquisition. The fallout from the project, however, continues to be felt to this day. In 2011, the Left Front government, led by the CPI-M, lost control of the state assembly after more than thirty years in power. Trinamool's Banerjee ascended to the chief minister position and to national political prominence. The Singur case has become grist for debate over the formation of new legislation to regulate the land-acquisition process.

Singur is often a reference point for scholars and analysts interested in controversies over land acquisition in India. In the account that follows, however, I will argue that this case in fact represents the culmination of the paradoxes of the government of West Bengal's strategy of land monetization through urban real estate megaproject development that unfolded throughout the first decade of the new millennium. On the one hand, the Left Front government's historically strong role in land regulation and acquisition (when compared to other Indian states) placed it in a relatively powerful position in the push for land monetization and urban development. As the discussion of the cases that follow will show, urban development projects in the Kolkata metropolitan region have reflected strong influence from the state in varying ways: through state regulation, through a strong role for state actors in public-private partnerships, and through the relative deference of private-sector actors to the interests of the state. On the other hand, the Left Front increasingly found itself torn between two competing prerogatives, a need to cultivate the Left Front's legitimacy through the deployment of a rhetoric of social justice and its growing interest in fully seizing the opportunities for economic growth through land monetization and the resulting political-economic influence. One Ahmedabad-based architect and planner interviewed for this research prior to the fall of the Left Front touched on this contradiction, obliquely and unwittingly, when describing why the Left Front had been

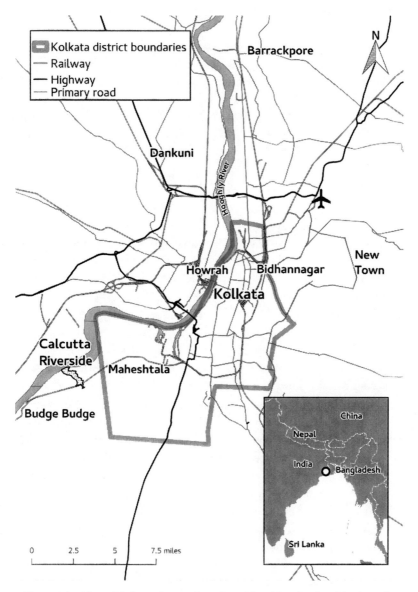

Figure 4.1. Map of Kolkata. Source: OpenStreetMap. Map developed by Antonio Vazquez Brust. Map data copyrighted OpenStreetMap contributors and available from http://www.openstreetmap.org.

relatively successful in acquiring land for megaprojects. In discussing the government's Rajarhat new town development, he stated:

> What are they doing? They [the West Bengal government] are basically taking up farmers land and eating up the land increment. Here in Ahmedabad, this is not possible. When you create a township, you sort of use your regulatory power to zone it, and to create development rights, and there are kickbacks and all involved in that, but at least you're not doing this sort of get in bed with the developer thing. Here it's not possible to do that. I think there it's possible because they're so secure, and because many of the top politicians are so clean.[3]

As the account that follows will reveal, this capacity to seize land increments proved a double-edged sword. As the Left Front deepened its strategy of land monetization through the commodification of space, questions over displacement, social fragmentation, food security, and state complicity in dirty land deals cut ever deeper into state narratives of legitimation. Singur simply functioned as a symbolic focal point of discontent over the Left Front's land agenda.

Urban development in preliberalization Kolkata was shaped fundamentally by the deployment of informality as a mechanism of governance. In Roy's (2003) analysis, the Left Front deliberately fostered ambiguity regarding property relations through state sanctioning of land invasions and the creation of resettlement colonies on lands of unclear ownership. The state further manipulated land markets through "vesting," or state acquisition. Vesting has been realized both through compulsory acquisition and through the taking of landholdings over the limits imposed by ULCRA and by the Left Front's own land-reform legislation. Until liberalization, this system was deployed in the service of state-driven urban developmental goals. Through the West Bengal Housing Board (WBHB), the state government built planned housing developments that, while targeted at moderate-income people, largely accommodated public-sector workers (Sengupta 2006). Given the regulatory restraints on private developers, such as the ULCRA and rent-control legislation passed by the Left Front, the WBHB emerged during this period as the largest developer in the state, while the private housing market was largely limited to mason-built single-family homes. For the majority of urban residents without access to WBHB housing or mason-built private housing, the state's resettlement

Figure 4.2. Election wall painting in Kolkata, 2010. Despite the CPI-M's strategy of rationalizing aggressive land acquisition as necessary for job creation, the party ultimately suffered electoral defeat in 2011. Source: Author

programs provided a housing solution that, while "mak[ing] possible claims to land, also make impossible rights to land" (Roy 2003 151–53).

In the aftermath of liberalization, the apparatus of vesting and the institutional machinery of urban planning, policy, and regulation came to be deployed in the interests of economic growth driven by speculative real estate development. This shift began with the development of several new upper-income housing developments through public-private partnerships between the WBHB and private developers in the late 1990s. Building on these experiments, the government of West Bengal launched the New Kolkata project, more popularly known as Rajarhat, a project of the West Bengal Housing Board. This project is slated to eventually accommodate about 700,000 people on 3,075 hectares adjacent to the Salt Lake development. Managed by the parastatal organization West Bengal Housing Infrastructure Development Corporation (HIDCO), the project is conceived as a satellite town to be developed through state land acquisition and leasing to private real estate developers and public-private partnerships, predominantly between developers and the WBHB (HIDCO 1999; Sengupta 2013). Similar to the Chinese model of state land acquisition and development, HIDCO is empowered to acquire land and lease it to developers, secure funds from capital markets, and build infrastructure at the site. During the mid-2000s the area saw significant development of office complexes and housing estates for predominantly middle- and upper-income households. The area has emerged as a major magnet for developers, including large Indian developers like DLF, Unitech, and Ambuja Realty, as well as foreign investors like Keppel, a Singapore-based developer.

Encouraged by the success of Rajarhat, in 2006 the state government put out bids for the Dankuni Township project, to be developed on almost two thousand hectares of land twenty kilometers northwest of Kolkata. The bid called for a town with an eventual population of 600,000 to 800,000, to be developed through a partnership between the KMDA and a private developer (Chakraborty 2009). Unlike Rajarhat, which is emerging piecemeal through the development of numerous projects on scales generally ranging from fifteen to one hundred hectares, Dankuni was intended to be planned and built by a single developer as a self-contained, master-planned new town (Chakraborty 2009). Dankuni was but the largest of a number of integrated urban real estate megaprojects conceived during this period; another included an agreement between the Kolkata Metropolitan Development Authority and a consortium of Indonesia- and Singapore-based developers to build a 160-hectare integrated project called Kolkata West International City. The Singur development, as we have seen, also emerged during this time.

During the decade from the late 1990s to the middle 2000s, therefore, the government of West Bengal embarked in stages on the transition from what Levien (2013) has referred to as a "regime of land for production" to what he calls a "regime of land for the market." This transition is marked by notable tensions:

> While land was previously expropriated to produce goods for the market, it is now increasingly being expropriated for its own market value. This new regime of dispossession, with its more expansive criteria of what justifies the use of eminent domain, or compulsory purchase, has significantly less public legitimacy and has proven to be more vulnerable to challenge than its predecessor. (Levien 2013b, 384)

These tensions became increasingly notable as farmers and other small landholders and landless ruralites became increasingly aware of the ability of state agencies and their private partners to realize eventual property values amounting in some cases to hundreds of times the amount of compensation they had received (Sengupta 2013). As Chakravorty (2013) notes, widespread media coverage of instances of dispossession also bred awareness both of the injustices associated with land acquisition and the legal and political rights of landholders with respect to eviction and resettlement.

The story of the Dankuni bid provides fascinating insight into the trials and tribulations of the Left Front as it navigated this transition. A number of developers from across India launched bids for the project, but the largest Kolkata-based developer to do so was Ambuja Realty. While Ambuja had emerged as a major force in Kolkata real estate as an early mover in developing partnerships with the WBHB, it was a small player relative to larger national developers. Many of the more prominent members of the new generation of Kolkata-based developers—figures like Harish Neotia of Ambuja Realty and Sumit Dabriwala of Hiland—were members of Kolkata's Marwari community, whose roots were in a migrant community from Rajasthan who had played a major role in the city's economy and industry since British colonial times and who had formed some of postindependence India's largest industrial houses (Hardgrove 2005). Long accustomed to operating within a regulatory and political context in which the predominantly Bengali Left Front dominated, and aware of the importance of relations with state government for access to land, Marwari developers have sought to frame their plans within the rubric of the Left Front's developmental goals (Roy 2003). It is perhaps partially for this reason that the rhetoric and plans of these developers resonate with a certain nationalism and evoke a social vision.

The implications of this orientation toward state social goals was notably represented in Ambuja's bid for the Dankuni project (Ambuja Realty 2006). Neotia mobilized a team of renowned Kolkata-based architects to launch the bid, and the plan that resulted reflected their interpretation of the environmental and social realities of the site. The plan consisted of a series of "sectors," each around fifty-seven hectares, subdivided into neighborhood units, each centered on a green. Houses were laid out so that each was within five hundred meters of a neighborhood bazaar that could be reached without crossing a road and which contained a range of stores and services. The plan contained an economic zone focused mainly on agro-industry rather than on information technology. This choice of economic sector, unusual for such integrated megaprojects, was seen as a means to maximize job creation. While the project was to be segregated at the neighborhood level, higher-, medium-, and lower-income socio-economic groups were to be integrated at the sector level. Housing for "economically weaker sections" (EWS), including those evicted from the project site, was to be provided in separate sectors, a measure intended to forestall the inevitable growth of informal settlements around the development by providing housing for service workers. Perhaps most remarkably, the Bengal Ambuja plan accommodated a population of 375,000, far lower than the maximum population stipulated in the bid documents. This was ostensibly to remain within the urban development plans formulation and implementation (UDPFI) guidelines of the government of India, which had been disregarded in the bid documents.[4]

Despite these extensive efforts to frame the development within the state government's ostensible goals of job creation and social equity, the bid was eventually won by Delhi-based DLF, which at the time was the largest property developer in the country. While state officials maintain that DLF prevailed because of its better score on technical criteria, those associated with the Bengal Ambuja bid maintain that it was because the higher density and more commercial orientation of its proposal allowed DLF to post a much higher bid. Several years after submitting its successful bid, however, DLF pulled out of the project, citing the government of West Bengal's lack of progress in land acquisition in the aftermath of the Singur conflagration. The state government has disputed this claim and has argued that DLF's real reason for backing out is the softening Indian real estate market.

Bengal Ambuja's apparent efforts to address social concerns in its Dankuni bid were not necessarily representative of broader trends in Kolkata's real estate industry. In the late 2000s, public perceptions of real estate megaproject developments shifted toward the inequities and injustices of the state and the corporate sector's push to acquire land. Media coverage increasingly drew attention to instances of coercion and violence in land acquisition. This issue notably came to public attention following an incident in August of 2009 when a group of villagers set fire to buildings in Vedic Village, an elite fifty-hectare resort complex east of Kolkata, following a shooting at a soccer match. Subsequent coverage revealed that the perpetrator of the shootings, Gaffar Molla, was a land broker whose henchmen had coerced farmers to sell their land for the development with threats of violence (Rajat Roy 2009). Raids conducted after the fire revealed caches of weapons. This high-profile case gave credence to assertions in the press and popular discourse that the threat and reality of violence frequently lay behind acts of land acquisition.

This background of growing media and popular attention to the Left Front's push toward an increasingly speculative agenda of land acquisition frames the controversy over Singur. Indeed, the May 2006 visit of state and private-sector officials to the Singur site came on the heels of a state government pronouncement of its intention to acquire thirteen thousand hectares of land for urban development, a figure that was to rise to more than twenty-eight thousand hectares later in the year. According to some commentators, the controversy was further heightened by the fact that it was middle-income farmers—a group that had gained relative benefit from the Left Front's regime of rural land redistribution—who lost the most under the terms of compensation for land acquisition. The Left Front had strayed too far from its core legitimizing narrative in its quest to gain control of the Kolkata metropolitan region's land markets. Attracted by the China model of an economic explosion triggered by state-planned land commodification and urbanization, the CPI-M had been lured into a massive land acquisition push. This effort, however, came at the expense of its core electoral constituencies, who consequently punished the CPI-M at the polls and reversed this experiment in urban transformation.

Calcutta Riverside

Because the Left Front experienced limited success in acquiring land for large, master-planned developments, there are few examples of urban real estate megaprojects to study in the Kolkata metropolitan region. Of the various experiments that emerged during the first decade of the new millennium, the Dankuni Township and Kolkata West International City notably failed to take root. The case of Calcutta Riverside is chosen here simply because at the time this research was beginning, it appeared to be the major developments of a master-planned enclave that had the best chance of coming to fruition. In fact, since the field research for this chapter started, the project has been slowed by changing economic and political circumstances in West Bengal. Nonetheless, it remains one of the largest such projects to have broken ground in Kolkata.

In the discussion that follows, I will focus on three aspects of the Calcutta Riverside project that highlight what we can learn from this case about broader changes to Kolkata's urban form brought about by the urban real estate megaproject model. The first is that the project was able to take root due in large part to exceptional circumstances. The unusual nature of the land claims on the site precluded the need for state or corporate land acquisition. The second aspect is the negotiated nature of the project. Despite the relative ease of land acquisition, the developer undertook extensive efforts to ensure public acceptance of the scheme, specifically by paying attention to the ecological and social impacts of the project. The modifications to the scheme that resulted have the potential to moderate some of these impacts to some degree, if in fact the scheme is ever fully completed. Finally, I will call attention to the ambiguity of the project's "success," both in terms of its commercial performance and as an urbanistic scheme. Despite what appears to be good intentions on the part of many architects and planners involved in the scheme, it appears poised to exacerbate many of the social and ecological ills associated with the commercial urban real estate megaproject model more generally.

Initiated in 2004, Calcutta Riverside is fifteen kilometers from central Kolkata on a 106-hectare site along the Hooghly River. It is a joint venture between the Bata Corporation, a Czech shoe manufacturer, and the Hiland Group. At the time the project started, Hiland was a small developer that had only recently completed its largest project to date, a 4.5-hectare condo development called Hiland Park. The land upon which the project took shape was part of a larger 125-hectare site that had been granted to Bata by the British colonial government on a 999-year lease on the condition that Bata continue to use it for manufacturing in perpetuity. By the late 1990s, however, Bata's industrial operation was foundering, and in 2001 the company put out a bid to develop a joint venture real estate project on the site. Hiland won the bid, and in 2006 formed a subsidiary, the Calcutta Metropolitan Group, which subsequently entered into a public-private partnership with Bata to develop the township. This was incorporated as Riverbank Holdings Pvt. Ltd (Government of West Bengal 2006). This arrangement required an order from the Ministry of Land and Land Reform of the government of West Bengal terminating the colonial-era lease and its contingencies. This was signed in 2006. The order stipulated a number of conditions for the change in land use, including providing hospital and school facilities on the new site and a minimum amount of land to be set aside for green space, infrastructure, and industrial development. The order also stipulated minimum amounts for Riverbank Holdings' investments in housing, retail, infrastructure, and industrial space, and it mandated penalties on Bata if it did not reach its benchmarks for land development within seven years.

The project was therefore unique from the start in that it did not involve the compulsory acquisition of land. Because of the existence of the Bata lease and the relative dearth of other claims to the site, resistance was relatively muted. Nevertheless, it was not a "greenfield" site, as it contained a number of structures, including worker housing, and a number of schools, medical clinics, and other public facilities. In addition, while Batanagar was relatively sparsely populated itself, the surrounding municipality of Maheshtala is a dense urban area with a population of close to 450,000. Residents of the area had long used parts of the Batanagar site for various functions, including soccer matches and the display of temporary statues

Figure 4.3.   Rendering of Calcutta Riverside. Source: Hiland Incorporated

and podiums for the Durga Puja, the most important festival in Bengali culture. The site's location along the Hooghly also placed the development between area residents and an important economic and aesthetic resource. Local residents had historically crossed the site to fish and recreate on the riverbanks. Pockets of housing and shops had also been built at the periphery of the settlement. Moving the project forward thus required active engagement with a range of users.

From its beginning, the planning process for the development of Calcutta Riverside sought to manage the tension between the goal of fully exploiting the potential commercial value of this relatively pristine riverfront site and the political sensitivities involved in negotiating with other stakeholders. Hiland was also accountable to the terms of the government order detailed above, further constraining its flexibility with respect to the planning process. Hiland's approach to these political calculations was inflected with a certain elite idealism, as articulated by Sumit Dabriwala, founder and CEO of Hiland:

> We are a strange country where we have all of these fancy townships, but at another level we have many who are abjectly poor. We can't wish them away. . . . In this case we will spend close to $750 million on a 262-acre site, and if people in and around it cannot see the benefit of that flowing to them, then it cannot be successful.
>
> We very strongly hold this view that unless we have the buy in and the, I'll call it the blessings of the surrounding communities, these developments cannot be successful. Like I said, we can temporarily be commercially successful, but ultimately the intervention that we create, and the social construct, will fail. Therefore, there necessarily needs to be a buy in from communities.[5]

Hiland's perceived need for community buy-in was reflected in the planning approach undertaken by Hiland's planning team. This team was composed largely of young recent graduates of the Center for Environmental Planning and Technology (CEPT) University, an Ahmedabad-based architecture and planning school founded in 1962 through a joint effort of the government of India and the Ford Foundation. True to the principles learned in the CEPT curriculum, Hiland staff members began their process with a series of meetings and public input sessions engaging a variety of important stakeholders, including Bata employees and union representatives, municipal councilors and the municipal chairman of Maheshtala, and representatives of the KMDA. Reflecting the environmental focus of their training at CEPT, the planning team also undertook a comprehensive survey of vegetation on the site, identifying 2,500 species.

In 2005, prior to government approval of the plan, Hiland had engaged the San Francisco–based architecture and planning firm HOK to develop a master plan for the site. The HOK plan divided the project into three zones, an institutional zone, a low-density golf community, and a dense commercial and residential zone on the riverfront. This plan paid little attention to the ecology of the site or to the surrounding communities. The HOK plan was almost immediately abandoned once the order approving the project was issued. In interviews, Hiland employees and the planners and architects involved in later stages of the project argued that the HOK plan had minimal influence on the final master plan for the development. A representative of one of the firms that worked on the final Calcutta Riverside plan, in discussing the interventions of foreign architectural firms in India more generally, framed the use of foreign architects as a deliberate political strategy.

> Exactly why are you hiring these firms? Because if you look at the way they put together a master plan, the degree of seriousness with which they look at the idea of the land is completely different. . . . They have a template. The developer is saying "look, we need it as a marketing document." So I said fine, if you need it as a marketing document, then why don't you only use it as a marketing document? Which is what Calcutta Riverside did. They hired an HOK to do a master plan, and finally that is not the master plan that is being built at all. We turned around that entire master plan. Completely. I mean their master plan and the master plan that is presently working, they have nothing to do with each other.[6]

Shortly after the order approving the project was issued, Hiland assembled a team of India-based architects, engineers, urban designers, and landscape architects to flesh out the final plan. This team of consultants included some of India's most renowned architects and planners, including Kolkata-based Dulal Mukherjee, Mumbai-based Kiran Kapadia, Chennai-based Pramod Balakrishnan, and Ahmedabad-based Bimal Patel, Prabhakar and Aniket Bhagwat, and Balakrishnan Doshi. Through a series of monthly design charrettes that brought these actors together over the course of 2006, the group refined a broad vision for the site, after which each was then given marching orders to do detailed designs for portions of the development.

The plan that emerged from this unusual process reflects a balancing act between fully exploiting the commercial potential of the site and ameliorating some of its potential ecological and social impacts. Reflecting the giddy atmosphere in India prior to the 2008 real estate crash in the United States and subsequent global economic slowdown, the plan was distinctly upmarket, focusing as other such projects do on delivering the "lifestyle aspirations" of an emergent Indian elite. The plan is laid out on a narrow strip of land running from the Hooghly to the Budge Budge Trunk Road, which connects Maheshtala municipality to Kolkata (Riverbank Holdings Pvt. Ltd. n.d.; Riverbank Holdings Pvt. Ltd. 2005). The central portion of the development consists of Mandeville and Golf Greens, twenty-six medium-rise residential structures and clusters of townhomes surrounding a nine-hole executive golf course. At the far northern edge of the development lies the Princep, a row of seven high-rise residential structures, sporting blue glass façades in renderings, densely clustered along the riverfront. A Crowne Plaza Hotel and convention center also sit along the river. Sandwiched between these two signature residential developments is Lake Town, a cluster of medium-rise condominium buildings that frame a set of small open spaces that marketing documents present as carefully manicured "public" spaces intended for leisure and strolling. The plan exploits the obvious aesthetic value of its location through the creation of a marina and a riverfront promenade with boutiques, art galleries, restaurants, and other consumer amenities. An information technology SEZ and retail mall are clustered at the other end of the development, along the Budge Budge Trunk Road. Amenities interspersed throughout the plan include a hospital, international school, and sports club. The transportation network focuses on maintaining pedestrian orientation within the residential clusters.

In addressing the requirements of the order creating the project, the Hiland plan took some care to address community groups' concerns about the project. It touted these elements of the plan in meetings with local political representatives and in promotional material. Perhaps most notably, and essential to the progress of the project, Hiland agreed to rehouse Bata workers living in Batanagar in medium-rise apartments located on the site;

workers began moving into these units early in 2010. Existing religious buildings (including two Hindu temples, a mosque, and a church) were to be retained, and schools were to be retained and physically upgraded. The plan identifies several points of egress across the site, a measure intended to diffuse accusations that Hiland was creating a "gated" community and to address concerns of local residents about loss of access to the river as an amenity and a source of livelihood. Existing vendors on the site were to be accounted for and rehabilitated at a market center located at the Budge Budge intersection, where Hiland would also develop a transportation node for public buses. A six-hectare portion of the site was to be set aside for the development of a maidan accessible to neighboring communities for the Durga Puja and other recreational and ceremonial uses.

It is in the ecological measures surrounding the development, however, that the plan evinces its most significant idealism (Bhagwat n.d.). Several of the architects and Hiland employees interviewed for this research argued that the project's focus on the ecology of the site transcended financial gain and was instead intended to reduce the ecological vulnerability of the development and maintain a sense of place. Initially, for example, residential portions of the site were to be accessible only to battery-powered and solar vehicles, a feature that was abandoned early on due to demands from local political leaders for bus access across the project. Perhaps the most remarkable ecological gesture was the removal and replanting of 330 trees that, according to plans, will eventually be brought back and replanted on the site. This effort was part of a larger plan to retain about two-thirds of the existing trees. These ecological measures can be explained in part as an effort to appeal to the environmental and aesthetic concerns of the elite residents of the project, yet it is far from obvious that the potential commercial benefits outweigh the costs associated with these measures.

Like many projects conceived during the period of hubris that marked the Indian real estate market of the mid-2000s, the Calcutta Riverside plan almost immediately fell victim to the excessive optimism of its market projections. In 2010 the plan was revised to increase the number of units—from 3,150 to a new target of between 4,500 and 5,000—and the average size of units was reduced substantially. At the time of this writing construction continues at a slow pace. It is too early as yet to determine to what degree the social and ecological intentions of the master plan will be met.

Calcutta Riverside is a case of a project developed under the watchful gaze of state actors accustomed to having a strong regulatory hand in the service of state narratives of social equality and developmentalism, and of a developer that chose to pay scrupulous attention to social and ecological concerns. Nevertheless, the project was destined to become an enclave, largely cut off from its context and providing little economic or social opportunity to the population of Maheshtala. Moreover, while the unique circumstances allowed for development without potentially difficult and controversial state land acquisition, this also meant that the project did not provide the state an opportunity to gain control of the value created by the project. While displacement from the site was relatively limited, Calcutta Riverside was nonetheless part of a larger process of urbanization that has dramatic implications for displacement and dispossession in the area. Of most immediate note, in 2005, at the moment when the Calcutta Riverside project was taking shape, the government of West Bengal announced plans to widen Budge Budge Trunk Road, an initiative that human rights organizations argued would result in the displacement of more than thirty thousand families (AHRC 2015). What appears as a "best case" scenario of urban integrated megaproject development, a plan with a relatively progressive planning vision, nonetheless has had the immediate impact of exacerbating the processes of exclusion and dispossession that have defined India's shift to neoliberal urban governance.

Conclusion

The India case differs fundamentally from the cases of China and Suharto-era Indonesia in one fundamental respect. While these two cases represent stories of authoritarian states that attempt to shape processes of land monetization to state goals, India represents a very different case in which the state itself is transformed by processes of land monetization. The formation of new power centers around land has challenged state actors, particularly at the state and municipal levels, to reframe their very rationale for existence and to reshape state narratives of legitimacy. The consequences of this shift have varied dramatically. While some locales have seen the emergence of radical new regimes of dispossession and urban transformation, others, including Kolkata, have witnessed a backlash that leaves governance in flux between preliberalization norms of social equity and state-sponsored modernization, and the drive for economic development through land commodification. The central government, meanwhile, seeks to mediate a process of reconciling the apparent contradictions between these two models, yet finds itself in a weak position.

The India case therefore provides an example of a much more distributed, localized, and bottom-up process of state rescaling and neoliberalization. State actors at various levels of government finds themselves subject to pressures, both from within and from without, to create new and more powerful institutions at the municipal level, to renegotiate questions of property rights, to define new political coalitions, and shift the balance of electoral influence. In the process, the very future of the model of urban politics and governance is undergoing transformation, with the outcome of this change uncertain. In this context, the Calcutta Riverside project indicates both the potential for a more negotiated and inclusive model of urban real estate megaproject in this context, and the political dangers posed by the inherent exclusions and inequities of these projects in such a dynamic political framework.

5

CHONGQING

The State Capitalist Growth Machine

In 2011, Chinese academics and policy makers engaged in a debate about "cake theory," the stakes of which were nothing less than the future of China's model of economic and social development (Godement 2011; Mulvad 2015). The debate was kicked off in earnest by Guangdong provincial party secretary Wang Yang, who famously stated in 2011 that the foremost mission of the Chinese Communist Party (CCP) was not to share the "cake" of wealth, but rather to ensure its size and quality. Eschewing an expressly redistributionist agenda, Wang staked Guangdong's developmental model on shoring up the legitimacy of CCP rule by building the province's economic competitiveness, enacting reforms to enhance the transparency and effectiveness of government, and engaging in environmental conservation (Cheng 2013). Wang's signature moment followed the protests over land grabs in the village of Wukan, which were widely covered in Western and Chinese media. Wang notably responded not by directly addressing concerns over unfair terms of land appropriation, but rather by holding secret-ballot elections for new village leaders with the objective of enhancing local government accountability. The problem was not the need for a greater focus on equity in policy; it was the need for more effective leadership.

The champion of the other side of this debate was Bo Xilai, Chongqing provincial party secretary and a purported aspirant to a Politburo standing committee spot and high-level national position (Cheng 2013). Beginning in 2007, Chongqing engaged in an aggressive experiment in dividing the "cake" of Chongqing's wealth, greatly expanding the state's roles in social welfare and economic management. The city committed to a massive infrastructure investment program, aiming to build 2,000 kilometers of express highways, 150 kilometers of subways, and 20 bridges and to improve 8,000 kilometers of rural roads (Huang 2011; Cheng 2013). In 2010 the municipality launched a public housing plan that sought to accommodate 30 to 40 percent of the city's urban population in affordable rental units (Lafarguette 2011). Chongqing also undertook audacious experiments in social reform, providing two million residents with urban *hukou* within a year, developing a new system for exchange of rural collective land, and developing a pension fund for migrant workers (Huang 2011).

The Chongqing and Guangzhou models represent very different approaches to managing the issues that have emerged with China's rapid economic growth and urbanization: massive dispossession, ecological degradation, growing inequality, destruction of the natural resources base, and burgeoning problems of food insecurity. Yet the question of *how* China should pursue growth has largely remained beyond question. Particularly since reforms to local public finance initiated in 1994, China's model of economic growth has rested solidly on what You Tien Hsing (2010, 1) has referred to as a "land-centered accumulation project."[1] Within this model, Hsing (2010, 1) states, the question of land management "shapes the restructuring of Chinese state power and radically impacts state-society relations." The state's ownership of all urban land, stipulated in the Chinese constitution, has allowed the state to capture rent gaps in the service of economic growth and urban development. Municipal governments have undertaken ambitious innovations in urban governance, creating new institutional vehicles to channel land-based finance into agendas of economic growth, infrastructural modernization, and in some instances (most notably that of Chongqing) social welfare delivery. These emergent models of state-driven land-based accumulation have underwritten the most dramatic process of urbanization and infrastructural transformation yet witnessed in history.

From a comparative perspective, the "China model" can perhaps best be explained as a model of urban planning under state capitalism. The term "state capitalism" has recently been repopularized by Ian Bremmer (2010, 5), who defines it as a system "in which the state functions as the leading economic actor and uses markets primarily for political gain." In the case of China, a primary market that has produced profits for reinvestment has been the market for land and property. China's systems of land development, local public finance, and macroeconomic management have been developed by the CCP through a combination of deliberate policy engineering and trial and error, as a coordinated set of mechanisms to induce municipal governments to pursue local accumulation and growth through state exploitation of real estate markets. This fusion of the interests of the state and the corporate sector in monetizing land and shaping urban space has proven extraordinarily powerful in China's urban transformation. By combining its monopoly control over land with a regulatory and planning function coordinated by the CCP, and with its control of financial markets and to a significant extent the rest of the corporate economy, the Chinese state has been able to realize a massive transformation of urban space in the interests of the state. Specifically, it has deployed these capabilities to maximize state powers through state enrichment, to build state legitimacy through a developmentalist agenda, and to engage in social engineering and political control.

Yet this model also creates a fundamental challenge for the CCP: how to incentivize state actors to embrace markets and aggressively pursue property development while protecting against the potential for political backlash that emerges with the social issues this model creates. The development of China's land-based accumulation model has seen intense competition among state actors—municipal governments, rural cadre, national state-owned enterprises (SOEs), and many others—to advance their own political causes by extending their territorial control through a ceaseless and tenacious push for land commodification and the development of high-profile signature projects. It has consequently posed distinct threats to the legitimacy of the CCP, as the state itself bears direct responsibility not only for the benefits of economic growth but also for rural and urban displacement, destruction of farmland and natural resources, and the development of dangerous speculative property bubbles. The CCP has gone through stages of centralization and decentralization of authority over land acquisition, land use, and the provision of public goods, as it has sought to strike the right balance between the incentivization of local entrepreneurialism and the exercise of central control over developmental outcomes (Xu and Wang 2012).

It is in the context of deepening social disenchantment over these issues that the "cake theory" debate arose. Between 1984 and 2008, China's urban built-up area expanded more than fourfold, an increase more than double the country's urban population growth, as land-thirsty municipalities engaged in a ceaseless drive of development (Lin and Yi 2011). Particularly in coastal areas that expanded most rapidly, urban development was increasingly cutting into cultivatable land, and farmer uprisings over the terms of land acquisition and displacement were steeply rising. At the same time, difficulties in land acquisition threatened to stifle real-estate-driven economic growth. The debate about the Chongqing and Guangdong "models" is framed around a central choice for China's future development: Should the CCP seek to mute resistance with the promise of perpetual economic growth and the expansion of a compliant consumer class, continuing the push for land-based accumulation while engaging in political reform and controlled liberalization to enhance local state accountability? Or should the state use its powerful role in the economy to position itself as a distributer of social goods, directly addressing concerns over urban poverty and dispossession? This debate was ultimately disrupted by Bo Xilai's dramatic fall from power and expulsion from the CCP in 2012 following accusations of corruption and conspiracy that emerged following a controversy instigated by his wife's alleged involvement in the murder of a British businessman. The questions it raised, however, remain central to the future of the "China model."

The terms of the cake debate also have important implications for the questions of central concern in this book, which focus on how models of land monetization, especially as realized through the development of urban real estate megaprojects, impact the spatial development of cities, and consequently social, political, and environmental relations. The development of new towns and the redevelopment of central city districts on a massive scale have been central elements of the Chinese model and have enabled a fundamental transformation of Chinese cities that has resulted in significant achievements in infrastructure provision, economic growth, and the creation of a new consumer class. In the distinctive case of Chongqing, this real-estate-driven model enabled a massive redistribution program, capped by perhaps the most rapid expansion of affordable housing in one city in human history. Yet by tying the incentives of local states to ceaseless market expansion and economic growth through the commodification of urban space, the China model in Chongqing and elsewhere creates powerful local political machines with a unslakable thirst for land and an instrumentalist perspective on urban form and the people who occupy urban space.

In focusing on the Chongqing case, this chapter does not attempt to present a representative case of Chinese urbanization. Rather, Chongqing is an exceptional case that illustrates both the potential for the state capitalist development model and its inherent pitfalls. Despite the best intentions and technocratic capabilities of many urban planners, architects, urban designers, urban policy makers, and engineers, the Chinese model tethers the policy and planning system to a real-estate-driven agenda of sprawl and spatial fragmentation and a habitual if not indiscriminate destruction of ways of life that do not adhere to the goals of growth and the commodification of urban space. It therefore etches issues of inequality, fragmentation, and social dislocation into the fabric of cities in ways that have unpredictable outcomes for the future development of Chinese society. This chapter will first examine the evolution of China's state capitalist model of urban planning, and will then examine the Chongqing case in greater depth.

Unpacking China's State Capitalist Model of Urban Planning

The China model stands in distinct contrast to the other models of urban development analyzed in this volume. As in Suharto-era Indonesia, political power in contemporary China flows almost exclusively from one source. In China, however, that source is the CCP, a party that has over the course of many decades developed deep institutional roots and a strong ideological foundation. Importantly, the CCP controls not only the realm of politics but also exercises significant control of the economy, so that it does not have to share power with nonstate economic oligarchs and remains relatively insulated from external economic influence. This unusual degree of political and economic control and relative autonomy from nonstate and noncorporate actors has lent the Chinese state an unusually strong hand in shaping urban development to state interests, as the state faces relatively little competition for control of urban space.

More specifically, there are four important factors that have allowed the CCP to exploit urban development in the interests of the state. The first is the state's dominance of land markets. The stipulation that the state owns all urban land, which was added to the constitution in 1982, emerged as a critical element of the urban political economy with the establishment in 1988 of the land leasehold system, which allowed state owners of urban land to lease it for private development (Lin 2009; Hsing 2010). As will be explained in detail later in this chapter, state land leasing was to emerge as a central element of local government finance, urban development planning, and economic growth. Another landmark moment came in 1994 with the formulation of a new tax sharing system, which simultaneously gave local governments greater leeway to raise revenue through local development and deprived them of powers of taxation and bond financing (Wu 2002; Sanderson and Forsythe 2013). Incentivized to seek innovative new mechanisms to create revenue streams, local governments engaged in a wave of innovation, formulating new institutional vehicles for financing urban development and infrastructure based on land leasing (Ding 2007). The combination of state land leasing and reforms to local government finance transformed China's urban development system, leading to an era of massive urban physical change, economic development, and state fiscal empowerment based on large-scale, state-sponsored, commodified development. It also fostered a period in which state actors, deploying their powers over land and the full weight of the rhetoric of modernization and economic growth, enacted an increasingly controversial wave of evictions.

The second major factor enabling the "China model" is the hegemonic role of the Communist Party in urban politics. The CCP's authority is rooted to a significant degree in its power to shape policy by appointing and promoting officials at the municipal and provincial levels, including mayors, governors, district leaders, secretaries of local party branches, and others through the Central Organization Department (COD) (McGregor

2010). Through this power the CCP establishes the criteria upon which local officials will be judged, and this is their almost exclusive point of accountability. The COD also appoints the heads of state-owned enterprises that are major players in urban land markets both through their investment in local economies and also through their ownership and development of urban land. These large state-owned enterprises dominate the national economy; forty-two of the forty-three Chinese companies on the 2010 Fortune 500 list of the largest companies in the world were SOEs (Peck and Zhang 2013). The overarching power of the Communist Party in local governance and the economy is arguably essential to the (notably incomplete) coordination of various actors and the consistency of national state goals with local growth-driven agendas. As will be discussed in greater depth later in this chapter, the CCP has sought at various junctures to exert control over urban development outcomes through the issuance of new regulations and through new policy initiatives. CCP control over appointment and promotion has been essential to holding state and corporate leaders accountable to these measures.

The third mechanism in the Chinese model of urban development is the central government's control of the banking system. China's finance sector is dominated by five state banks, with the China Development Bank playing a leading role. In a relatively short period these banks have emerged as some of the largest financial institutions in the world as their bonds have become a major outlet of investment for commercial banks flush with consumer savings generated by China's economic growth. Since the early 1990s, and particularly since the restrictions on taxation and bond financing imposed by the reforms of 1994, local governments have depended heavily on these state banks to finance their urban development and infrastructure projects (Sanderson and Forsythe 2013). Cities have specifically turned to the development of local government financing vehicles that have used state-owned assets, notably including land, as collateral for state bank loans to finance infrastructure and commercial property development. These state banks have consequently become a critical mechanism for economic planning. In the aftermath of the financial crisis of 2008, for example, a significant amount of the Chinese government's program of fiscal stimulus consisted of 1.7 trillion yuan (or about US$250 billion at the time) in investment from the state banks to local government financing vehicles. State bank lending is also a powerful tool to direct urban development spending in other ways, for example to encourage the growth of underdeveloped regions. The critical issue such lending raises, of course, is whether such huge amounts of debt have been lent in a financially sustainable manner, a question that has become the subject of increasing speculation and concern as this debt has mounted. To date, however, the central government's backing of the financial sector, realized most specifically through the central government's occasional instructions to the state banks to roll over local government debt, has forestalled the potential for a crisis in the financial sector that could impinge on urban growth machines (Sanderson and Forsythe 2013).

The fourth factor that has enabled the Chinese state to maintain control of urban property markets is the state's ability to control the rural-urban transition through the *hukou*, or household registration system. The difference in the provision of social services and different rights to claim a stake in collective land ownership between rural and urban *hukou* holders provides the Chinese state a powerful mechanism to manage the process of urbanization. The *hukou* system has acted as a constraint on the movement of ruralites to urban centers, thereby muting the informalization of urban space and facilitating the state's maintenance of spatial control (Ding 2003). As we will see in the case of Chongqing, the large-scale provision of urban *hukou* can also be used as a mechanism to access urban land by divesting rural *hukou* holders of their claims, and therefore it can be used as a powerful administrative means to accelerate urbanization and generate new sources of finance to build infrastructure and urban space.

While there is some debate concerning how conscious and deliberate the push toward land monetization as a central strategy of development, state building, and economic growth has been, there is less debate among scholars of Chinese urbanization that this was indeed the eventual outcome. Two early reforms in particular set the foundation for the system that was to emerge. The first was a 1988 revision of the Land Law of 1986, which separated ownership rights to urban land from land-use rights, and stipulated for the first time in the history of the People's Republic that land-use rights could legally be transferred from one entity to another (Ding 2003). This reform was rooted in several years of policy experimentation. In 1984 the city of Fushun experimented with charging state enterprises usage fees for land, and in 1987 this experiment was extended to the rapidly growing coastal cities of Shenzhen and Shanghai, with the explicit goal of generating revenue for infrastructure development (Wang, Zhang, Zhang, and Zhao 2011). Building on these experiments, the 1988 modification of the Land Law set the foundation for land leasing to emerge as an essential tool of state finance. While the initial adoption of land leasing was slow in the aftermath of the Tiananmen crackdown and resulting political turmoil, increased state support for the real estate industry led to an explosion of land leasing between 1992 and 1994, as land-owning government entities—state-owned enterprises, military units, hospitals, local governments, and others—sought to cash in on their land holdings. According to Wu (2001), housing investment nearly quadrupled in Shanghai between 1993 and 1994. The resulting property bubble, and rising vacancies in many markets, led to a slowdown in the property sector in the mid-1990s. The immediate response to this crisis was the Urban Real Estate Management Law of 1994, which attempted to rein in uncontrolled speculation by standardizing the procedures for land leasing, requiring municipalities to develop plans specifying lands to be made available through leasing, and ensuring that leases accord with city plans (Huang and Yang 1996).

The second foundational reform was contained in changes in 1994 to the tax-sharing system between the central and local governments. This reform dramatically increased the proportion of local revenue that was remitted to the center, and it fixed remissions as a set proportion of local government revenue, measures intended to improve the central government's fiscal standing (Lin and Yi 2011). This new system, however, also essentially resulted in a set of defunded mandates, as local government sources of tax-based revenue were now severely restricted, while their responsibilities for local infrastructure and services remained in place. Whether this outcome was an explicit intention of fiscal recentralization or not, the almost immediate outcome was a focus in municipalities on the development of "off budget" sources of revenue, most specifically land conveyance fees from land leasing. The Urban Real Estate Management Law, mentioned above, specified that land for purposes outside military uses, infrastructure, resource management, and other public purposes could only be assigned through land leasing and that land for commercial development would be allocated through bidding or auctions. These measures were seemingly intended to increase transparency and maximize revenue from land leasing. Between 1999 and 2012 municipal revenue from conveyance fees rose more than fifty-fold, and by the latter date these revenues amounted to 2.69 trillion yuan, or 44 percent of local budgetary revenue (Liu and Lin 2014).

The early reforms in land leasing and municipal finance briefly described in the preceding pages established the foundation for the political economy of urbanization as it has unfolded today. In China's contemporary model of urban entrepreneurialism, municipal leaders act as "virtual CEOs of 'urban development corporations,'" viewing urban planning and land monetization through commercial property development as mutually supporting goals (Wu 2015, 80). Held accountable to centrally mandated targets for economic growth, municipal leaders deploy many of the same economic development tactics that are used throughout the capitalist world, such as providing low-cost land as an inducement to corporate investment. Yet this strategy coexists with an interest in maximizing revenue from land monetization as a means to finance infrastructure and provide services. In fact, evidence indicates that municipalities tend to view these two strategies as interrelated and deploy them in mutually reinforcing ways. In other words, economic growth created by providing incentives for corporate investment generates consumer and corporate demand, which in turn is viewed as a means to increase in the value of state-owned land. Land development also generates increased economic growth, at least in the short and perhaps medium term (Whiting 2011; Liu and Lin 2014; Wu 2015).

Municipal governments have proven quite innovative in their land strategies, and there are perhaps as many institutional models of land monetization as there are municipalities in China. One notable form many cities have adopted, however, is the urban development investment corporation (UDIC). These are state-owned enterprises that borrow from state or commercial banks, often using land granted to the corporation by the municipality as collateral for these loans, to build infrastructure and service land and then lease it to private developers or state entities (Wang, Zhang, Zhang, and Zhao 2011; Wu 2015). The revenue generated from the land lease is then used to repay the lender. The UDIC model has provided municipalities with a prodigious engine for infrastructure and urban development. Yet this system raises some concerns in that it ties urban development to a never-ending quest for land and for debt financing. This not only arguably leads to an institutional impetus to encourage ceaseless urban expansion and possible overdevelopment, but it also potentially leaves the infrastructure development system prone to fiscal crisis in the event of a downturn in property markets.

This review of the basic history and functioning of state-driven land monetization in contemporary China helps to frame the two axes of conflict over land that have largely defined China's urban politics. The first of these conflicts emerges from competition between municipal authorities and other major state landowners, which Hsing (2010) refers to as "socialist land masters." The latter are often powerful, large, state-owned enterprises, military units, government agencies, and other state entities that, as a legacy of a socialist-era bias in favor of industrial and state administrative functions, control large amounts of land located in choice locations in central cities. These central state entities have themselves sought to capitalize on land price increases by creating development companies or by selling land-use rights to private developers, despite a 1998 revision of the Land Management Law that specifies municipal governments as the sole state representatives responsible for acquiring, servicing, and leasing administratively assigned land.

The central government, recognizing the implications of fragmented control of land among competing state entities for the state's ability to exert regulatory control, sought in 2002 to consolidate municipal control over land by requiring that land transfers occur only through open auctions and tenders organized by municipalities. In implementing this measure, the Ministry for Land Resources sought to ensure that private developers paid full value for the land and that proposed projects complied with land-use regulations and urban plans. Yet this only partially successful measure, intended to strengthen state regulatory capacity, also has the paradoxical effect of deepening the contradictions inherent in the role of municipalities. It positions municipal leaders both as the lead regulators of urban land and as lead market actors jockeying to use their regulatory and administrative authority to maximize their territorial control and therefore their land-based revenue. The result of these mixed incentives and mandates, Hsing argues, is as much a degradation of the municipality's adherence to rational planning and regulation as a consolidation of its capacity to plan and regulate. Municipalities have become key agents in a process of relentless competitive territorial expansion, launching ambitious plans for new towns, special economic zones, prestige housing and office developments, and landmark megaprojects in an effort to increase land values. Municipal leaders have come to:

> identify themselves as city promoters and devote themselves to boosting property value. Property prices are used to measure the success of urban development, and are openly referenced by local leaders as a primary political mandate. Mayors don suits and embark on road shows to promote real estate projects in their cities, and compete with one another to hire advertising gurus to help in developing "urban strategic development plans" aimed at improving the image of their cities and boosting property values. (Hsing 2010, 8)

This tendency of municipal officials has apparent implications for the dislocation of urban residents. This contradictory stance has engendered property rights protests as urban residents have perceived coercive municipal land appropriations and inadequate compensation packages as acts of corruption and misuse of state power.

The second set of conflicts over land emerges from municipal efforts to expand their territorial control through the acquisition of land at the periurban fringe. As land within municipal boundaries has become scarce, the quest to expand these boundaries has become a critical tool for the local state to maintain the momentum of its land-driven accumulation machine. Although all urban land belongs to the state, Chinese law stipulates that rural land belongs to village collectives and that collective land can only be acquired by municipalities for urban development based on the existence of a "public interest" in the resulting project. Yet there are important aspects of rural collective ownership that render it subordinate to municipal interests. First, rural collective land can only be legally leased to a developer by a state owner, meaning that it must first be transferred to urban use (Hsing 2010). In practice, therefore, the constraints on collective ownership set up a similar dualism in China's land market to that between registered and unregistered land in Suharto-era Indonesia, as rural land can only be fully commodified after acquisition by an urban government and redesignation for urban use. As in periurban Jakarta, this leaves rural land users in a relatively weak bargaining position. Urban governments are further empowered in their negotiations by the ambiguity of the meaning of collective ownership of land; the law is unclear on the question of who represents collective interests (Ho 2001). In practice, according to Lin (2010, 29), the default is often that "collective ownership works in reality as local cadres ownership," as village-level political leaders collude with municipalities in land deals.

Issues surrounding municipal acquisition of rural land have proven particularly politically explosive in recent years. Researchers estimate that three to four million rural residents have been losing their land rights yearly and that at least fifty-two million have been displaced since land leasing began (Chuang 2014). Research has further indicated that most of those displaced have received inadequate or even no compensation and that they report a decline in average income, as well as poor quality relocation housing and housing insecurity. Of course they also lose ways of life and community connections built up over generations, a loss that can be significant to some, notably middle aged and older ruralites, who may have difficulty integrating into urban economic and social life (Ong 2014). By 2008, the Chinese government recorded more than 120,000 "mass protest incidents," with many of these being localized disputes over land (Tong and Lei 2010).

Driven by their need for land, municipalities have attempted to overcome rural resistance though a combination of coercion and concession. Inducements to rural residents to divest of their landholdings include grants of land, relocation housing, provision of urban *hukou*, or the promise of jobs in the new developments. One bargaining chip that has been used extensively in southern China is the reversion of a portion of serviced land in an area acquired by a municipality back to the village residents, who then form shareholding companies to develop this land. This practice has led to the development of *chengzhongcun*, or villages in the city, which exist as village-owned portions of urbanized areas that have developed outside municipal regulation. The dense urban settlements exist, in the words of Hsing (2010, 126), as "a physical expression of a territorial pact between villages and city government," which allows village residents to participate in the process of land commodification in exchange for the sacrifice of their land to municipal expansionism.

The preceding discussion has argued that land-based accumulation is a central arena of strategic state action and interstate competition, and it has outlined some of the contradictions and conflicts that emerge around land development. With this analysis as background, I now turn to a discussion of the issues that have driven academic debate and urban policy and planning: ecological destruction, food insecurity, social inequality, and spatial fragmentation. Each of these issues has implications for the legitimacy of the state. In the urban arena, the legitimacy challenge for the CCP lies in the contradiction between the central state's interest in providing local state functionaries with strong incentives and leeway to maximize land-centered accumulation and pursue economic growth, and the need to maintain leverage for the center so it can manage the damage to CCP prestige and legitimacy caused by the social and ecological impacts this strategy entails. The policy response to this contradiction has been a consistent effort to rescale state action, tacking between efforts to consolidate municipal power over land acquisition and conversion and the reinforcement of central government influence over matters such as land-use planning, farmland preservation, or regional development (Lin 2010; Li and Wu 2012; Cartier 2015). In the past decade in particular, there has been a marked shift toward an empowerment of the center, as concerns over dispossession, ecological damage, and loss of farmland have deepened (Cheung 2013). Despite meticulous policy engineering, however, the relationship between the pursuit of growth and the social and ecological damage this pursuit causes remains at the center of Chinese politics.

Policy debates about the ecological impacts of urbanization have largely focused on the contradiction between the goal of maximizing state-driven accumulation and the need to maintain the agricultural and resource base required for national development. Lin (2010) argues that, particularly since the late 1990s, concerns over the political implications of the loss of arable land have been of particular concern in the framing of national land-management policy. This loss has been most notable along the southeastern coast, an area that has seen rapid urbanization but also contains some of the country's most fertile land. The CCP Central Committee issued a notice mandating a one-year freeze on farmland conversion in 1997, and in 1998 the Land Administrative Law vested the central government with enhanced regulatory tools to manage land conversion (Cartier 2001; Wang et al. 2010). Under this law, the central government develops land-use plans for provinces that regulate annual amounts of farmland that can be converted to urban uses, and it also places severe restrictions on conversion of prime farmland. The farmland preservation effort was reinforced in 2005 when a national minimum of land needed for grain production was established (Ong 2014). Regulations on farm-land conversion have led to a number of innovations at the provincial level, including the development of markets in the transfer and trade be-tween municipalities of development rights to farmland. When combined with strong incentives to develop commodified urban space and industrial zones, the quota system has also seen a push in many municipalities to relocate scattered rural residences and industry into denser new develop-ments, or "concentrated villages," thereby creating new farmland that can be counted toward the quota (Ong 2014; Tian 2015).

The issues of social inequality and spatial fragmentation emerge from the state's direct stake in the primacy of exchange value over the use value of urban space. This contradiction plays out with the push to carve out ex-clusive residential spaces to cater to consumer elites, and with the creation of exclusive and exclusionary spaces of consumption. With the consolida-tion of powers over land conversion at the municipal level since the early 2000s, these forces have taken shape most notably in the formulation of schemes for urban real estate megaprojects in various forms, including state-driven new towns, or *xincheng*, as well as smaller-scale privately de-veloped elite enclaves and new urban districts like the high-end Xintiandi residential, commercial, and office district in the old French Quarter of Shanghai (He and Wu 2005). Such large, integrated projects have become central to the territorial ambitions and economic development strategies of municipal governments. They are also critical to the fiscal strategies of municipal governments, for as Wu (2015, 163) notes, "first and foremost, the new town is an investment and financing platform." In Shanghai alone, six new town projects accommodated an increase in population of more than a million between 2000 and 2010, and these towns were eventually slated to accommodate 4.2 million people. This example is only illustra-tive; new town plans have emerged as a driving force of urbanization in all major cities in China. A nonexhaustive web search conducted for this research in 2011 documented more than a hundred *xincheng* projects na-tionwide, with a total planned population likely in excess of 50 million.

The push toward the development of *xincheng* and other large real estate megaprojects has had implications for urban spatial change. Re-searchers have paid the most attention to their implications for spatial fragmentation (He 2013). As many commentators have gone to pains to note, the phenomenon of "gating" has historically been a feature of

Chinese urbanism and was notably a feature of *danwei*, or work unit housing that characterized the period of preliberalization socialist planning (Webster, Wu, and Zhao 2006; Hogan et al. 2012; He 2013). A number of studies, however, have pointed to the class-stratified nature of contemporary gated enclaves, as the relatively wealthy gravitate into commodity housing estates equipped with concentrations of services such as security, health care, and recreational facilities, while migrants and less socially mobile residents are concentrated in low-rent *chengzhongcun*, older neighborhoods, and privatized work unit housing (Douglass, Wissink, and Kempen 2012; He 2013).

Developed as they often are by state-owned corporations and public agencies that pursue both political and commercial objectives, the *xincheng* also shape urban spatial development in ways that reflect a curious combination of market and state logics. These projects tends to reflect a focus on showcase projects—stadia, concert and exhibition halls, and megalithic municipal buildings—alongside a certain functionalist logic that focuses on density and transportation efficiency intended to maximize the market viability of commercially developed residential, commercial, and office districts. Less attention is paid to questions of public space or walkability. There has been disproportionate media and research attention to elite residential developments that openly mimic Western neotraditionalist forms of suburban development, such as Thames Town outside Shanghai, modeled on a turn-of-the-century British suburb, and Orange County outside Beijing, named for the Southern California county that has become a global template for suburban development. Yet as Shen and Wu (2012) reveal in the case of Thames Town, this showcase development was created explicitly as a promotional "welcome gesture" (in the words of the head of the district government) for the much larger Songjiang New Town of which it is a part. Most of the residential areas in Songjiang evince built forms that are better attuned to the prevailing densities and prices of the Shanghai housing market. It is indeed these high-rise, high-density developments that have a stronger market and deliver higher land rents for the corporation. The prevalent form is high-rise condominium buildings built in functional rows along street grids that are connected to highway networks. On the whole, therefore, the development of *xincheng* has largely replaced the small-scale fabric of old urban neighborhoods and low- or medium-rise work unit housing with superblocks composed of high-rise residential districts, office parks, university campuses, high-tech zones, and prestige projects like concert halls, exhibition halls, supertall high rises, vast artificial lakes, and monumental government buildings (Xue, Wang, and Tsai 2013).

The flip side of the commodified *xincheng* has been the development of spaces of displacement and transition that have emerged through processes of rural dispossession. One has been the municipal push toward the development of "consolidated villages," developments that seek to free up land for development under the increasingly stringent farmland conversion quotas by consolidating rural industry and settlements in dense, medium-rise developments (Ong 2014; Long et al. 2012). Accompanied as it is by an increased costs of housing and commodities associated with the new style of living, and a frequent loss of livelihood, the consolidation of villages creates financial difficulties for many who experience displacement (Ong 2014). Another is the *chengzhongcun*, discussed above, which provides shelter and business spaces for many, particularly rural *hukou* holders, largely outside the municipal planning and regulatory regime. These *chengzhongcun* have in many instances emerged as major residential and industrial centers that function in opposition to the municipal government's regulatory regime (Wu, Zhang, and Webster 2013).

The central government's primary concern about this evolving process of urban fragmentation has been with the inequities of rural dispossession and displacement. These dynamics have led to considerable unrest that has raised concern about questions of state legitimacy while also increasingly acting as a constraint on municipal land acquisition. In response, the Eleventh Five Year Plan released in 2006 introduced the idea of "coordinated rural-urban development," or *chengxiang yitihua*, as part of a broader effort framed in the plan as "Building a New Socialist Countryside." The ostensible goal of this new policy push was to foster economic and social development in the countryside as a means to deal with disenchantment over the exclusion of rural residents from the benefits of growth. Strategies outlined in the plan include modernizing agricultural production, providing public goods to rural residents, and relocating rural communities to "urbanized" settings, denser urban settlements with urban services (Ahlers and Schubert 2013).

This new national planning agenda has led to a wave of policy and planning experimentation; as we will see in the next section Chongqing has been a major center for such experimentation. The outcomes of this experimentation, however, reflect the multiple, sometimes conflicting goals of both national and municipal governments. As Wu (2015) argues, *chengxiang yitihua* is intended not only to address social inequality, but also to jump-start stalling economic growth. Bringing rural residents into the urban fold creates new markets for consumer durables in particular, thereby stimulating the growth of the domestic consumer market. It could also free up new land for development by facilitating the shift of rural dwellers into urban housing and labor markets. This move thus leaves open the question of whether "harmonious development" can be sustained within a framework that is premised in large part on a downmarket shift of the model of land-based commodification and the expansion of urban labor and consumer markets. Will job opportunities continue to expand sufficiently to absorb rural migrants at an accelerated rate, given the vagaries of global trade and investment? Will rural migrants integrate into urban economies and provide the desired boost to consumer demand?

As with many central government initiatives in urban development, the details of policies and programs to achieve the goals of the *chengxiang yitihua* campaign are left to local governments. For municipal governments, the goals pursued by the central authorities are layered on other objectives. One notable objective in many municipalities is the consolidation of rural industrial and residential land uses, which municipalities have used to free land for agricultural production to meet quotas on farmland preservation. Municipal plans in response to the push to coordinate rural and urban development have consequently often focused aggressively on the displacement of farmers and their relocation in "modern" housing blocks. Chuang (2014) details the issues that emerge in one such scheme in Chongqing. Local township officials utilized a combination of coercion and incentive to compel rural residents to relocate, offering modest compensation for early movers with the threat of loss of land rights and much lower compensation for those who held out. Subsidized housing units that were initially used to entice the move to resettlement areas sold out quickly, and many of those relocated were compelled to purchase more expensive units. Many experienced a serious decline in disposable income and quality of life. Chuang (2014, 667) argues that this new regime is resulting in the "muting of rightful resistance" to dispossession, as "protestors are demobilized through internal ranking and division" by fiscally challenged townships that seek to meet state goals for relocation within budgetary constraints.

While the preceding pages have characterized China's contemporary urban development system in broad strokes, it is important to note that this system differs substantially between cities. This chapter will now turn to an examination of the Chongqing case. As the pages that follow will reveal, the Chongqing case represents a particular variation of the China model that has developed in a distinct regional, administrative, and political context. The city has been the setting of a notable experiment that provides unique insight into the opportunities and contradictions faced by the Chinese government.

Chongqing's Experiment in "Coordinating Rural and Urban Development"

What came to be known as the "Chongqing model" emerged from one of the most ambitious efforts to address the contradictions of the China model of urban development. In Chongqing, the CCP deployed all its available tools—administrative, financial, territorial, political, discursive—to formulate a model of state-driven land commodification intended to achieve its stated objectives of "coordinated rural-urban development." The model was further championed by a powerful and politically ambitious leadership team that exhibited remarkable creativity in its policy experimentation. Particularly during the period from 2007 to 2011, Chongqing emerged as a laboratory for the creation of a new model of urban development that could employ the land-based financing model in new ways to address social goals. Through this model, economic growth was to continue, and indeed accelerate, through the aggressive use of land-based financing for infrastructure development. At the same time, the rural-urban dichotomy was to be ameliorated through the development of more equitable models of land monetization and the application of land-based financing to address social issues. Moreover, this redistributionist agenda was accompanied by a vigorous cultural campaign, the "singing red" campaign, which mobilized Chongqing citizens to sing revolutionary and patriotic songs in deliberate evocation of Mao-era efforts at social mobilization. The symbolism was clear: in its social reform and its cultural

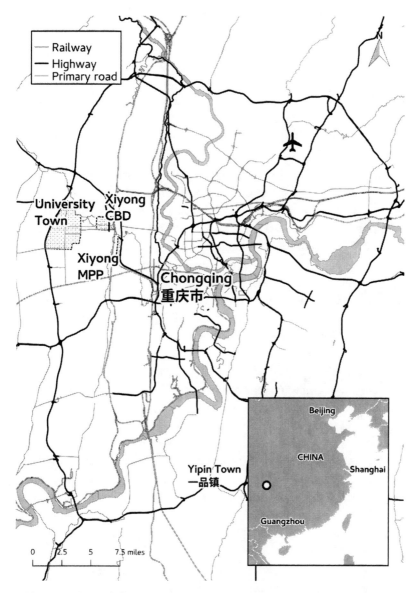

Figure 5.1. Map of Chongqing. Source: OpenStreetMap; Jones Lang Lasalle 2013; Arup 2016. Map developed by Antonio Vazquez Brust. Map data copyrighted OpenStreetMap contributors and available from http://www.openstreetmap.org.

program, the Chongqing municipal government was reclaiming the CCP's historical mantle as agent of social justice and moral rectitude.

Ultimately, the Chongqing experiment was to remain uncompleted. In March of 2012 Bo Xilai, the primary architect of the experiment, was removed as party chief of the city and was eventually expelled from the party. His removal came at the end of a series of events that was initiated by the murder of a British businessman in Chongqing, a crime for which Bo's wife Gu Kailai was eventually convicted. Nevertheless, I will argue in the pages that follow that some of the contradictions of the Chongqing model were already becoming apparent at the time of Bo's fall.

An important piece of the groundwork for the Chongqing model, which started in earnest a decade later, was laid in 1997. This was the year that the city was carved out of Sichuan Province and designated as one of a handful of province-level cities, on par with Beijing, Shanghai, and Tianjin. This designation placed Chongqing directly under central government supervision and gave the city greater political autonomy (since it did not have to deal with province-level authorities) and more direct access to national-level financing (Hong 2004).[2] Coinciding with an emerging policy agenda of "Opening Up the West"—drawing investment inland from the rapidly growing cities along the coast to the poorer inland provinces—the intent was to provide the city with the resources and autonomy needed to spur growth and development. With the designation the central government dramatically increased funding to Chongqing, notably for infrastructure to build the city's manufacturing economy. The designation also expanded the city's boundaries to include a very large area—roughly equivalent in size to Austria or Taiwan—that included an overwhelmingly rural population. In 2009, while the municipal population stood at about 33 million, about two-thirds of this population was classified as rural, and the population of the urbanized area of the central city stood at about 7.5 million (Huang 2011; Jones Lang Lasalle 2013). Hence while it has sometimes been cited as the "largest city in the world," its urban area still does not approach that of Shanghai or Beijing. The consolidation of a region of this size under one urban administration positioned the city as a potential site for the experiment in "coordinated rural-urban development" and regional-scale infrastructure investment that was to occur a decade later. The city also had less than half the per capita income of Shanghai and Beijing, far lower than the national average, positioning it as a test case for accelerated development in the inland provinces (Bo and Chen 2009).

In 2001, the CCP evinced further commitment to Chongqing's development when it appointed Huang Qifan as vice mayor and later party secretary for the Chongqing State Assets Supervision and Management Commission (SASAC), which represents state interests in the management of the city's state-owned enterprises. Huang was former deputy district head of Shanghai's iconic Pudong development district and an architect of the seminal land-based financing models of infrastructure and urban development that were developed there (Huang 2011). Under Huang, the Chongqing SASAC restructured debt-ridden state-owned enterprises, consolidating firms and reallocating land and other resources to relatively successful firms (Rithmire 2013). Huang was also instrumental in developing the framework for urban and infrastructure development in Chongqing that was established in 2002 with the formation of eight major UDICs. The Chongqing UDICs are state-owned local development financing vehicles that are each allocated responsibility for development of specific categories of infrastructure such as water, energy, or expressways (World Bank 2010b). Under this model, the Chongqing municipal government allocates lands to these companies to finance the municipality's infrastructure priorities. The companies then use the land as collateral for loans from the China Development Bank, other central state banks, and other sources, both to build infrastructure and to develop the granted land on a commercial basis. Ideally, these loans are to be paid down using the revenue stream from land development. The Chongqing SASAC was also an early innovator in the development of risk-management mechanisms to maintain the fiscal solvency of the eight UDICs.

In 2007, following several years of rapid economic growth, Chongqing and the city of Chengdu in Sichuan Province were designated as a "pilot zone" for policy experimentation in "Urban-Rural Integrated Development and Reform," a designation that established these two cities as critical sites for the development of a "new socialist countryside" (Cai et al. 2012). This new agenda was clearly motivated by a desire to develop new models of urbanization that learned from the conflicts that had arisen in rapidly growing coastal cities. November of that year saw the appointment of Bo Xilai, former minister of commerce and mayor of Dalian, as the party secretary of Chongqing. Bo was a rising figure and aspirant to the CCP Politburo Standing Committee. His appointment signaled the party's push to position Chongqing as a major new development center, and it brought significant new resources to Chongqing. In April of 2008 the central government approved substantial new infrastructure funding along with a package of reforms requested by the Chongqing government, including preferential tax policies, new social and environmental programs, and a new land-exchange system that will be explained below (Rithmire 2013).

In the ensuing years, Huang Qifan engineered an aggressive campaign to dramatically accelerate Chongqing's economic growth by wooing major corporate investment. His pitch to investors focused on three incentives: the city's lower corporate tax rate, which stood at 15 percent, about 10 percent below the average rate; dramatically improved transportation infrastructure, including 150 kilometers of subways and 7,000 kilometers of highways; and large amounts of land at much lower cost than coastal cities (Huang 2011). In addition, there were plans to link Chongqing into a larger national and international transport network that would allow passengers and goods to reach key destinations in the Yangtze Delta and Southeast Asia within eight hours by rail (Cheng 2013). The city further invested in improved rail links to Europe via Russia and Kazakhstan and negotiated customs agreements that allowed the city to market itself as having much more rapid access to Western markets than coastal cities had. Huang's pitch attracted major new investments from Hewlett Packard, Chang'an Automobile Company, BASF, and FoxConn, the Taiwanese maker of iPods and iPhones, among other companies. As a result, while China's growth slowed in the aftermath of the global financial crisis, Chongqing's accelerated, reaching 16.5 percent annually during the first half of 2011 (Cheng 2013).

Another boost to Chongqing's economy, also provided by central government action, was the creation of the Liangjiang New Area in 2010. This development followed on the creation of the Pudong New Area and the Tianjin Binhai New Area, which were conceived by the central government as focus areas for infrastructural investment to create major industrial centers that could act as development drivers for their regions. Covering an area of 550 square kilometers and with a population of 2.2 million, the area was designated in the Twelfth Five Year Plan for the development of a new commercial, logistic, and financial center as a way to further spur economic growth inland and reduce the economic gap between the inland and the coast.

Part of the Chongqing story, therefore, is the robust economic growth that was made possible by a particularly innovative, well-resourced, and ambitious agenda of economic development. What makes the city's experience distinct, however, is reforms intended to address social and ecological issues by attempting to engineer the process of rural to urban transition. The state used its role in the market to encourage this transition and spread its benefits more equitably, and it engaged in broad-based redistribution of benefits to rural migrants and the urban poor. One important element of this effort was the development of a new land certificate exchange system, a novel form of transfer of development rights designed to allow rural dwellers whose land was acquired by the state to gain access to urban *hukou* and recoup some of the value of their land (Cai et al. 2012; Rithmire 2013). With their change in *hukou* status, households would be provided a certificate representing the amount of land they had relinquished to the state. This certificate would then be purchased at auction by a developer, who would gain rights to develop an equivalent amount of land elsewhere in the city. This mechanism theoretically provided compensation to farmers at closer to market rates while ensuring no net loss of arable land. According to Huang (2011), the going price for certificates reached 100,000 yuan per mu, many times higher than the compensation farmers had previously been receiving.[3] It was also intended to provide the city with a steady supply of developable land while avoiding social conflict, thus avoiding a significant constraint on urban development in coastal cities like Shanghai and Guangzhou, where land acquisition continued to occur through contentious bargaining.

Along with the land certificate exchange, Chongqing simultaneously undertook one of China's most ambitious efforts at reform of the *hukou* system. In 2010 Chongqing announced its intention to provide urban *hukou* to all of the 3.38 million rural *hukou* holders who were already residing in the city of Chongqing. This was to be followed by providing urban *hukou* to an additional seven million in the countryside, for a total of more than ten million new urban *hukou* holders by 2020 (Cai et al. 2012; Rithmire 2013). This initiative would raise the proportion of urban dwellers in Chongqing from less than a third to about two-thirds, thus achieving a massive urban transition. Given that these newly minted urbanites would lose their rights to rural collective land, this transition was more than conceptual and would require their integration into urban labor and housing markets.

While this process of *hukou* conversion experienced some early success with the conversion of *hukou* of urban migrants, progress in converting *hukou* of existing rural dwellers has been considerably slower. Rural *hukou* holders have proven reluctant to give up the sources of livelihood provided by rural landholdings (although they are allowed to maintain these rights for three years after *hukou* conversion) and unable to resist the growing attractiveness of the social benefits provided by the national government to rural *hukou* holders, benefits intended to encourage rural dwellers to stay in place as a means to shore up food security.[4] Huang Qifan has attempted to play up the enticements of *hukou* transition, encouraging peasants to "take off three pieces of clothing" (rights to agricultural land, forest, and housing land) so they can "put on five," a reference to a list of health and social benefits available through the urban *hukou* (CCTV 2010). As Chuang (2014) documents, however, their continued reluctance has led some local officials to resort to coercion to meet the program's goals.

Together, the *hukou* and land certificate exchange are engineered to cope with a number of the contradictions in Chongqing's rural-to-urban transition and current economic circumstance. In addition to assuring the supply of land, the reforms are also intended to ensure a continued supply of workers for urban labor markets, as people are essentially administratively assigned away from agricultural occupations and therefore must integrate into the urban labor market. The potential for tightness in labor markets is a matter of concern for Chongqing's economic expansion because Chongqing is a significant net loser of workers to migration to labor markets in the coastal cities. This strategy nevertheless sets up a delicate balancing act as the municipality comes under pressure to fill demand for jobs created by the many new urban *hukou* holders recently cut off from rural sources of income and subsistence. The reforms appear to take as given an endless wave of job expansion and an endless need for land for property development despite the massive amount of construction that has already taken place to date. Some analysts express the more immediate concern that while younger new *hukou* holders can find their way into urban labor markets, and older people might enjoy the social benefits provided by the urban *hukou*, the middle aged are likely to experience the greatest trouble with the transition (Lafarguette 2011).

These issues apparently have yet to fully come home to roost with Chongqing's continued economic growth. The potential threat becomes tangible, however, given FoxConn's recent maneuvers to explore the development of manufacturing facilities in India, Indonesia, and the United States (Hung 2014; Bhattacharjee 2015). Planners also hope that providing urban *hukou* and integrating rural dwellers into an urban lifestyle will foster a surge in consumerism that will open up new economies that will bolster job creation, helping to prevent or ameliorate any possible downturn. A significant slowdown in investment, however, or the loss of manufacturing jobs through disinvestment, could create a cascading effect by lowering consumer demand. In sum, it is apparent that the dramatic expansion of *hukou* reform entails considerable risk.

The "Chongqing model" also involved significant investments in social welfare services. Most notable here was a public rental housing program, which emerged as a nationally discussed model for affordable housing provision when launched in 2011. Through this program Bo Xilai aspired to rapidly increase the per capita residential square footage from 27.34 square meters in 2008 to 35 square meters in 2017 (Cheng 2013; Xiang and Wu 2013). In contrast to the normal trend of public housing investment, which has tended to scale down over time, the Chongqing program gradually expanded in scope throughout the planning process and eventually involved a planned two hundred billion yuan investment in the development of forty million square meters of public rental housing, amounting to a total of about 800,000 units in twenty-one planned communities. The program aspired to build housing for more than 30 percent of the urban housing market (Huang 2011; Xiang and Wu 2013). Units were intended to be available only to lower-income residents of Chongqing, although this requirement has proven difficult to enforce due to difficulties in documenting people's income. Moreover, renters will eventually be able to purchase usership rights to their rental units after a period of five years; full ownership rights are withheld so that regulators can maintain the affordability of the units through restrictions on resale.

The public rental housing is built by two UDICs using a model that, as Huang (2011, 591) states, is "substantially the same method as the infrastructural construction projects." The municipality provides land grants, and the UDICs take loans for development, then repay the loans through a combination of rental revenue, revenue from the sale of units, other land sales and property taxes, and revenue from commercial development on a portion of the land. While full financial information on the development is difficult to obtain, Chongqing-based academics interviewed for this research who have studied the project believe that the expectations are that its costs are to be overwhelmingly covered by the various revenue streams listed above, and that expected public subsidy (aside from the grant of land) will be limited.[5] However, the low rate of return of the projects, the likely rising costs of maintenance, and the heavy debt load incurred in their development raise questions as to the future financial burden of the projects on local government (Lafarguette 2011; Li et al. 2014).

By the summer of 2015 the construction of these twenty-one public rental housing communities was largely complete, despite the political earthquake that had accompanied the fall of the program's architect. Initial evaluations of the project were mixed. The program has successfully injected a large amount of affordable housing onto the market, and some of these communities are almost fully occupied and have emerged as vibrant urban centers (figure 5.2). But many of the project locations are in far-flung periurban areas and lack convenient transportation connections to major employment centers (Luo and Zeng 2015). This has restricted access to jobs and has led to high commuting costs and significant increases in times of commutes to work. As a result, concerns have begun to emerge among scholars about the high vacancy rates in some of these developments, which could be an indication of the possibility of longer-term issues of vacancy and social problems (Li et al. 2014). Moreover, by concentrating lower-income urban residents in urban enclaves cut off from the rest of the urban environment, public rental housing doubles down on the powerful trend toward class-based enclavization that is inherent in the pursuit of large-scale commodified urban development in the new towns.[6] As with so many other aspects of the Chongqing experiment, the consequences of this move have been muted by a frothy economy. But questions of access to economic opportunity are likely to shape the sociospatial development of public rental housing units in the instance of a significant slowing of the city's economy.

How do we assess the "Chongqing model"? In terms of its ambitions and quantitative achievements, the experiment has indeed been remarkable. Chongqing has used land-based financing to achieve one of the most rapid

Figure 5.2. Min Xin Jia Yuan public rental housing complex. Min Xin Jia Yuan was the first public rental housing complex built and is the closest to central Chongqing at about eight kilometers distance. Its central location and access to transport has made it one of the more successful public rental housing developments. Source: Author

interventions in public housing on such a scale in human history. *Hukou* reform has helped the city to take steps toward rapid urban transition through administrative mandate, although not yet on the scale that was intended. The land certificate program has emerged as an important model for more equitably distributing the land windfall resulting from urbanization.

These achievements have been analyzed by scholars as a distinct experiment in governance with potentially dramatic implications for China and beyond. The number three has frequently been deployed in efforts to capture the combination of market and state forces at play in the Chongqing experiments. Huang Qifan has referred to this as a model of "third hand" financing, something distinct from Adam Smith's "invisible hand" of the market and the state hand in planning the economy, a model of state-managed markets deployed in the service of development. Similarly, Huang (2011) and Szelenyi (2011) have debated whether this model might represent a potentially transformational "third way" between the alternatives of an economy governed by the market or by the state. It may be, as Szelenyi (2011, 678) states, a model in which state control of the economy is used in a system that "aims at the satisfaction of public needs, not maximization of redistributive power (as under the state socialist redistributive economy) nor maximization of profits of publicly owned enterprises (as is the case in market socialism)." Using similar numerology, Wang Shaoguang has termed the Chongqing experiment "Socialism 3.0," a model that reconciles the objectives of Maoist socialism and Deng's market-oriented reforms by seeking to combine the powers of state planning and the market (Freeman and Yuan 2011).

Yet the Chongqing experiment is also fraught with perils that highlight the contradictions of China's authoritarian state capitalist model of land monetization and urban development. The competing state imperatives of market maximization and legitimization through developmentalism and social equity consistently undermine each other, threatening program failure and social and political fallout. The issue of the location of public rental housing provides one illustration of this dynamic. The municipality seems to have responded to strong disincentives to allocate land deemed highly valuable by the market for the housing program. Yet in consigning much of the affordable housing stock to areas that have lower land values precisely because of their poor access to urban economies and amenities, the program risks creating sites of social marginalization and stigma.[7] At the same time, by adding such a massive stock of affordable housing to the market in such a short time, the state also risks undercutting the private residential market that provides much of the value that drives the land-based accumulation machine.[8] With *hukou* reform, the state seeks to refuel the urban economy by cutting people off from rural economies and reassigning them as urbanites and would-be consumer citizens. Yet in doing so it risks creating a massive urban underclass of people who have lost their sources of livelihood yet are structurally cut off from opportunities in the urban economy.

The Chongqing experience reveals another contradiction of China's urban development: Urban development agendas are inevitably shackled to the political ambitions of urban leaders. The success of these leaders in turn depends on mandates from faraway bureaucrats. This link leads to two imperatives. The first is a need for speed, as measured by the setting and achieving of quantifiable goals in urban spatial development. The second is a focus on visible impacts on the urban landscape. Hence the public rental housing project builds benchmarks that lead to the infusion of a massive amount of housing without the ability to gauge the viability of individual projects or to assess the program's impacts on the housing market over time. With regards to *hukou* reform, some studies indicate that the push to meet the program's quantitative goals has led to some chicanery and coercion on the part of local officials in the effort to divest people of their rural *hukou* (Chuang 2014).

Municipal officials are conscious of many of these contradictions and have paid some attention to addressing them. For example, there have been efforts to improve transit services to public rental housing sites. The factor that has played a more significant role in forestalling a greater reckoning, however, is that Chongqing's economy has remained one of the fastest growing for a city of its size in the world for the better part of the past decade. This growth in turn is largely an artifact of the Chinese government's financial and political commitment to the city, which through massive infrastructure investment and economic policy has successfully repositioned the city as a major new manufacturing and financial center. As long as sales at Chongqing outlets of Tiffany's, Prada, and Dolce & Gabbana remain brisk, and as long as workers continue to stream into the factories of FoxConn, HP, and Chang'an Motors, the state will maintain a strong wherewithal to pay down at least some of the social bills of its policies. Land values will continue to support the distribution of benefits to farmers, state revenue will continue to allow for investments in the infrastructure needed to continue growth, and, importantly, people will be able to continue to find sources of livelihood. An economic slowdown would reverberate across the social, economic, and political landscape with consequences that are difficult to fully anticipate. The potential for a significant slow in the rise of land values could potential lead to a collapse of the land-based financing system that has underwritten so much of Chongqing's development (Szelenyi 2011).

Until these changes come, however, Chongqing's accomplishments cannot and should not be dismissed lightly. For the many problems they engender, they stand as one of the most significant efforts to develop a redistributive model of land monetization in the world.

Western Chongqing's Urban Real Estate Megaprojects and the Spatial Logic of the Chongqing Model

While referred to in the media as "Western New City," the developments occurring to the west of Chongqing city proper are more accurately thought of as a cluster of planned developments containing varied functions intended to provide Chongqing with a major new growth engine. These developments, located in Shapingba District, include Xiyong Microelectronics Production Park, Chongqing University Town, Chongqing Modern Logistics Park, and Xiyong Central Business District. With a total planned area of twelve thousand hectares, this massive set of developments located immediately west of central Chongqing demonstrates the kind of large-scale, integrated initiative that the municipal government has been able to imagine with the expansive territory it has at its disposal.

As is typical of many other Chinese urban megaprojects, the western developments were master-planned by the Chongqing municipal government, which then employed the UDICs to build out the needed infrastructure. The municipality set out in planning the area to create an economic hub that will drive much of the city's economic and residential expansion in the coming years. The design and planning of these projects reflects the imperatives driving the Chinese urban development model, to foster rapid economic growth by creating enclaves for corporate investment and by engaging in speculative land development. Each of the projects listed above is intended both to create an economic presence while also cultivating a robust property market that will create financial opportunity for state actors. As Wu (2015, 163) notes, "first and foremost, the new town is an investment and financing platform." New towns are a means to achieve growth goals through the monetization of land at the urban periphery. Their planning thus reflects what Wu (2015) refers to as a "business model of planning," the planning of urban spaces to cater strategically to market niches, with the intention of ensuring the marketability and commercial viability of the resulting development. Yet the consequence, in Wu's (2015, 165) view, is that "[p]lanning is thus becoming more project-led instead of formulating a comprehensive land use plan."

The initial wave of development in the Western New Town development area played a central role in Chongqing's emergence is a major economic growth center. Notably, the Xiyong Micro-Electronics Industrial Park was established in 2005 and was approved by the central government as a provincial-level development zone, making it the largest duty-free zone in China's inland provinces (Jing 2010). This thirty-seven-square kilometer development zone has become a major economic growth and job generator for the region, with investment from major technology firms like FoxConn, Hewlett Packard, and Acer. In 2010 the central government further approved the Xiyong Integrated Free Trade Zone, a bonded zone that allows goods to be manufactured, packaged, and shipped without the imposition of duties. The municipality's heavy investment in infrastructure and the lower labor costs in Chongqing combined to quickly attract substantial investment, a trend that accelerated from 2008 on. Employment in the park in recent years has been estimated by the government at between 300,000 and 500,000, and total annual output was estimated in 2015 at 500 billion yuan (Tan 2015). In an additional effort to lure industrial investment, the municipality developed dormitories, medium-rise, densely built structures that accommodate as many as eight workers per room. Another critical economic development initiative is the Chongqing Logistics Park, a thirty-three-square-kilometers collection of intermodal transit, logistics, and shipping facilities that links Chongqing industry to the world by rail, air, and by sea via the Yangtze River. Established in 2007, the area contains a bonded logistics zone, cargo storage, and an intermodal transfer area. Finally, Chongqing CBD is 7.4 square kilometers in size and is intended as the major office and entertainment district.

Chongqing University Town is another important component of the western Chongqing projects, which is intended both to drive population growth in the area and to position the Shapingba developments as knowledge-based drivers of economic growth. The 3,300-hectare area is planned for 500,000 residents and will contain campuses of fourteen universities. Chongqing University Town follows a trend of the development of university towns across China; according to Li, Li, and Wang (2014) more than one hundred such towns were developed during the first decade of the 2000s. These authors further argue that the spate of development of such towns is one element of the model of "speculative urbanism" that defines contemporary Chinese planning. Indeed, these projects are intended both to provide a developmental rationale for the conversion of rural land and to generate new markets for urban real estate products, both by manufacturing a market for real estate products in growth areas and in the longer term by generating knowledge-based economic growth. The university campuses that have been relocated to Chongqing University Town were already estimated in 2015 to contain 200,000 staff and faculty members and students, so this element of the project has been a central component of efforts to foster the area as a major new population center. This has been important to generating markets for residential and commercial developments built by private developers in areas surrounding the university campuses. The municipality has also sought to develop cooperation between the universities located in the town and the Chongqing Microelectronics Industrial Park by establishing research and development centers within the park.

The spatial logic of the Shapingba developments is typical for such developments elsewhere in China. The built area is defined by multilane highways that connect largely monofunctional superblocks that are leased out to developers for the construction of residential districts, office complexes, shopping malls, and industrial zones. Residential developments consist for the most part of rows of high-rise, twenty- to forty-story condominium towers, set in developments that often also contain primary schools, shopping centers, and other basic facilities. These areas are sometimes gated and usually restricted to automobile access due to limited pedestrian access from major roads. There has been a modest effort to integrate the planned development areas with mass transit; Chongqing University Town is connected by an elevated rail system that transports passengers to central Chongqing in about forty-five minutes. The number of residents and workers within walking distance of this line, however, is quite limited. In the office districts, the scale of blocks and the dearth of commercial spaces means there is little pedestrian activity on the streets. Commercial functions are concentrated in shopping malls.

The Shapingba developments are planned as fragmented, strongly automobile-oriented urban spaces in which pedestrian activity is largely limited to the carefully landscaped green areas of subdivisions. One aspect of the new town model in Chongqing that is distinct, however, is the inclusion of two large public affordable rental housing complexes. Yet, as noted earlier, these developments lie in a relatively inaccessible portion of Xiyong, several kilometers from the rail line and the major centers of employment. Moreover, the spatial division between elite enclaves and densely built public rental housing developments, and even denser worker dormitories, ensures that residential areas within the new town remain segregated. As with sprawled suburban settings everywhere, it appears that in Chongqing's western fringe the car will come to serve as a major class divider, shaping the way that residents experience this new urban fabric, providing some residents with access to the amenities and opportunities provided by the town while excluding others.

Conclusion

The case of Chongqing, and of China more generally, raises the most pointed challenges to theories of neoliberalization of the three cases examined in this book. Despite a wealth of literature on the political economy of China's urbanization, this model has not been adequately analyzed and theorized in comparison to other models of urban development. This chapter has argued that viewing China's urban development as a model of state capitalist urban planning helps interpret the distinct interactions between institutions of land management, property relations, and urban planning and policy that shape urban outcomes. These variables also help interpret the distinct patterns of adaptation of market reform that have emerged, the transformation of political and social patterns wrought by these reforms, and the spatial implications of these changes.

In their 1987 book *Urban Fortunes*, John Logan and Harvey Molotch set an agenda for urban research in describing cities as growth machines, driven by shared interests in land development among corporate elites, property developers, and representatives of the local state. The China case is different, for here the separation between these groups breaks down, and the state stands not only as regulator and planner, but also as developer and as corporate head. Land development emerges as the central thrust of state, and specifically of CCP strategy. As the Chongqing case illustrates, land commodification not only becomes the central objective of urban politics, but it also becomes a tool that the state applies to a range of social and ecological problems.

To state this in terms of current debates about the neoliberalization of cities, it is the powers over land and economy that allow the Chinese state to so readily deploy neoliberal policy as a "technology of governing" in the sense discussed by Ong (2006). Ong argues that neoliberal policy ideals should not be viewed as imposed whole cloth on Asian societies by Western powers and international agencies, but rather as deployed selectively by Asian states in the pursuit of their own interests. States use market-oriented modes of governance with the intention to achieve economic growth by "induc[ing] an enterprising subjectivity in elite subjects," through a strategy of "separating some groups for special attention, and carving out special zones that overlap, but do not coincide, with the national terrain" (Ong 2006, 5, 6). Indeed, this argument seems to explain much about the direction of policy in Singapore and China, where the construction of subjectivities is apparent in the creation of new models of urban spatial production and in the re-engineering of labor relations, which seems clearly intended to establish incentives and new privileges that encourage entrepreneurialism and reward a highly educated elite. It is the state's ability to control land and economy that puts such goals of social engineering within reach.

This chapter has outlined some of the issues that emerge with this model. Not only does the state's complicity in urban development implicate the state in the social and ecological problems that arise with capitalist urbanization, but the state also becomes addicted to land development, as further development through land-based finance comes to be viewed as an elixir for all urban problems. This is apparent in the applications of land-based finance to the problems of social inequality and rural-urban integration discussed in this chapter. It is also apparent in the spate of eco-city projects that have emerged throughout China in recent years and that are projected in the media as China's primary response to ecological degradation and global warming.

The paradox in all these cases is the same; in attempting to build its way out of crises, the state perpetuates the endless agenda of profit-driven growth that created these crises in the first place. In the case of eco-cities, the approach involves the appropriation of land to build elite enclaves employing renewable energy, recycling, composting, and other environmentally sustainable technologies. Yet the measure of the ecological footprint of these new urban spaces misses the ecological impacts of the large urban development process that created these spaces, which may include displacement of rural communities, loss of ecosystems and arable land, disinvestment from existing built environments, expansion of urban regions and consequent increasing reliance on cars, and reliance of these eco-cities on larger carbon-intensive industries (Caprotti 2014).

In sum, China's model of urban development grants great powers to the state to realize a variety of goals. The question remains, however, as to how this power might be managed and tempered within a framework that allows for a broad discussion and debate concerning what goals this model should be applied to.

Conclusion

Interpreting the Theoretical and Practical Implications of the Real Estate Turn

As the new millennium took shape, Jakarta and many other Asian coastal megacities became conscious of a potentially devastating new threat: climate-change-induced flooding. Yet even as projections of sea level rise have taken shape, Jakarta has already begun to experience dramatic floods for a mix of reasons related both to climate change and to entrenched social and political problems: land subsidence due to groundwater extraction, increasingly intense rains due to changing weather patterns, and deforestation and increased impervious surface due to uncontrolled development in upland areas (Marfai, Sekaranom, and Ward 2015; Padawangi and Douglass 2015). In 2014 the Indonesian government, drawing on technical expertise from the Dutch, responded by launching the National Capital Integrated Coastal Development Plan, known colloquially as the Great Garuda plan (Government of Indonesia 2014). This initiative sought to forestall the permanent inundation of parts of the city due to sea level rise through the construction of a massive seawall along which 1,250 hectares of land, crafted in the shape of Garuda, the mythical Hindu bird, would be reclaimed from the sea. This US$40 billion initiative would be financed in part through the development of this reclaimed land as a new city of 1.5 million residents, with the body of the Garuda containing a new central business district for the region and the wings zoned as dense new residential areas. The formation of the Garuda would create a giant lake between the reclaimed land and Jakarta's north shore to retain water from rivers that drain the highlands that surround the city. Giant pumping stations, the largest in the world, would pump excess water from low-lying areas; in 2014, 40 percent of the city's land area already lay below the high-tide mark.

The Great Garuda plan stands as a useful conceptual bookend to the Boeung Kak plan that framed the beginning of the introduction to this book. Unlike that plan, the Great Garuda project was conceived in a democratic political setting, and the project goes to some pains to limit displacement. As argued earlier, land reclamation has increasingly been deployed as a means to manufacture developable land unencumbered by claims of ownership or usership that confound so many efforts at land acquisition. The project further seeks to transcend the focus on economic development that defines most urban real estate megaprojects, and instead is framed as an infrastructure of urban resilience and sustainability with broad societal benefits. In many ways this project represents urban real estate megaproject 2.0, representative of a new generation of such projects, often developed in democratized political contexts, that claim the mantle of a better, smarter, and more sustainable form of urbanism.[1]

Such claims aside, the Great Garuda plan also embodies what this volume has argued are the inherent flaws of the urban real estate megaproject model. While ostensibly a defense against flooding, the project turns its back on the inland problems that are the immediate generators of this threat, many of which are themselves a consequence of the real-estate-driven model that has defined Jakarta's urban development since the late New Order period. These include a sprawled pattern of development facilitated by the massive permitting of land, and dramatic land subsidence caused by groundwater extraction, an infrastructural-cum-governance failure that is inextricably linked to the concentration of Jakarta's population in "unregistered" *kampung* settlements that remain largely excluded from the city's piped water infrastructure. Moreover, the Great Garuda may in the end fail to meet its heroic goals precisely because of the urban real estate megaproject model it embraces. The glut of land previously permitted for other developments may undermine the market viability of this project. As long as developers sit on tens of thousands of hectares of development permits, Jakarta's development will continue to unfold in a sprawled and fragmented pattern, and a market saturated with a supply of developable land due to state intervention may determine the fate of the Great Garuda plan's real estate ambitions.

Despite the tactical embrace of ideals of ecological sustainability by a new generation of urban real estate megaprojects, therefore, the model itself exhibits inherent issues. Embraced by states that have been pulled toward the adoption of an entrepreneurial urban politics by the forces of competition and fiscal austerity, these projects have formed around the convergence of state, corporate, and real estate interests. Their central premise is the extraction of emergent rent gaps as a source of profit for corporations and power for states. Yet as enclaves built by profit-driven and politically influential actors, these projects exhibit an inherent tendency toward exclusion and elitism, as developers seek to create self-enclosed spaces of corporate capital accumulation. As impositions on densely populated and intensely used spaces, their footprints inevitably lead to displacement of existing residents, in addition to displacement through ancillary infrastructure development and the destruction of economies and social spaces their development creates. These projects are also haunted by the specter of failure, as the coalescence of state and corporate interests creates a policy push toward increasingly speculative ambitions for urban transformation and financial gains. The consequences and costs of this potential for failure inevitably radiate outward into the broader society in the form of blight, ecological damage, and lost economic and financial opportunity. Examples of failure include Bangkok's Muang Thong Thani, a significant portion of which was completed in 1998 but which remains largely abandoned to this day, and China's famous ghost towns, which have received international media attention.

This book has sought to develop a comparative understanding of the political dynamics that shape state agendas of urban real estate megaproject development and the challenges these politics present to governments and communities. It has sought to move beyond generalizations about the neoliberalization of urban policy and to question perspectives on neoliberalization as an externally imposed force that imposes a homogenous set of changes on urban social, political, and spatial change. It has done so by exploring the particular ways states strategize efforts to transform market relations around property as a means to enable the development of these privatized projects. It has further focused attention on how the degree of pluralization of sources of influence over urban real estate megaprojects, particularly through legal, political, and social structures of property rights and planning and policy, influences the ability of different actors to shape the outcomes of these developments. The book has specifically analyzed the explanatory power of two variables: the extent of autonomy of land managers from social and economic interest groups, and the extent of the state's direct control over land markets.

The case studies of Kolkata, Jakarta, and Chongqing, chosen based on their differences along these two variables, do indeed show dramatic differences in the politics of urban real estate megaproject development and in their spatial outcomes. In each case we see the real estate turn in urban politics emerge as a suite of reforms in the areas of property rights, land markets, urban governance, land use planning, banking and finance, and urban economic development policy. Yet in each case these shifts are at apparent normative odds with still extant (although often problematic) state narratives arising from the postcolonial and socialistic roots of states, of the state as custodian of citizenship and inclusiveness, and of the state's role in defending threatened ecologies and ways of life. Across the case studies, we see state actors tack between a defensive, discursive stance, seeking to justify their role in massive land transfers to for-profit actors, and a muscular effort to force through such transfers in the face of public opprobrium over the resulting social and ecological dislocation.

The case studies reveal substantial differences in the spatial outcomes of these contestations. Jakarta, an authoritarian state with an almost complete monopoly on political power, was able to reshape property rights and land-management regimes to realize a massive and regressive transfer of land wealth to a handful of oligarchs who formed a critical part of the foundation of New Order rule. Yet even in this case of strong central control, the regime felt compelled, in the interests of political legitimacy, to frame the spate of new town planning that accompanied the late New Order period in terms of technocratic and rhetorical aspirations to equitable and ecologically sustainable development. China, a state that monopolized both political power and property markets, was able to translate those powers into a massive urban transformation that directly enriched and empowered the state and granted it enormous powers of social and political control. Here too, however, the state found itself embroiled in the issues of social displacement, ecological destruction, and runaway corruption that this model engendered, and it sought aggressively to reassert central control in the interest of managing these issues (with Chongqing emerging as one model for doing so). Kolkata, a state with a highly pluralistic political milieu, met substantial resistance to its agenda of urban real estate megaproject development from the very beginning. Despite an effort by the ruling CPI-M to frame its land-acquisition push as necessary to the economic and political transformation of the state of West Bengal, this disjuncture led to the fall of a government and the end of any immediate aspirations for an ambitious agenda of new town development.

This conclusion will begin by revisiting some of the theoretical starting points outlined in the introduction, particularly theoretical debates about the neoliberalization of urban governance, and will seek to summarize what the analysis of the case studies adds to our understanding of these theories. It will then examine some of the specific political dynamics and contestations that emerge as crosscutting themes across the cases, exploring how these themes elucidate both commonalities and differences in the political challenges presented by each case. These crosscutting themes are the controversies created by the uses and abuses of the land value increment produced by urban real estate megaprojects, the construction of dualisms as a means to rationalize dispossession, the varied ways in which the act of dispossession is legitimized through developmental discourses, and the dynamics of economic and social exclusion produced by these projects.

The Real Estate Turn and Urban Theory

This book began by framing the real estate turn in Asia's urban politics within the larger literature on neoliberalization and urban governance. This literature asks how we interpret contemporary urban political and social change in a context of intensified global interconnectivity and competition. Is the adoption of market-oriented governance by Asian states attributable to the rote adoption of ideals promulgated by Western governments and international institutions? Such an interpretation of neoliberalism as a "thought virus," an ideology that passes from society to society through the institutional and intellectual influence of the West, implies a passive role for states in the Global South (Peck and Tickell 2002). In this view, states are seen as borrowing from an abstract playbook of market-oriented reform in a callow effort to court investment, subsuming immediate state and national interests in urban development to the desires of global capital (Peck and Tickell 2002). Or, instead, does the adoption of neoliberal ideals reflect a more purposive adaptation of market-oriented governance to local interests, producing a variegated *process* of "neoliberalization" that reflects the interaction between global rule regimes and local institutions (Brenner, Peck, and Theodore 2010)? Or, alternatively, are scholars wrongly privileging accounts of neoliberalization and associated concepts (gentrification, entrepreneurial governance) simply because these phenomena are more easily understood by anglophone scholars accustomed to theories rooted largely in American and British experiences (Parnell and Robinson 2012). Jennifer Robinson has been a particularly eloquent voice in calling for scholarship to move beyond concepts of globalization and neoliberalization. She calls on scholars to reengage with the distinct issues, struggles, challenges, and opportunities of cities that may have taken shape more through historically embedded social, cultural, and political institutions than through globalizing forces (Robinson 2006; Parnell and Robinson 2012).

The analysis in this book favors the middle interpretation, of a systematic trend toward market-oriented shifts in urban development that nonetheless takes utterly distinct forms based on differences in local political economies, particularly around institutions of property and land management. The case studies reviewed here reveal state actors across levels of government shaping political economic agendas less out of any abstract desire to adhere to neoliberal ideology than out of an interest in exploiting markets (particularly markets in land) to achieve specific state goals of regime consolidation, vote bank cultivation, and sometimes personal enrichment. The specificity of the tools they have available and constraints they face (e.g., extant property relations, state landholdings, and cultural and political norms around land) lead to very different strategies that do not cohere into a legible "playbook" of neoliberal reform. Indeed, many of the policy innovations documented in the cases, while focused on breaking down communal and statist modes of land regulation and creating new markets in land, nonetheless fly in the face of accepted global norms of neoliberal practice and are sometimes undertaken despite opposition from the World Bank and other ostensible guardians of the neoliberal world order. What emerges most clearly from the cases examined here, therefore, is the ways that questions of land are subject to struggles for power that can only be understood in the context of debates over property and social rights that have deep roots in colonial and post-colonial histories.

Yet the case studies do not indicate a need to shift our focus away from processes of neoliberalization, as suggested by Parnell and Robinson (2012). In their insightful article, which focuses on African cases, they paraphrase James Ferguson in suggesting that neoliberal regulatory logics remain "socially thin" in most African cities. They see these logics as confined to global enclaves that are points of connection to the global economy, while the rest of society is subject to "models of national development that framed the post-independence era in many African countries" (Parnell and Robinson 2012, 601). The cases examined in this book, however, reveal the limitations of such an either-or framing, which separates populations between those who reside within spaces of neoliberalization and those who do not. The case studies focus attention on how the process of neoliberalization of land management and property rights has broad implications across scales and across a range of social and political issues, including questions of urban poverty, environmental justice, and social welfare. This is most notable in Chongqing, where the state's keen interest in land monetization shaped policies and regulations concerning *hukou* reform, agricultural development, and affordable housing. The Jakarta case shows how state interventions in the realm of property rights that were intended to transfer rent gaps to cronies of the state played out in the political and spatial marginalization of *kampung* settlements more generally. While "unregistered" claims to land rooted in customary tenure relations do constitute a space of autonomy to some degree, in the context of their subordination through the permitting system these customary relations also become a mechanism of exclusion and dispossession. Hence what appears as the persistence of non-neoliberal dynamics is in fact being reshaped by new forces of market-oriented governance.

The analysis in the case studies, therefore, supports an understanding of the neoliberalization of urban governance as a "variegated" process that unfolds unevenly as coalitions of corporate and state actors seek strategic advantage through the invention or reframing of markets, in this case markets for land. As Peck and Theodore (2012, 21) argue, ostensibly neoliberal "(p)henomena like the decentering of nation-state power, the rise of multilateral agencies, and the transnationalization of expert networks should not be taken as mere precursors to global homogenization, but rather as complex and contradictory spaces ripe for critical interrogation." The obvious question that emerges from this observation is, how do we begin to unpack this complexity and contradiction? In the case of the real estate turn in urban politics, what are the key institutional and political sources of variation among cases? How do historically formed relations of property, embedded in institutions, laws, and social and cultural norms, shape the capacity of states to monetize land and the strength of the social opposition they face in doing so? How do dynamics of displacement and spatial inequality, which inevitably accompany this process of land monetization, play out in political and legal strategy? How do communities respond? The remainder of this conclusion will attempt to summarize some of the insights into these questions that emerge from the case studies, organizing this analysis around several crosscutting themes that emerge throughout the cases.

Uses and Abuses of the Land Value Increment

A central premise of this book is that one important state objective in the pursuit of urban real estate megaprojects is the exploitation of emergent rent gaps in Asian cities for purposes of state enrichment and empowerment. The three case studies document quite different models through which this exploitation takes place: through the transfer of land development rights to cronies in Jakarta, through the state's direct appropriation of rent gaps in Chongqing, and through the use of land transfers as a means to incentivize the creation of new urban space in Kolkata. The primary tools states have used in each case have included development permitting in Jakarta, providing land grants to state-owned corporations in

Chongqing, and state compulsory acquisition of land for transfer to developers in Kolkata.

In each of the three case studies, the assertion of new powers over land presents a moment of stark opportunities and significant dangers. The question of the distribution of costs and benefits is inherent in any urban change. However, when state actors play a central role in land transfers that involve the loss of livelihoods and ways of life on a such a massive scale, and when they do so in the interest of creating windfall profits for powerful individuals and corporations, questions of fairness and equity present a potentially destabilizing political challenge. It is notable that in two of the cases examined in the preceding three chapters, issues surrounding the management of land development and the distribution of resulting revenue brought about seismic political shifts that arguably played a role in the fall of urban political regimes. In each case this occurred during the period when field research for the book was being conducted.[2] In Kolkata, as we have seen, concerns over the government of West Bengal's forcible acquisition of land played a significant role in the Left Front's loss of its electoral mandate after thirty years in power. In Chongqing, some commentators have speculated that Bo Xilai's redistributive policies, which, as analyzed in chapter 5, were based in part on a redistributionist use of land-based revenue, may have posed a threat to high-level national leaders of the CCP who were invested, ideologically and perhaps financially as well, in the continuation of China's real estate binge and the larger project of growth-driven economic management (Li 2012; Mulvad 2015). Some have argued that this ideological turn may have played a role in Bo's dismissal, which more immediately resulted from revelations surrounding the murder of a British businessman, which instigated the chain of events that led to his fall from power (Fenby 2012).

How, then, have state actors sought to frame their appropriation of land value increments in political terms? What sources of opposition have they experienced, and how have they sought to counter this opposition? The most coercive approaches among the cases examined in this book are those of Suharto-era Indonesia and contemporary Cambodia. In chapter 2, I characterized these as cases of a "political economy of the land grab," in which authoritarian regimes and an oligarchic economic and political elite sought to incorporate urban land, the claims to which were spread broadly across society, into their political machines. In both cities, what appears to have resulted is a growing exploitation of mechanisms of land acquisition as land values rose and become an increasingly important source of wealth. In the Jakarta case this built into a feeding frenzy that transformed the Jakarta Metropolitan Region in ways that will continue to be felt for generations.

The Jakarta case study reveals the blunt sociospatial logic of the Indonesian version of this model. The orgy of land permitting that accompanied the real estate shift in the New Order oligarchy has created an urban landscape that is remarkably fragmented even by the standards of other neoliberalizing Asian cities. Permitting has created not only spatial but also political path dependencies, as the continued control by developers of massive land banks serves to perpetuate the political influence of companies that have descended from Suharto-era oligarchies. This influence is arguably evident in approaches to flooding evinced in the Great Garuda plan, which chooses to deal with flooding problems partially caused by the sprawled pattern of developer-driven spatial change by reclaiming yet more land to be permitted to these same developers.

Hence the cases of states like Indonesia and Cambodia demonstrates the use of land monetization for what I referred to in the introduction as a *strategy of accumulation* and as a *tactic of rent seeking*. That is, land management has been deployed in these cases as a means to pursue the particularistic interests of rent-seeking individuals, and to a lesser degree to realize a broader agenda of accumulation by a corporate elite. I discussed these terms in the introduction in relation to Ong's (2006) argument that, particularly in East Asian settings like Singapore and China, neoliberal policy has been deployed as a "technology of governing," a more developmental effort to produce entrepreneurial subjects as part of a new regime of globalization-driven economic development. These strategies of rent seeking and corporate accumulation present a different set of legitimization challenges.

The challenge for authoritarian states like those in Indonesia and Cambodia is to frame massive economically and politically regressive land transfers as acts of development. These authoritarian regimes strive to exert sufficient control over discourses of property rights and the objectives of development to frame urban real estate megaprojects in ways that key constituencies—notably foreign aid donors and trade partners—can find palatable. In Cambodia and New Order Indonesia state actors did so by evoking state claims to land in ways that were deeply rooted in colonial and postcolonial histories. In Phnom Penh, a city forged from wetlands and water bodies by Cambodian kings and French colonial rulers, the Hun Sen regime seized on this legacy by engaging in a politically opportunistic, and in the case of Boeung Kak ecologically destructive, agenda of land reclamation. In the Jakarta Metropolitan Region, the state reinvented a colonial-era land dualism as a mechanism for land appropriation. That the displacements in Jakarta moved forward with relatively little organized opposition is likely attributable to the effectiveness of the New Order state's control of the media and of civil society and the strong support the regime received from an international community that viewed Suharto's regime as a bulwark against communism. In contrast, the Boeung Kak project eventually faltered in the face of international opprobrium. International support for local opposition was built through the canny use of web-based media outlets through which opponents of the project could alert larger publics in Cambodia and beyond to the displacement and abuses that were occurring. It was only through an appeal to international donors based on a human rights claim of unfair imprisonment that the Boeung Kak project was eventually stopped, although too late to stop the evictions. Despite the availability of channels through which to express dissent in contemporary Phnom Penh, however, such movements have failed to halt several other cases of land grabs for real estate projects.

The case studies of Kolkata and Chongqing in chapters 4 and 5 reveal highly contrasting cases of much more nuanced approaches to state legitimization of land appropriation. In the "state capitalist" models of Chongqing and Singapore, state actors have attempted to legitimize their capacity to directly appropriate land-based revenue by translating this capacity into an aggressive agenda of infrastructure modernization, economic development, and the creation of symbolically charged urban spaces designed to signal the arrival of these cities as globally relevant urban centers. In both cases land monetization was also used for the delivery of public goods. Both countries have also sought through new town development to cater to the lifestyle aspirations of their citizens through the creation of consumer enclaves.

To an even greater extent than is true of Chongqing, Singapore represents the ideal typical manifestation of this strategy. Here the state has used its dominance of land ownership not only to generate revenue, but also to dominate the housing sector and therefore the physical form and social functioning of community life (Shatkin 2014). The Singaporean government also uses its control of urban space to exert powerful control in directing the trajectory of economic growth, investing heavily in incubators and other new spaces for biotechnology and other perceived growth sectors, and in the cultural economy of the city (Yeoh 2005; Wong and Bunnell 2006). When combined with an assiduous campaign of intimidation of opposition politicians, dominance of the media, and the manipulation of the electoral map through controls on the ethnic mix of public housing estates, the legitimacy accorded by the distribution of economic benefits has allowed the ruling People's Action Party to maintain electoral dominance since Singapore's independence. The Singapore case illustrates the power of state control over land markets as a tool for legitimation and regime construction through a combination of the strategic distribution of economic benefits and social and political engineering.

While it provides opportunities for legitimation and empowerment that are the envy of other states, however, the state capitalist model of urban planning also creates notable contradictions. The central challenge, more notable in the Chinese than in the Singaporean case, is to create incentives for entrepreneurialism among local state actors, to instill in them the predatory urges of capitalists so they will craft agendas of economic growth, while reining in the inherent potential for rapacity, corruption, and state violence that can result. This contradiction is muted in the Singapore case because Singapore is a small city-state with an area close to that of New York City and a citizen and permanent resident population currently standing at less than four million. This context has allowed Singapore to outsource some of the social and ecological issues that accompany its rapid growth. Neighboring areas of Malaysia and Indonesia have seen dramatic ecological and social transformations with new industrial, commercial, logistical, and residential areas supporting Singapore's growth, and the city-state's low-wage service economy employs migrants from across the region at living standards far below those of the average Singaporean citizen. Singapore's small scale also means that there is full integration of national and local governance, so that the state can more directly administer urban governance in forwarding state goals.

In contrast, the Chinese Communist Party has had to take full ownership of the ecological and social dislocations attending rapid state-driven capitalist urbanization, including disruptive periurban transformations, massive rural-urban migration, and ecological damage. Moreover, the intense competition among state entities, including that between national ministries and state-owned corporations, municipal bodies, and village collectives, has increased both the potential for conflict and the incentives for predatory behavior. The inequalities, exclusions, and displacements accompanying the resulting processes of land development have given rise to popular movements that have contested state agendas, using strategies such as assertions of property rights by people living in houses slated for demolition, refusal of the terms of compensation for eviction, and formation of cross-neighborhood networks to engage in mass protest against dispossession (Hsing 2010). In response, the national government has been compelled to recentralize land administration, and to intervene persistently to rein in social dislocation, loss of farmland, and environmental damage. China has been at the forefront of deploying eco-city developments as a way to reframe new town development as drivers of ecological sustainability, yet the ecological goals of projects like Sino-Singapore Tianjin Eco-City and Caofeidian Eco-City are ultimately undermined by the overwhelming trends toward urban expansion, car-oriented development, and energy-intensive industrialization that drive the regional economies in which they are embedded (Caprotti 2014). As China's supply of land and labor for economic growth dwindles, and as the vagaries of the global economy continue to shift the country's competitive position, the local state's addiction to land as a source of economic growth and competitiveness will continue to shape its interaction with urban space and with urban and periurban communities in unpredictable and potentially destabilizing ways.

In the India case, as in other cases of democratic states with diffuse land-ownership systems (such as the Philippines), states have faced the challenge of building political coalitions around an agenda of land appropriation for urban development. What emerges in such cases is a nascent urban regime politics in which elected leaders seek to mobilize various constituencies, most notably a growing consumer class and corporate elites, around state efforts at land acquisition, transfer or sale to developers, and public-private partnerships in land development. In mobilizing coalitions, state actors frame land monetization as a strategy of accumulation, an effort to carve out spaces for the realization of corporate investment. Yet in India such coalitions generally remain weak, and where projects have experienced some modest success, this has largely been due either to the exercise of considerable political capital by state actors, the aggressive deployment of rationales of economic growth, or careful negotiation of the terms of compensation and relocation of those displaced. The question of the terms through which land appropriation occurs has emerged as a controversial political issue, one that in India has shaped political dynamics not only at the municipal but also at the state and national levels.

But while state-sponsored megaprojects like the Dankuni Township project discussed in chapter 4 have foundered, developers in India have nonetheless been able to gain traction in the development of small and mid-sized developments. Rouanet and Halbert (2015) argue that they are able to do so by positioning themselves both as mediators who can manage negotiations over land acquisition on behalf of global and domestic capital, and as agents of symbolically powerful models of world-class city development. Their account indicates that the process of land commodification in Indian cities is ongoing and that developers and other interests connected to property development are gradually gaining political traction through the realization of urban transformations at smaller scales. In the longer term, therefore, the issue of the political implications of the state thrust toward land monetization continues to unfold, and these politics are worthy of considerable further investigation.

The Construction of Dualisms: Destabilizing Nonstate and Nonfreehold Claims to Land

A notable common feature among all three of the case studies is the state's exploitation of legal and institutional dualisms in claims to land as a means to cultivate and capture rent gaps. In each case these dualisms have deep roots in colonial and postcolonial histories and serve to structure the ability of various actors to acquire, use, develop, and exchange land. The restrictions placed on certain categories of land claims—the unregistered *hak girik* and *hak garapan* claims in Indonesia, "informal" claims in India, and collective claims in periurban areas of Chinese cities—inhibit their commodification and therefore suppress their market value. This presents an opportunity for the capture of windfall gains with a change in category that enables their market exchange and redevelopment. A central dynamic in each of the case studies is the presence of a legal and institutional reform movement focused, implicitly or explicitly, on reinforcing these dualisms and asserting the control of the state and allied actors in adjudicating processes of regularization.

In each of these cases, the agenda of constructing and policing dualisms has emerged in an ad hoc manner in response to a growing understanding of the political importance of land markets and of the possibilities presented by a stronger state hand. In China, the state notably intervened to reinforce this dualism when it mandated state ownership of all urban land in the 1982 constitution. Whether the Chinese Communist Party was conscious of the implications of this move for the state's later role in commercial real estate development is a matter for further investigation and debate. Nevertheless, the state's interest in land markets deepened dramatically in the ensuing decades, leading to a series of increasingly contentious reforms intended to assert municipal governments' ability to urbanize rural collective land. In Jakarta, land permitting predated the state-driven real estate boom that began in the mid-1980s, but this mechanism became increasingly politicized during the last thirteen years of the New Order regime as its potential as a tool for land monetization became apparent. It was during this period that massive permits were issued to politically connected developers. In India, where a multiparty electoral political system dictates a more contested, decentered, and deliberate process of reforms to institutions of property, and where significant political support exists for informal claims, state governments have undertaken a more gradual approach to reform. Over the past two decades coalitions of state and corporate actors have gradually come to view the Land Acquisition Act of 1892 as the most feasible available mechanism to acquire land for transfer to developers, and they have backed initiatives like the Dharavi Redevelopment Program as means to transform "slum" settlements through the agency of property developers. The passage of the Land Acquisition, Rehabilitation, and Resettlement Act of 2013 represents a significant recent chapter in the ongoing negotiations over rights to property.

The argument for the political centrality of dualisms presented here has strong resonance with Ananya Roy's (2009, 82) argument framing "informality" as a "mode of governing," a category of activities created through "purposive action and planning, and one where the seeming withdrawal of regulatory power creates a logic of resource allocation, accumulation, and authority." Much as argued here, Roy sees legal and regulatory systems that subordinate certain claims as constructed through deliberate action in the interests of state power. Where the argument presented in this book differs subtly from Roy's argument is in pointing to a variety of dualisms, beyond those delineating the formal from the informal. The comparative case studies presented here reveal a wide range of institutional, legal, and political claims to land in varied political environments, beyond the legal dichotomy that frames certain claims as outside the law and other claims as inside the law. In the Indonesian and Chinese cases, property claims that are legally recognized are nonetheless subordinate and have been subject to gradual degradation and destabilization despite their recognition within "formal" regulatory and legal structures (as noted in the case of Indonesia in Leaf 1993).

It is important to note the variation in the legal, institutional, and political origins of dualisms because these differences have led to substantial variation in the strategies of state and corporate actors in exploiting these dualisms. In each case the objectives have been the same: to undermine the legal and political basis of alternative claims to urban space and to sow doubt in the public conscience about the legitimacy and justice of these alternative claims. These objectives have been pursued through varied means. In India's relatively pluralistic political environment, this has unfolded through contestations in a variety of realms, including shifts in court decisions and in structures of governance and in legislation seeking to weaken the political power of "informal" users of urban space. This has notably played out, as discussed in chapter 4, through public interest litigations (PILs) launched by middle-class associations against informal claims to space. It has also occurred through political reforms like the Bhaghidari scheme, intended to subject lower-level politicians and bureaucrats, seen as too beholden to the poor, to direct accountability to middle-class citizens. In another instance, Bjorkman (2013) describes the "reslumming" of Shivajinagar, a Mumbai community that despite its origins in a state resettlement program, found itself relegated by bureaucrats to the category of "slum" due to its illegal tapping of the piped water system, a move itself born of necessity due to state infrastructural neglect. Yet these shifts toward the delegitimization of urban spatial claims of the poor are subject to substantial contestation, as communities deploy a number of political and legal strategies to protect their claims. They embrace caste-based politics, conduct demonstrations to counter the claims of the state, and launch their own PILs to assert their rights to urban space.

In the cases of China and Indonesia, questions of the legality of settlements play a much more muted role for two reasons. First, the state's primary claims to powers of land acquisition rest not on the illegality of alternate claims, but rather on the state's ostensible role in social modernization and urbanization. Second, the authoritarian nature of these regimes seems to leave little scope for questioning or contesting the legal basis of state land takings or of state machinations in the area of land rights. Contestations over land in China focus not on questions of the legality of claims, but on administrative questions. These include concerns over the predatory practices of local governments and the lack of popular representation in rural areas that belies the idea that rural land decisions reflect collective ownership.

In Jakarta, it is notable that dissension over the inequities associated with the dualism between registered and unregistered land continues to be surprisingly muted in the current era of democratized government. Despite news accounts of the predatory practices developers have deployed in wresting unregistered lands from both periurban and urban communities—including walling off such communities as discussed in chapter 3—there has been little legal effort to strengthen the property claims of such communities, to contest the obstacles that prevent them from registering their claims, or to question the transfer of development rights through the mechanism of location permits. Where legal efforts have challenged dualisms in post–New Order Indonesia, these efforts have focused on defending the informal communities that make up a much smaller proportion of the population but are subject to more immediate threats of summary eviction. This lack of political challenges to dualisms and to the continued practice of providing location permits to developers is perhaps partially attributable to the increased political sway of *kampung* communities within the democratized, decentralized political framework, which provides communities greater leeway to negotiate the terms of land sale to permit holders.

Given the centrality of legal and institutional dualisms to state strategies of land acquisition, it is apparent that a clear understanding of the historical construction of such dualisms is critical to how we understand the issues of equity and justice that emerge with the dispossession of poor communities. Across the case studies there seems to be a dearth of public understanding of these histories, which enables states to exercise a great deal of control over discourses of land development and to frame the claims of the poor as standing in the way of urban and national progress. Further research on this topic is needed to inform these debates and to increase understanding of the potential strategies of poor communities in asserting their rights in questions of legality and legitimacy.

Framing the Dispossessed

The question of what happens to those dispossessed by urban real estate megaprojects—residents of periurban villages, squatter settlements, age-worn residential areas, bazaars, and industrial districts that find themselves in the path of development and infrastructure schemes—constitutes another moment of contestation and political mobilization. How do state and corporate actors attempt to strike what is sometimes a delicate balance between their strategic and financial interests in the dispossession of substantial populations, their pursuit of the public benefits that sometimes accrue from such projects, and the need to maintain the legitimacy of the state as an arbiter of historical ideals of universal citizenship? There is little systematically gathered empirical data to answer the very basic question of what happens to populations that have been displaced. Where do they go? How do they reintegrate into urban or periurban life? What social and economic impacts do they experience? Indeed, this is a critical area for additional research. What does emerge as a clear crosscutting theme in the case studies is the ways that state actors frame the process of dispossession and reintegration of the dispossessed as part of the larger ideological project of urban redevelopment. In each case state actors rationalize these processes of dispossession as part of an ideological project of ecological and social transformation through urbanization. Such rationalizations are, however, sometimes flawed in coherence and logic and therefore provide an opportunity for contestation and the development of counternarratives.

In the case of the Jakarta Metropolitan Region, Kusno (2012b) has linked the process of dispossession of periurban farmers to a larger New

Order project of managing the peasantry. Peasants, he argues, have always been seen by the state as a potential source of dissent and violence that needs to be modernized in the interests of both stability and of economic and social progress. While the New Order state had sought early on to close Jakarta to rural-urban migrants, its perspective evolved with the expansion of the metropolitan region and the clear need for a reserve pool of labor for the city's economy, which was increasingly important to national development. During the 1970s and 1980s, therefore, regional planning for what came to be termed by the state as the Jabotabek (later Jabodetabek) region focused on creating a periurban zone of "transition" (*transisi*). This was explicitly framed as a space in which migrants, instead of coming into the city, could be transitioned to urban life at the fringe while contributing to the metropolitan region's burgeoning industrial and service economy. Curiously, according to Kusno, in 1984 (at the precise moment that the Bumi Serpong Damai project was being conceived) the minister of agriculture announced the objective of eradicating farms of less than half a hectare across the country. Doing so would free smallholder lands for other uses and contribute substantially to the flow of migrants. In this context, it appears that the spate of land permitting that ensued in the coming years was rationalized in part by a parallel state agenda of transforming rural smallholders into a "floating mass," ostensibly with the ultimate goal of assimilating them into urban modernity. The highly speculative and fragmented nature of the resulting development, and its failure to provide either a strong basis for broad-based industrial development or to contribute appreciably to the stock of affordable housing, seems to have undercut this agenda.

The Chongqing case represents an even more aggressive agenda of engineering the urban transition, enabled by the Communist Party's control of land and economy, which has allowed it to bypass partial measures and to imagine the rapid and almost complete urbanization of the country. The twin agendas of constructing a "new Socialist countryside" and of "coordinating rural and urban development" are explicitly intended to achieve this objective. This agenda is precisely about incorporating ruralites into the urban fabric through efforts to "initiate agricultural modernization . . . strengthen the provision of public goods (most notably, social welfare and basic education), relocate peasants to new villages or urban neighborhoods, [and] expand vocational training and create new job opportunities" (Ahlers and Schubert 2013, 833). Yet an important question in this case, as indeed in the Indonesian case as well, is what motivations truly drive the agenda of urbanization. Is the urbanization agenda truly driven by technocratic ideals of integrating rural dwellers into the infrastructural, social, and economic benefits of the urban economy? Or is the urbanization of peasants instead being pursued in a bid to perpetuate a model of land monetization and economic growth premised on real estate development and expanded consumer spending. The truth most likely lies in some combination of the two. To the extent that the latter motivation prevails, however, and particularistic interests operating at the nexus of real estate and politics hold sway in driving urban development, the disjuncture of interests between the state and the peasantry is likely to exacerbate political tensions as the push for mass urbanization proceeds.

In India, an environment of political pluralism has ensured that questions of dispossession and the urban transition have played out in cacophonous public debate. Indeed, the dispossessed (or dispossessable) slum dweller and periurban ruralite has emerged as a divisive figure at the heart of both policy and popular discourse and elite and subaltern collective action. In an influential article, Baviskar (2003) relates the story of a young man's murder in a public park in Delhi by a middle-class vigilante mob, ostensibly due to suspicion that the bottle of water he was carrying was intended to be used to wash himself after defecating on the park grounds. Benjamin (2008) cites the rant of a participant at the Federation of Indian Chambers of Conference and Industries who argued that local elected councilors who provide political cover for slums should be lined up and shot for their crimes against India's globalizing economy. Yet public debates also reflect an ambivalence about the implications of modernization and urbanization amongst a public whose thinking has also been shaped by Gandhian notions of the sanctity of agriculture and of India's artisanal traditions. In 2014, newly elected prime minister Narendra Modi faced intense criticism over a record number of suicides by farmers caught in webs of debt resulting from their integration into commodity and capital markets. These suicides notably included that of a farmer who hanged himself in the very public forum of a rally against a new land acquisition bill sponsored by Modi's government. This incident was widely reported in national and international media.

Everywhere the politics of dispossession plays out in a vacuum of knowledge. State actors position themselves as agents of a progressive urban transformation, through which their task is to purposively transform rural and slum dwellers into fully integrated and "productive" members of urban society. In the popular conscience, and particularly among emerging consumer classes, understandings of the situation of the dispossessed often takes the form of anecdotes that focus on their failed efforts to integrate into urban life. An anecdote I encountered in numerous cities during field research is of the farmer who experiences a windfall of cash from selling his land. He buys a pick-up truck, a flat screen television, and other consumer goods. Ultimately, however, he proves incapable of managing his newfound wealth or of seizing the economic opportunities of the city and finds himself and his family sliding into the ranks of the urban poor. Such anecdotes belie what is usually a much more complex reality, in which the terms of compensation often fall short of the loss of livelihood from dispossession, and in which the low-wage job opportunities presented by urban real estate megaprojects accommodate the employment needs of only a tiny fraction of those displaced. Such narratives, however, help to shift the blame for the destabilizing effects of dispossession to the dispossessed themselves. In doing so, they play a role in muting critiques of land-acquisition practices.

Constructing Exclusion

The final common theme between the three case studies is the dynamics of exclusion that these projects inevitably create, as developers' interests in maximizing property values leads to a strong push to maintain urban real estate megaprojects as spaces for the highest-income market segments. The deepening of social segregation fostered by urban real estate megaprojects is a cause for concern beyond the apparent normative preferences of many urban scholars for social integration as a central value of progressive urbanism. As major sites for investment in high-quality infrastructure and services, urban real estate megaprojects are places of concentrated economic growth and opportunity. In most Asian cities, income groups have historically lived in relatively close proximity, and mutual cross-class economic reliance has generally been the norm. In such contexts, urban real estate megaprojects have tended to replace economies of small shops, bazaars, and household businesses and manufacturing facilities, which sustain the livelihoods of a broad segment of urban populations, with office towers and shopping centers that operate as profit centers for global brands.

It is notable that in each of the case studies, issues of socioeconomic segregation and exclusion emerged as explicit sources of concern. Each of the cases witnessed thoughtful efforts by at least some architects and urban designers from within these societies to create urban visions that attempted to reconcile the goals of wholesale commodification of urban space with their own more inclusive design norms. Some of the architects and urban designers discussed in this book were quite reflexive in doing so, attempting to transcend inherited pedagogies of urbanism derived from American and European examples to create designs that attended to the demands of local ecologies and cultures. At least to some extent and in some instances, architects and urban designers sought to integrate these projects socioeconomically, to encourage pedestrian and transit orientation, to mitigate their ecological impacts, and to integrate these projects into the larger urban fabric. In each case, however, these measures were partial, often weakly implemented, and of limited impact. The primacy of the corporate developer's interest in profit maximization, and failure of the state's political will to regulate development, ultimately ensured that most urban real estate megaprojects gravitated strongly toward the development of models that mimicked ideals of "global" urbanism and exacerbated enclavization and the exclusion of poorer groups. Hence in the two cases (Jakarta and Chongqing) where urban megaprojects have been built at significant scale, they have inscribed a separation between car-dependent enclaves in far-flung suburbs, inner-city elite gated enclaves and condominium developments, and excluded settlements of lower-income city residents.

Jakarta perhaps best represents this tension between the tempered idealism of architects and urban designers of new town projects and the crass reality of state-corporate collusion that ultimately ensured their contribution to a deepening geography of exclusion. Just as the New Order regime used the development of an indigenous industrial base as a rationale to justify monopoly control of key economic sectors by cronies of the regime, so too the regime argued for the creation of new towns as engines of modernization to rationalize the permitting of massive lands to these same cronies. The 6:3:1 formula mandating the provision of smaller and more affordable units, and the deployment of regional plans that espoused internationally accepted planning principles, provided these projects with a veneer of developmentalism. Yet the early embrace of these guidelines by an idealistic team of young architects—for example through the inclusion of substantial amounts of affordable housing in BSD City—proved to be an exception. The new town model has on the whole powerfully reproduced the inequalities in Indonesian society that emerged in large part due to the the economic priorities of the New Order regime. The logic of intensely consumer-oriented and profit-maximizing development built on artificially cheap land provided through land permitting has played out in the development of sprawling gated residential areas, shopping malls, and office complexes catering to the wealthiest sliver of Jakarta society.

In Chongqing, the fusion of state and market interests in urban development produced a much more robust planning and regulatory push to integrate goals of broad-based economic and social opportunity in new towns. Yet this same fusion also led state planners to actively pursue an agenda of social segregation within the new towns in the interests of maximizing corporate revenue. The China model is premised on the state's ability to engineer the urban transition in the interests of state fiscal empowerment and economic growth. This dual focus on fiscal and developmental objectives leads new town planners to focus both on strategic infrastructure investment and on the creation of "highest and best use" consumer enclaves. Hence, while Chongqing undertook one of the most ambitious expansions of public housing in human history, the revenue-maximizing logic of residential and commercial development in the new towns dictated that these affordable housing projects be isolated from consumer enclaves in the least accessible areas with the lowest land values. It is reasonable to hypothesize that many of these projects will eventually emerge as sites of blight, stigmatization, and marginalization due to their economic and social isolation.

In Kolkata, despite the presence until 2011 of a democratically elected government that espoused a socialist ideology, the state in fact expressed little intent to ensure social inclusion in new urban developments. The main measure intended to mitigate social segregation in the state of West Bengal is an "inclusionary zoning" regulation, modeled on similar regulations in the United States and elsewhere, that mandates that 10 to 15 percent of housing in public-private partnership schemes be affordable to lower- or middle-income groups. Implementation of this measure, however, has been weak.[3] Efforts to address issues of social exclusion at the Calcutta Riverside project emerged not through state planning or regulation, but rather through the developer's interest in avoiding conflict with communities surrounding the site. While the Calcutta Riverside development itself remains unabashedly elite in its orientation, it has addressed questions of exclusion and segregation by making some concessions to enhance access to the site from surrounding communities and by providing spaces for community needs. These limited measures help to mitigate some of the economic impacts of the project on surrounding communities, but the aggregate impact of Calcutta Riverside is to make a substantial contribution the ongoing spatial polarization of the city.

In an insightful article, Hogan et al. (2012) question the analytical focus of much of anglophone literature on critiques of the privatization of "public" space and of the "gatedness" of communities in contemporary Asian cities. They question the universal relevance of these framings by pointing to historical antecedents of gating in much of Asia and to the historical prevalence of privately built spaces in many Asian urban contexts. They further question narratives of dystopia, arguing that privatized urbanism may actually enhance public amenities, as developers step in to create such amenities where governments have been unable to do so. The analysis contained in this book supports their argument to some extent, but it also leads to two important counterpoints. The first is that while there are certainly precedents for social segregation in Asia, and indeed in all urban contexts, the question of scale is important to understanding the meaning of this segregation. With the creation of massive, commodified urban spaces, as with gentrification in some globalizing cities in the United States and Europe, the wealthy and the poor are increasingly segregated at unprecedented scales, rendering social and economic interactions across classes increasingly difficult. This change has the potential to cut off economic and social opportunity for communities already struggling to find a place in increasingly competitive urban environments. Second, while privatized planning may not uniformly result in a loss of public amenities like parks, hospitals, and schools, within urban real estate megaprojects access to these amenities is often policed in ways both formal and informal. Moreover, the extent to which these amenities are available to broader publics is strongly correlated to the capacity of communities to place pressure on state actors to effectively enforce requirements for them, and also to support planning processes that require developers to negotiate the terms of community access to these amenities. Historicizing the question of the privatization of public space in Asia should therefore not come at the expense of evading increasingly critical questions that emerge with new restrictions on urban space and with constraints on political representation realized through spatial change.

Final Reflections: The Remaking of Asian Cities

In an influential essay on the concept of the right to the city, David Harvey (2003b, 939) frames this issue as one of people's inherent interest in retaining the ability to shape their own sociality, indeed to define themselves and their relations to the world:

> The right to the city is not merely a right of access to what already exists, but a right to change it after our heart's desire. We need to be sure we can live with our own creations (a problem for every planner, architect and utopian thinker). But the right to remake ourselves by creating a qualitatively different kind of urban sociality is one of the most precious of all human rights. The sheer pace and chaotic forms of urbanization throughout the world have made it hard to reflect on the nature of this task. We have been made and re-made without knowing exactly why, how, wherefore and to what end. How then, can we better exercise this right to the city?

The precise intent of this book has been to reflect on this task in the context of Asia's rapidly urbanizing and globalizing cities, to ask how cities and their residents have been remade and are being remade, and toward what end. That this is a moment of tremendous opportunity has been stated repeatedly. But it is also a time of danger, when institutions, laws, politics, and acts of collective action are congealing into infrastructures, spatialities, and economies defined by new forms of segregation and exclusion that will shape people's lives for decades and perhaps centuries to come. The real estate turn may or may not continue to define urban policy in the coming decades, but it is inscribing these dynamics of segregation and exclusion further into urban form in ways that will have lasting consequences.

If there is one central argument that emerges from this book, it is that powerful actors with interests in urban real estate are reframing the political, legal, and institutional structures that govern urban life and the creation of urban space. In doing so, they are bending to their own interests interpretations of the histories of these societies, of the role of the postcolonial state as an arbiter of citizenship, and of social values around land as a resource. The central intent of this book has been to shed light on the models of urban governance, design, and planning pursued by state actors, with the hope that doing so will inform a critical assessment of the interpretations of social life and the history of cities and nations that underlie them. In doing so, the book hopes to inform the formation of alternative interpretations. As Asian societies continue their historically unprecedented process of urban expansion, such reflection is an urgent task.

NOTES

Introduction

1. This review uncovered area data for only sixty-three of these projects and projected population data for only fifty-four, so these figures are significant underestimates of the total projected size and population of these projects.

2. Among the projects I visited during this period were Muang Thong Thani in Bangkok; Lippo Karawaci, Kota Modern, and Bumi Serpong Damai in Jakarta; Shanghai Harbour City, the new towns of Songjiang and Anting, and Shanghai Xintiandi in Shanghai; Kolkata West International City and Rajarhat in Kolkata; Bonifacio Global City and Eastwood City in Metro Manila; and Bandar Utama Damansara in Malaysia.

1. Origins and Consequences of the Real Estate Turn

1. The website of the Prime Minister's Department of Malaysia contains a particularly direct expression of this idea, referring to Malaysia Incorporated as "jointly owned by [the public and private sectors] working together in a common pursuit of the nation."

2. Entities such as the State Railway of Thailand, the National Housing Authority, the Port Authority of Thailand, and the Treasury Department of the Ministry of Finance (which alone controlled two million hectares of land in the country) sought to develop commercial projects on state land as part of a strategy of fiscal revitalization (Prinya 1998; Wichit 2004).

2. Comparing State Agendas of Land Monetization

1. Examples of Asian cities where public-sector owners own more than 25 percent of urban land include Ho Chi Minh City, Pusan, and Chennai (Peterson and Kaganova 2010).

3. Planned Grab

1. During the 1980s and 1990s the JMR was referred to as Jabotabek; Depok was added to the definition of the JMR later, hence the change to Jabodetabek.

2. In fact, colonial land law elucidates a much more nuanced range of claims within the two broad categories of *hak girik* and *hak garapan*, including rights of cultivation, of commercial use, of building, and others. See Leaf (1992), Winarso (2000), and Struyk, Hoffman, and Katsura (1990) for more extended discussions.

3. The term Pancasila means five principles and refers to the five core principles that the state promotes as the framework for the nation. These are: monotheism, just and civilized humanity, national unity, democracy, and social justice.

4. Field notes, representative of Ministry of Public Works, government of Indonesia, interview, June 6, 2014.

5. Two developers interviewed for this study spoke openly about the relative readiness of many state-owned enterprise heads to agree to sell plantation land at below-market costs in exchange for bribes. This readiness, according to these informants, was all the more pronounced during the Suharto era, when new town developments were often backed by powerful businessmen with strong connections to the Suharto regime.

6. An extended discussion of this unrest is beyond the scope of this book. In brief summary, the Suharto regime emerged in the aftermath of the massive slaughter of suspected communists and communist sympathizers, an orgy of violence that swept across the country in 1966 and resulted in an estimated 300,000 to 400,000 deaths. The army tacitly supported and sometimes participated in this violence (Schwarz 2004). This precedent of state-supported extreme violence against elements of opposition set the tone for state-society relations throughout the Suharto period.

7. Field notes, employee of Bumi Serpong Damai Ltd., interview, June 1, 2014.

8. Field notes, former employee of Bumi Serpong Damai Ltd, interview, June 2, 2014.

9. Field notes, representative of Sinar Mas Land, interview, December 12, 2013.

10. Field notes, former employee of Bumi Serpong Damai Ltd., interview, June 1, 2014.

11. Field notes, former employee of Bumi Serpong Damai Ltd., interview, June 2, 2014.

12. Field notes, employee of Bumi Serpong Damai, interview and site visit, December 13, 2013.

13. Field notes, Jakarta developer, interview, June 3, 2014.

4. Experiments in Power

1. Field research notes, representative of Ahmedabad-based planning and architecture firm, interview, March 15, 2010.

2. The law requires compensation equal to two times the market value of the land in urban areas and four times the market value in rural areas.

3. Field research notes, representative of Ahmedabad-based planning and architecture firm, interview, March 15, 2010.

4. Field notes, executive at the West Bengal Housing Board, interview, April 12, 2010.

5. Field notes, Sumit Dabriwala, interview, April 20, 2010.

6. Field notes, Calcutta Riverside architect, interview, March 23, 2010.

5. Chongqing

1. This chapter is influenced by Hsing's excellent analysis of the China model in *The Great Urban Transformation: Politics of Land and Property in China*. The debate about the Chongqing and Guangzhou models emerged precisely as alternate state responses to the contradictions Hsing identifies in her book. In this respect, the debate shows how China's larger urban political economy has continued to transform and evolve since Hsing's seminal study was published in 2010.

2. The designation was also motivated in part by the Three Gorges Dam project, which required a tremendous amount of investment in infrastructure and in the resettlement of 1.2 million people.

3. The mu is a unit of measurement used in China that is equivalent to about one-fifteenth of a hectare. During field interviews conducted for this research in August of 2015, respondents gave figures for the per mu cost of land certificates much higher than those quoted by Huang, with some estimating prices in excess of 200,000 yuan per mu.

4. Field research notes, August 3, 2015.

5. Field notes, faculty at Chongqing University, interviews, August 4, 2015.

6. In fact, the implications of public rental housing for social segregation are likely to be complex. Income restrictions have proven difficult to enforce, with the result that some projects have a greater income mix than anticipated. But due to variation in the accessibility of the projects, and therefore their desirability, it is likely that there will be some sorting within these projects that will lead to differentiation in the socioeconomic mix of these settlements over time.

7. Discussions with Chongqing residents unearthed numerous stories centered on the stigma that has already come to be associated with residence in the public rental housing.

8. Chongqing-based scholars interviewed for this research framed the suppression of rents as a deliberate outcome, part of the public rental housing project's overall objective of maintaining housing affordability. They nonetheless did also view this as a factor in a slow-down in housing construction across the city.

Conclusion

1. For another prominent example, see recent scholarship on the "smart city" push in India (for example Datta 2015).

2. In fact, issues surrounding land monetization arguably played a significant role in the fall of the Suharto regime in Indonesia, although this was not related to questions of distribution of benefits and costs. Massive land permitting, along with financial sector liberalization, led to a spasm of real estate development that eventually left banks with massive nonperforming loans. This was a central factor in the Asian financial crisis of 1997 and 1998, which in turn precipitated Suharto's fall in February of 1998.

3. The laxness of implementation of inclusionary zoning requirements in Kolkata was evident when, during a field research visit to a condominium development in the Rajarhat new town, a marketing agent for the developer tried to sell me one of the units set aside for affordable housing. When I asked him about documentation requirements to purchase one of these units, he conveyed that these were quite easy to evade.

BIBLIOGRAPHY

Acharya, Ballabh. 1989. *The Indian Urban Land Ceiling Act: A Critique of the 1976 Legislation.* Washington, DC: World Bank.

Ahlers, Anna, and Gunter Schubert. 2013. "Strategic Modeling: 'Building a New Socialist Countryside' in Three Chinese Counties." *China Quarterly* 216: 831–849.

Ahluwalia, Montek. 2007. "Economic Reforms in India Since 1991: Has Gradualism Worked?" In *India's Economic Transition: The Politics of Reform*, edited by Rahul Mukherji, 87–116. New Delhi: Oxford University Press.

Ahuja, Sanjeev. 2008. "NCR to Get 14 New Townships." *Hindustan Times*, January 14.

Akosoro, Lana W. 1994. "The Effects of the Location Permit on Urban Land Market: A Case Study in the Jabotabek Area, Indonesia." Master's thesis, Massachusetts Institute of Technology.

Alterman, Rachelle. 2010. *Takings International: A Comparative Perspective on Land Use Regulations and Compensation Rights.* New York: American Bar Association.

Ambuja Realty. 2006. "Dankuni Township Development Proposal." Unpublished document.

Angel, Shlomo, Jason Parent, Daniel Civco, and Alejandro Blei. 2012. *Atlas of Urban Expansion.* Cambridge: Lincoln Land Institute.

Anjaria, Jonathan. 2009. "Guardians of the Bourgeoisie City: Citizenship, Public Space, and Middle-Class Activism in Mumbai." *City & Community* 8, no. 4: 391–406.

——. 2011. "Ordinary States: Everyday Corruption and the Politics of Space in Mumbai." *American Ethnologist* 38, no. 1: 58–72.

Appadurai, Arjun. 2000. "Spectral Housing and Urban Cleansing: Notes on Millennial Mumbai." *Public Culture* 12, no. 3: 627–651.

Arabindoo, Pushpa. 2011. "'City of Sand': Stately Re-imagination of Marina Beach in Chennai." *International Journal of Urban and Regional Research* 35, no. 2: 379–401.

Arai, Kenichiro. 2001. "Only Yesterday in Jakarta: Property Boom and Consumptive Trends in the Late New Order Metropolitan City." *Southeast Asian Studies* 38, no. 4: 481–511.

Argo, Teti, and Aprodicio Laquian. 2004. *Privatization of Water Utilities and its Effects on the Urban Poor in Jakarta Raya and Metro Manila.* Paper presented at the Forum on Urban Infrastructure and Public Service: Delivery for the Urban Poor, Regional Focus: Asia. India Habitat Centre, New Delhi: Woodrow Wilson International Center for Scholars, National Institute of Urban Affairs.

Arup. 2016. "Chongqing Xiyong Integrated Planning." http://www.arup.com/projects/integrated_planning_chongqing_xiyong_subcentre. Retrieved August 2, 2016.

AHRC (Asian Human Rights Commission). 2015. "India: New Eviction Case in the Name of Road Expansion, West Bengal." Unpublished document.

Attaporn Bianpoen. 2005. "Dindaeng Redevelopment Project." In *Urban Renewal and New Town Development: Proceeding of the Seminar on 11 March 2005,* edited by Siriwan Silapacharanan, 65–74. Bangkok: Faculty of Architecture, Chulalongkorn University.

Badan Penghargaan dan Sayembara IAI Jakarta. 2014. "Masterplan Project @ BSD City." Jakarta: Ikatan Arsitek Indonesia Jakarta. Available at http://sayembara-iai.org/gallery/documents/sinar-mas-land-young-architect-competition-2014/Masterplan.

Balakrishnan, Sai. 2013. "Land Conflicts and Cooperatives Along Pune's Highways: Managing India's Agrarian to Urban Transition." PhD dissertation, Harvard University.

Bandyopadhyay, Ritajyoti. 2011. "Politics of Archiving: Hawkers and Pavement Dwellers in Calcutta," *Dialectical Anthropology* 35, no. 3: 295–316.

Banerjee, Parthasarathi. 2006. "Land Acquisition and Peasant Resistance at Singur." *Economic and Political Weekly* 41, no. 46: 4718–4720.

Bases Conversion Development Authority. 2013. "BCDA-Administered Economic Zones." http://www.bcda.gov.ph/freeport_and_ecozones. Accessed May 9, 2013.

Baviskar, Amita. 2003. "Between Violence and Desire: Space, Power, and Identity in the Making of Metropolitan Delhi." *International Social Science Journal* 55, no. 175: 89–98.

Baviskar, Amita, and Nandini Sundar. 2008. "Democracy Versus Economic Transformation?" *Economic and Political Weekly* 43, no. 46: 87–89.

Bello, Walden. 1998. "East Asia: On the Eve of the Great Transformation? "*Review of International Political Economy* 5, no. 3: 424–444.

Benjamin, Solomon. 2008. "Occupancy Urbanism: Radicalizing Politics and Economy Beyond Policy and Programs." *International Journal of Urban and Regional Research* 32, no. 3: 719–729.

Bertaud, Alain. 1989. *The Regulatory Environment of Urban Land in Indonesia: Constraints Imposed on the Poor.* Washington, DC: World Bank Technical Department.

Bhagwat, Prabhakar. N.d. "Environmental Assessment of Water Bodies and Flora, Calcutta Riverside, Maheshtala, Kolkata." Unpublished PowerPoint presentation.

Bhan, Gautam. 2009. " 'This Is No Longer the City I Once Knew': Evictions, the Urban Poor, and the Right to the City in Millennial Delhi." *Environment and Urbanization* 21, no. 1: 127–142.

———. 2013. "Planned Illegalities: Housing and the 'Failure' of Planning in Delhi, 1947–2010." *Economic and Political Weekly* 48, no. 24.

Bhattacharjee, Nivedita. 2015. "iPhone maker Foxconn in Talks to Build First Apple Plant in India." *Reuters*, June 11. http://www.reuters.com/article/2015/06/11/us-foxconn-india-idUSKBN0OR1M720150611. Accessed August 15, 2015.

Bianpoen. 1990. "Urban Land Management: The Case of Jakarta." Proceedings of an International Workshop on Asian Urban Land, June 8–10, University of Malaya, Kuala Lumpur.

Biddulph, Robin. 2014. "Cambodia's Land Management and Administration Project." United Nations University, WIDER Working Paper 2014/086.

Bjorkman, Lisa. 2013. "Becoming a Slum: From Municipal Colony to Illegal Settlement in Liberalization Era Mumbai." In *Contesting the Indian City: Global Visions and the Politics of the Local*, edited by Gavin Shatkin, 208–240. Oxford: Wiley-Blackwell.

Bo, Zhiyue, and Chen Gang. 2009. "Bo Xilai and the Chongqing Model." EAI Background Brief No. 465.

Borras, Saturnino, Ruth Hall, Ian Scoones, Ben White, and Wendy Wolford. 2011. "Towards a Better Understanding of Global Land Grabbing: An Editorial Introduction." *Journal of Peasant Studies* 38, no. 2: 209–216.

Bremmer, Ian. 2010. *The End of the Free Market: Who Wins the War Between States and Corporations.* New York: Portfolio.

Brenner, Neil. 2004. *New State Spaces: Urban Governance and the Rescaling of Statehood.* Oxford: Oxford University Press.

Brenner, Neil, Jamie Peck, and Nick Theodore. 2010. "After Neoliberalization?" *Globalizations* 7, no. 3: 327–345.

BSD City. 2015. "BSD City: Big City, Big Opportunity." http://www.bsdcity.com/site/?lang=en. Accessed June 15, 2015.

Bugalski, Natalie, and David Pred. 2011. "Formalizing Inequality: Land Titling in Cambodia." In *Defending the Commons, Territories, and the Right to Food and Water, Land Struggles.* LRAN Briefing Paper Series No. 2, 73–82.

Bunnell, Tim, and Anand Maringanti. 2010. "Practising Urban and Regional Research Beyond Metrocentricity." *International Journal of Urban and Regional Research* 34, no. 2: 415–420.

Burrows, Edwin, and Mike Wallace. 1999. *Gotham: A History of New York City to 1898.* New York: Oxford University Press.

Cai, Jianming, Zhen Yang, Douglas Webster, Tao Song, and Andrew Gulbrandson. 2012. "Chongqing: Beyond the Latecomer Advantage." *Asia Pacific Viewpoint* 53, no. 1: 38–55.

Cahyafitri, Raras. 2013. "Bakrieland to Make Sentul City Full Owner of Bukit Jong-gol." *Jakarta Post*, Business Section, September 17. http://www.thejakartapost.com/news/2013/09/17/bakrieland-make-sentul-city-full-owner-bukit-jonggol.html. Accessed August 14, 2004.

Caprotti, Federico. 2014. "Eco-urbanism and the Eco-city, or, Denying the Right to the City?" *Antipode*. Online first. doi: 10.1111/anti.12087.

Cartier, Carolyn. 2001. "'Zone Fever', the Arable Land Debate, and Real Estate Spec-ulation: China's Evolving Land Use Regime and its Geographical Contradictions." *Journal of Contemporary China* 10, no. 28: 445–469.

——. 2015. "Territorial Urbanization and the Party-State in China." *Territory, Politics, Governance*. Online first. doi: 10.1080/21622671.2015.1005125.

Chakraborty, Ajanta. 2009. "It's Curtains for DLF Project at Dankuni." *Times of India*, January 18.

Chakravorty, Sanjoy. 2013. *The Price of Land: Acquisition and Consequence*. New Delhi: Oxford University Press.

Charoen, L. 2004. "Transforming Public Transport. *Bangkok Post Year-End Economic Review*.

Chatterjee, Partha. 2004. *Politics of the Governed*. New York: Columbia University Press.

Chatterji, Tathagata. 2013. "The Micro-politics of Urban Transformation in the Con-text of Globalization: A Case Study of Gurgaon, India." *South Asia: Journal of South Asian Studies* 36, no. 2: 273–287.

Cheng, Joseph. 2013. "The 'Chongqing Model': What it Means to China Today." *Jour-nal of Comparative Asian Development* 12, no. 3: 411–442.

Cheung, Peter. 2013. "China's Changing Regional Development: Trends, Strategies and Challenges in the 12th Five-Year Plan (2011–2015) Period." *Asia Pacific Viewpoint* 53, no. 1: 1–6.

CCTV (China Central Television). 2010. Interview with Chongqing Mayor on Hukou Reform." *China 24 News*. http://english.cntv.cn/program/china24/20100817/100896.shtml. Accessed August 12, 2015.

Chua Beng Huat. 1997. *Political Legitimacy and Housing: Stakeholding in Singapore*. London: Routledge.

Chuang, Julia. 2014. "China's Rural Land Politics: Bureaucratic Absorption and the Muting of Rightful Resistance." *The China Quarterly* 219: 649–669.

Cowherd, Robert. 2002. "Cultural Construction of Jakarta: Design, Planning and De-velopment of Jabotabek, 1980–1997." PhD dissertation, Massachusetts Institute of Technology.

Cowherd, Robert, and Eric Heikkila. 2002. Orange County, Java: Hybridity, Social Du-alism and an Imagined West. In *Southern California and the World*, edited by Eric Heikkila and Rafael Pizarro, 195–220. Westport, CT: Praeger.

Das Gupta, Moushumi. 2008. "Five New Mega-cities in Delhi by 2021." *Hindustan Times*, January 7, 1.

Datta, Ayona. 2015. "New Urban Utopias of Postcolonial India: 'Entrepreneurial Ur-banization' in Dholera Smart City, Gujarat." *Dialogues in Human Geography* 5, no. 1: 3–22.

Department of Industrial and Policy Promotion. 2008. Fact Sheet on Foreign Direct Investment (FDI): From August 1991 to January 2008. Delhi: Ministry of Commerce and Industry, Government of India.

——. 2010. Fact Sheet on Foreign Direct Investment (FDI): From August 1991 to January 2010. Delhi: Ministry of Commerce and Industry, Government of India.

——. 2011. Fact Sheet on Foreign Direct Investment (FDI): From August 1991 to July 2011. Delhi: Ministry of Commerce and Industry, Government of India.

Dick, Howard, and Peter Rimmer. 1998. Beyond the Third World City: The New Urban Geography of South-east Asia." *Urban Studies* 35, no. 12: 2303–2321.

Dieleman, Marleen, and Wladimir Sachs. 2008. "Coevolution of Institutions and Corporations in Emerging Economies: How the Salim Group Morphed into an Institution of Suharto's Crony Regime." *Journal of Management Studies* 45, no. 1: 1274–1300.

Ding, Chengri. 2003. "Land Policy Reform in China: Assessment and Prospects." *Land Use Policy* 20, no. 2: 109–120.

——. 2007. "Policy and Praxis of Land Acquisition in China." *Land Use Policy* 24, no. 1: 1–13.

Douglass, Michael. 1989. "The Environmental Sustainability of Development: Coordination, Incentives, and Political Will in Land Use Planning for the Jakarta Metropolis." *Third World Planning Review* 11, no. 2: 211–238.

Douglass, Michael, and Pornpan Boonchuen. 2006. "Bangkok: Intentional World City." In *Relocating Global Cities: From the Center to the Margins*, edited by Mark Amen, Kevin Archer, and Martin Bosman, 75–100. Lanham, MD: Rowman and Littlefield.

Douglass, Michael, Bart Wissink, and Ronald van Kempen. 2012. "Enclave Urbanism In China: Consequences and Interpretations." *Urban Geography* 33, no. 2: 167–182.

Doxiadis Associates, John Portman and Associates, and PT Encona Engineering Inc. 1995. *Bumi Serpong Damai New City: Revised Master Plan and Central Business District Planning: Preliminary Master Plan Report*. Jakarta, Indonesia: PT. Bumi Serpong Damai.

Dupont, Veronique. 2007. "Conflicting Stakes and Governance in the Peripheries of Large Indian Metropolises: An Introduction." *Cities* 24, no. 2: 89–94.

Economic Planning Unit. 2013. *Malaysia Incorporated Policy*. Prime Minister's Department Malaysia website. http://www.epu.gov.my/en/dasar-pengkorporatan-malaysia. Accessed July 28, 2013.

Economic Times. 2015. "PM Narendra Modi Launches Smart Cities Mission, Says Centre Committed to Urban India." *India Times*, June 26. http://articles.economictimes. indiatimes.com/2015-06-26/news/63862339_1_prime-minister-narendra-modi-real-estate-regulatory-bill-urban-india. Accessed July 17, 2015.

Economist. 2012. "Justice in Cambodia: The Boeung Kak 13." *The Economist*, http:// www.economist.com/blogs/banyan/2012/06/justice-cambodia. Accessed July 25, 2014.

Expert Group on the Commercialization of Infrastructure Projects. 1996. *The India Infrastructure Report: Policy Imperatives for Growth and Welfare*. New Delhi: Ministry of Finance.

Fainstein, Susan. 1995. "Politics, Economics, and Planning: Why Urban Regimes Matter." *Planning Theory* 14: 34–41.

——. 2001. *The City Builders: Property Development in New York and London, 1980–2000.* Lawrence: University of Kansas Press.

Fenby, Jonathan. 2012. "The Rumour Machine: Wang Hui on the dismissal of Bo Xilai." *London Review of Books,* May 10.

Fernandes, Leela. 2004. "The Politics of Forgetting: Class Politics, State Power and the Restructuring of Urban Space in India." *Urban Studies* 41, no. 12: 2415–2430.

Firman, Tommy. 1997. "Land Conversion and Urban Development in the Northern Region of West Java, Indonesia." *Urban Studies* 34, no. 7: 1027–1046.

——. 2004. "New Town Development in Jakarta Metropolitan Region: A Perspective of Spatial Segregation." *Habitat International* 28, no. 3: 349–368.

——. 2009. "The Continuity and Change in Mega-urbanization in Indonesia: A Survey of Jakarta-Bandung Region (JBR) Development." *Habitat International* 33, no. 4: 327–339.

Firman, Tommy, Benedictus Kombaitan, and Pradono Pradono. 2007. "The Dynamics of Indonesia's Urbanization, 1980–2006." *Urban Policy and Research* 25, no. 4: 433–454.

Fischer, Dominique. 2000. "Indonesia's Real Estate Disturbance: An Ineluctable Outcome." In *Asia's Financial Crisis and the Role of Real Estate,* edited by Koichi Mera and Bertrand Renaud, 219–243. New York: M.E. Sharpe.

Freeman, Charles, and Wen Jin Yuan. 2011. *China's New Leftists and the China Model Debate after the Financial Crisis.* A Report of the CSIS Freeman Chair in Chinese Studies. Washington DC: Center for Strategic and International Studies.

Ghatak, Maitreesh, Sandip Mitra, Dilip Mookherjee, and Anusha Nath. 2013. "Land Acquisition and Compensation: What Really Happened in Singur?" *Economic and Political Weekly* 48, no. 21: 32–44.

Ghertner, Asher. 2008. "Analysis of New Legal Discourse Behind Delhi's Slum Demolitions." *Economic and Political Weekly,* May 17, 57–66.

——. 2011a. "Rule by Aesthetics: World-Class City Making in Delhi." In *Worlding Cities: Asian Experiments and the Art of Being Global,* edited by Ananya Roy and Aihwa Ong, 279–306. Oxford: Blackwell.

——. 2011b. "The Nuisance of Slums: Environmental Law and the Production of Slum Illegality in India." In *Urban Navigations: Politics, Space and the City in South Asia,* edited by Jonathan Anjaria and Colin McFarlane, 23–49. New Delhi: Routledge.

——. 2011c. "Gentrifying the State, Gentrifying Participation: Elite Governance Programs in Delhi." *International Journal of Urban and Regional Research* 35, no. 3: 504–532.

Ghosh, Archana, Lorraine Kennedy, Joel Ruet, Stephanie Lama-Rewal, and Marie-Helene Zerah. 2009. "A Comparative Overview of Urban Governance in Delhi, Hyderbad, Kolkata, and Mumbai." In *Governing India's Metropolises,* edited by Joel Ruet and Stephanie Lama-Rewal, 24–54. New Delhi: Routledge.

Glassman, Jim. 2004. *Thailand at the Margins: Internationalization of the State and Transformation of Labor.* Oxford: Oxford University Press.

——. 2007. "Recovering From Crisis: The Case of Thailand's Spatial Fix." *Economic Geography* 83, no. 4: 349–370.

Glasze, Georg, Chris Webster, and Klaus Franz, eds. 2006. *Private Cities: Global and Local Perspectives*. London: Routledge.

Godement, Francoise. 2011. "Introduction." In *One or Two Chinese Models?*, edited by Francoise Godement, Chan Yang, Jean-Pierre Cabestan, Jerome Doyon, and Romain Lafarguette, 1–2. European Council of Foreign Relations: China Analysis. Available from: http://www.ecfr.eu/page/-/China_Analysis_One_or_two_Chinese_models_ November2011. pdf. Accessed July 20, 2015.

Goldman, Michael. 2011. Speculative Urbanism and the Making of the Next World City: Speculative Urbanism in Bangalore." *International Journal of Urban and Regional Research 35*, no. 3: 555–581.

Gotsch, Peter. 2009. "NeoTowns: Prototypes of Corporate Urbanism." PhD dissertation, Karlsruhe Institute of Technology.

Gorvett, Jon. 2011. "Cambodians Evicted in 'Land Grab.'" *Guardian Weekly*, March 29. http://www.guardian.co.uk/world/2011/mar/29/cambodia-evictions-land-rights-gorvett. Accessed April 30, 2013.

Government of India. 2009. "Thirteenth Finance Commission, 2010–2015: Volume 1: Report." December.

——. 2013. "National Land Record Modernization Program." Ministry of Rural Development, Department of Land Resources. http://www.dolr.nic.in/land_reforms1. htm. Accessed October 7, 2013.

Government of Indonesia. 2014. *Master Plan: National Capital Integrated Coastal Development*. Jakarta: Coordinating Ministry for Economic Affairs.

Government of West Bengal. 2006. *Memo No. 1063-LR/3M-130/05/GH(M)*. Kolkata: Department of Land and Land Reforms.

Halbert, Ludovic, and Hortense Rouanet. 2014. "Filtering Risk Away: Global Finance Capital, Transcalar Territorial Networks and the (Un)Making of City-Regions: An Analysis of Business Property Development in Bangalore, India." *Regional Studies* 48, no. 3: 471–484.

Halim, Haeril. 2014. "KPK Arrests Sentul City Boss for Graft." *Jakarta Post*, National Section, October 1. http://www.thejakartapost.com/news/2014/10/01/kpk-arrests-sentul-city-boss-graft.html. Accessed January 31, 2015.

Han Sun Sheng. 2005. Global City-Making in Singapore: A Real Estate Perspective." *Progress in Planning* 64: 169–175.

Hardgrove, Anne. 2005. *Community and Public Culture: The Marwaris of Calcutta, c. 1897–1997*. New York: Columbia University Press.

Harsono, Andreas. 1999. "Jakarta's Dispossessed." *UNESCO Courier*, June 26–28.

Harvey, David. 1989. From Managerialism to Entrepreneurialism: The Transformation in Urban Governance in Late Capitalism." *Geografiska Annaler. Series B, Human Geography* 71, no. 1: 3–17.

——. 2003a. *The New Imperialism*. Oxford: Oxford University Press.

——. 2003b. "The Right to the City." *International Journal of Urban and Regional Research* 27, no. 4: 939–941.

——. 2005. *A Brief History of Neoliberalism*. Oxford: Oxford University Press.

——. 2009. "The 'New' Imperialism: Accumulation by Dispossession." *Socialist Register* 40: 63–87.

Hasan, Mirza. 2003. "Sustainable Development in a Metropolitan Region in a Developing Country: A Case Study of the New Town Bumi Serpong Damai (BSD), Greater Jakarta, Indonesia." PhD dissertation, University of South Australia.

He, Shenjing. 2013. "Evolving Enclave Urbanism in China and its Socio-spatial Implications: The Case of Guangzhou." *Social & Cultural Geography* 14, no. 3: 243–275.

He, Shenjing, and Fulong Wu. 2005. "Property-Led Redevelopment in Post-reform China: A Case Study of Xintiandi Redevelopment Project in Shanghai." *Journal of Urban Affairs* 27, no. 1: 1–23.

Heeks, Richard. 2010. "Indian IT Sector Statistics." Centre for Development Informatics, University of Manchester. www.manchester.ac.uk/cdi. Accessed June 25.

Herlambang, Suryono. 2013. "25 Years of New Town Development in Jakarta: An Evaluation." Unpublished presentation at the Workshop on Spatial Justice in Asian Cities, Universitas Tarumanagara, Jakarta, January 26.

Herring, Richard, and Susan Wachter. 1998. "Real Estate Booms and Banking Busts: An International Perspective." Paper presented at Wharton Conference on Asia's Twin Financial Crises. University of Pennsylvania, Philadelphia, March 9–10.

Hewison, Kevin. 1989. *Bankers and Bureaucrats: Capital and the Role of the State in Thailand.* New Haven, CT: Monograph Series 34, Yale University Southeast Asian Studies.

HIDCO. 1999. "New Town, Calcutta: Project Report." West Bengal Housing Infrastructure Development Corporation.

Hiland Incorporated. N.d. "Community Initiatives at Calcutta Riverside Development at Batanagar." Unpublished brochure.

Hirsch, Philip. 2011. "Titling Against Grabbing? Critiques and Conundrums Around Land Formalization in Southeast Asia." Paper presented at the International Conference on Global Land Grabbing, University of Sussex, Brighton, April 6–8.

Ho, Peter. 2001. "Who Owns China's Land? Policies, Property Rights, and Deliberate Ambiguity." *China Quarterly* 166: 394–421.

Hogan, Trevor, Tim Bunnell, Choon Piew Po, Eka Permanasari, and Sirat Morshidi. 2012. "Asian Urbanisms and the Privatization of Cities." *Cities* 29, no. 1: 59–63.

Hogan, Trevor, and Christopher Houston. 2002. "Corporate Cities—Urban Gateways or Gated Communities Against the City: The Case of Lippo, Jakarta." In *Critical Reflections on Cities in Southeast Asia*, edited by Tim Bunnell, Lisa Drummond, and Ho Kong Chong, 31–53. Singapore: Times Academic Press.

HOK. N.d. *Fort Bonifacio Global City Master Plan.* HOK: San Francisco.

Hong, Lijian. 2004. "Chongqing: Opportunities and Risks." *China Quarterly* 178: 448–466.

Hsing, You Tien. 2010. *The Great Urban Transformation: Politics of Land and Property in China.* Oxford: Oxford University Press.

Huang, Philip. 2011. "Chongqing Equitable Development Driven by a 'Third Hand'?" *Modern China* 37, no. 6: 569–622.

——. 2012. "Profit-Making Firms and China's Development Experience: 'State Capitalism' or 'Socialist Market Economy'?" *Modern China* 38, no. 6: 591–629.

Huang, Yanzhong, and Dali Yang. 1996. "The Political Dynamics of Regulatory Change: Speculation and Regulation in the Real Estate Sector." *Journal of Contemporary China* 5, no. 12: 171–185.

Hudalah, Delik, and Tommy Firman. 2012. "Beyond Property: Industrial Estates and Post-suburban Transformation in Jakarta Metropolitan Region." *Cities* 29, no. 1: 40–48.

Hudalah, Delik, and Johan Woltjer. 2007. "Spatial Planning System in Transitional Indonesia." *International Planning Studies* 12, no. 3: 291–303.

Hung, Faith. 2015. "Foxconn Eyes Factories in U.S., Indonesia as China's Luster Fades." Reuters, June 11. http://www.reuters.com/article/2014/01/27/us-foxconn-taiwan-idUSBREA0Q01F20140127. Accessed August 15, 2015.

Jakarta Globe. 2013. "Bumi Serpong Damai to Sell Land for $208 Million to Joint Ventures," *Investor Daily*, January 22. http://jakartaglobe.id/archive/bumi-serpong-damai-to-sell-land-for-208-million-to-joint-ventures/. Accessed November 21, 2016.

Jakarta Post. 1996. "Soeharto Gives Green Light to Jonggol Project," City News, December 19, 3.

Jing, Meng. 2010. "High Tech Companies Go West." *China Daily*, November 5.

Johnson, Ian. 2013a. "New China Cities: Shoddy Homes, Broken Hope." *New York Times*, November 9.

Johnson, Ian. 2013b. "Picking Death Over Eviction." *New York Times*, September 8.

Jones Lang Lasalle. 2013. *China's City Winners: Chongqing City Profile*. World Winning Cities: Global Foresight Series. Singapore: Jones Lang Lasalle.

Kalbag, Chaitanya. 2011. "The Method Man." *Business Today Online Edition,* January 23. http://businesstoday.intoday.in/story/gujarats-chief-minister-on-governance/1/11910.html. Accessed October 17, 2013.

Karmali, Nazneen. 2006. "Lords of the Land." *Business India*, May 21, 42–49.

Kawai, Masahiro, and Ken-ichi Takayasu. 1999. "The Economic Crisis and Financial Sector Restructuring in Thailand." In *Rising to the Challenges in Asia: A Study of Financial Markets in Thailand*. Metro Manila: Asian Development Bank, 37–103.

Kotaka, Tsuyoshi, and David Callies. 2002. *Taking Land: Compulsory Purchase and Regulation in Asian-Pacific Countries*. Honolulu: University of Hawai`i Press.

Kusno, Abidin. 2004. "Whither Nationalist Urbanism? Public Life in Governor Sutiyoso's Jakarta." *Urban Studies* 41, no. 12: 2377–2394.

——. 2010. *Appearances of Memory: Mnemonic Practices of Architecture and Urban Form in Indonesia*. Durham, NC: Duke University Press.

——. 2012a. "Housing at the Margin: Perumahan Rakyat and the Future Urban Form of Jakarta." *Indonesia* 94 (October): 23–56.

——. 2012b. "Peasants in Indonesia and the Politics of Periurbanization." In *Global Capitalism and the Future of Agrarian Society*, edited by Arif Dirlik, Roxann Prazniak, and Alexander Woodside, 193–220. London: Paradigm Publishers.

Kusno, Abidin, Melani Budianta, and Hilmar Farid. 2011. "Editorial Introduction: Runaway Cities/Leftover Spaces." *Inter-Asia Cultural Studies* 12, no. 4: 473–481.

Labbe, Danielle, and Clement Musil. 2013. "Periurban Land Redevelopment in Vietnam Under Market Socialism." *Urban Studies*. doi: 10.1177/0042098013495574. Accessed November 1, 2013.

Lafarguette, Romain. 2011. "Chongqing: A Model for a New Economic and Social Policy?" In *One or Two Chinese Models?*, edited by Francoise Godement, Chan Yang, Jean-Pierre Cabestan, Jerome Doyon, and Romain Lafarguette, 13–15. European Council of Foreign Relations: China Analysis. Available from: http://www.ecfr.

eu/page/-/China_Analysis_One_or_two_Chinese_models_November2011.pdf.   Accessed July 20, 2015.

Landler, Mark. 1999. "Year of Living Dangerously for a Tycoon in Indonesia." *New York Times*, May 16.

Leaf, Michael. 1992. "Land Regulation and Housing Development in Jakarta, Indonesia: From the 'Big Village' to the 'Modern City.'" PhD dissertation, University of California at Berkeley.

——. 1993. "Land Rights for Residential Development in Jakarta, Indonesia: The Colonial Roots of Contemporary Urban Dualism." *International Journal of Urban and Regional Research* 17, no. 4: 477–491.

——. 2005. "The Bazaar and the Normal." In *Service Industries and Asia-Pacific Cities New Development Trajectories*, edited by Peter Daniels, Ho Kong Chong, and T. A. Hutton, 111–130. New York: Routledge.

——. 2015. "Exporting Indonesian Urbanism: Ciputra and the Developmental Vision of Market Modernism." *South East Asia Research* 23, no. 2: 169–86.

Leisch, Harold. 2002. "Gated Communities in Indonesia." *Cities* 19, no. 5: 341–350.

Leitner, Helga, Jamie Peck, and Eric Sheppard. 2007. *Contesting Neoliberalism: Urban Frontiers*. New York: Guilford Press.

Levien, Michael. 2012. "The Land Question: Special Economic Zones and the Political Economy of Dispossession in India." *The Journal of Peasant Studies* 39, no. 3–4: 933–969.

——. 2013a. "The Politics of Dispossession: Theorizing India's 'Land Wars.'" *Politics & Society* 41, no. 3: 351–394.

——. 2013b. "Regimes of Dispossession: From Steel Towns to Special Economic Zones." *Development and Change* 44, no. 2: 381–407.

Li, Cheng. 2012. "The Battle for China's Top Nine Leadership Posts." *Washington Quarterly* 35, no. 1: 131–145.

Li, Xiao, Xiang Gu, Yue Teng, and Pan Li. 2014. "Sustainable Supply Model Design of Public Rental Housing: Case Study of Chongqing." *Frontiers of Engineering Management*. Online first. doi: 10.15302/J-FEM-2014050.

Li, Yi, and Fulong Wu. 2012. "The Transformation of Regional Governance in China: The Rescaling of Statehood." *Progress in Planning* 78: 55–99.

Li, Zhigang, Xun Li, and Lei Wang. 2014. "Speculative Urbanism and the Making of University Towns in China: A Case of Guangzhou University Town." *Habitat International* 44 (October): 422–431.

Lin, George Chu-Sheng. 2010. *Developing China: Land, Politics and Social Conditions*. London: Routledge.

Lin, George Chu-Sheng, and Fangxin Yi. 2011. "Urbanization of Capital or Capitalization on Urban Land? Land Development and Local Public Finance in Urbanizing China." *Urban Geography* 32, no. 1: 50–79.

Lippo Group. 2015. "The St. Moritz Penthouses and Residences." http://www.thestmoritz.com/#. Accessed June 14.

Liu, Tao, and George Chu-Sheng Lin. 2014. "New Geography of Land Commodification in Chinese Cities: Uneven Landscape of Urban Land Development Under Market Reforms and Globalization." *Applied Geography* 51: 118–130.

Logan, John, and Harvey Molotch. 1987. *Urban Fortunes: The Political Economy of Place*. Berkeley: University of California Press.

Long, Hualou, Yurui Li, Yansui Liu, Michael Woods, and Jian Zou. 2012. "Accelerated Restructuring in Rural China Fueled by 'Increasing vs. Decreasing Balance' Land-Use Policy for Dealing with Hollowed Villages." *Land Use Policy* 29, no. 1: 11–22.

Low, Linda. 2002. "Rethinking Singapore Inc. and the GLCs." *Southeast Asian Affairs* 2002: 282–302.

Luo, Lizi, and Deheng Zeng. 2015. "Jobs-Housing Spatial Mismatch Condition in Public Rental Housing in Chongqing, China." In *Proceedings of the 19th International Symposium on Advancement of Construction Management and Real Estate*, edited by L. Shen, 521–530. Berlin: Springer-Verlag.

Mahadevia, Darshini. 2006. "NURM and the Poor in Globalizing Megacities." *Lok Samvad Newsletter*, October 1.

Marfai, Muh Aris, Andung Bayu Sekaranom, and Philip Ward. 2015. "Community Responses and Adaptation Strategies toward Flood Hazard in Jakarta, Indonesia." *Natural Hazards* 75, no. 2: 1127–1144.

Marshall, Richard. 2003. *Emerging Urbanity: Global Urban Projects in the Asia Pacific Rim*. London: Spon Press.

McFarlane, Colin. 2009. "Translocal Assemblages: Space, Power and Social Movements." *Geoforum* 40, no. 4: 561–567.

McGregor, Richard. 2010. *The Party: The Secret World of China's Communist Rulers*. New York: Harper.

McKinsey & Company. 2012. *Urban World: Cities and the Rise of the Consuming Class*. McKinsey Global Institute.

Mera, Koichi, and Bertrand Renaud. 2000. "Introduction." In *Asia's Financial Crisis and the Role of Real Estate*, edited by Koichi Mera and Bertrand Renaud, 1–27. New York: M. E. Sharpe.

Mgbako, Chi, Rijie Ernie Gao, Elizabeth Joynes, Anna Cave, and Jessica Mikhailevich. 2010. "Forced Eviction and Resettlement in Cambodia: Case Studies from Phnom Penh." *Washington University Global Studies Law Review* 9: 39–76.

Ministry of Commerce and Industry. 2002. "Press Note No. 3: Guidelines for FDI in Development of Integrated Townships Including Housing and Building Material." New Delhi: Government of India.

Ministry for Economic Affairs. 2014. "Master Plan: National Capital Integrated Coastal Development: Draft." Government of Indonesia and Government of Netherlands.

Mitra, Sanjay. 2002. "Planned Urbanization Through Public Participation: The Case of New Town, Kolkata." *Economic and Political Weekly*, March 16, 1048–1052.

Monkkonen, Paavo. 2013. "Urban Land Use Regulation and Housing Markets in Developing Countries: Evidence from Indonesia on the Importance of Enforcement." *Land Use Policy* 34, no. 3: 255–264.

Mulvad, Andreas. 2015. "Competing Hegemonic Projects Within China's Variegated Capitalism: 'Liberal' Guangdong vs. 'Statist' Chongqing." *New Political Economy* 20, no. 2: 199–227.

Murakami, Akinobu, Alinda Zain, Kazuhiko Takeuchi, Atsushi Tsunekawa, and Shigehiro Yokota. 2005. "Trends in Urbanization and Patterns of Land Use in the Asian

Mega Cities Jakarta, Bangkok, and Metro Manila." *Landscape and Urban Planning* 70, no. 3–4: 251–259.

NESDB (National Economic and Social Development Board). 2005. *Thailand's Mega-Projects: Investment for the Future and Business Opportunity*. Bangkok: NESDB.

Nielsen, Kenneth. 2010. "Contesting India's Development? Industrialisation, Land Acquisition and Protest in West Bengal." *Forum for Development Studies* 37, no. 2: 145–170.

Nurfiyasari, Efi. 2013. "Sentul City to Lift Stake in Bukit Jonggol to 100% for Full Control." *Jakarta Post*, September 20.

Oi, Jean. 1992. "Fiscal Reform and the Economic Foundations of Local State Corporatism in China." *World Politics* 45, no. 1: 99–126.

Ong, Aihwa. 2006. *Neoliberalism as Exception: Mutations in Citizenship and Sovereignty*. Durham, NC: Duke University Press.

——. 2007. "Neoliberalism as a Mobile Technology." *Transactions of the Institute of British Geographers* 32, no. 1: 3–8.

——. 2011. "Introduction: Worlding Cities and the Art of Being Global." In *Worlding Cities: Asian Experiments and the Art of Being Global*, edited by Ananya Roy and Aihwa Ong, 1–27. Cambridge: Blackwell.

Ong, Lynette. 2014. "State-Led Urbanization in China: Skyscrapers, Land Revenue and 'Concentrated Villages.'" *The China Quarterly* 217: 162–179.

OpenStreetMap. https://www.openstreetmap.org/.

Oren, Michelle, Rachelle Alterman, and Yaffa Zilbershatz. 2013. *Housing Rights in Constitutional Legislation: A Conceptual Classification*. SSRN Scholarly Paper. Rochester, NY: Social Science Research Network.

Orueta, Fernando, and Susan Fainstein. 2008. "The New Mega-projects: Genesis and Impacts." *International Journal of Urban and Regional Research* 32, no. 3: 759–767.

Padawangi, Rita, and Michael Douglass. 2015. "Water, Water Everywhere: Towards Participatory Solutions to Chronic Urban Flooding in Jakarta." *Pacific Affairs* 88, no. 3: 517–550.

Pamuntjak, M. 1990. "Private Sector Responses to Urban Planned Development in Indonesia." Proceedings of an International Workshop on Asian Urban Land, June 1989, University of Malaya, Kuala Lumpur.

Parnell, Susan, and Jennifer Robinson. 2012. "(Re)Theorizing Cities from the Global South: Looking Beyond Neoliberalism." *Urban Geography* 33, no. 4: 593–617.

Pasadilla, Gloria, and Melanie Milo. 2005. "Effects of Liberalization on Banking Competition." Philippine Institute for Development Studies Discussion Paper Series no. 2005–03.

Pasuk Phongpaichit. 2003. "Financing Thaksinomics." Unpublished article.

Pasuk Phongpaichit and Chris Baker. 1995. *Thailand: Economy and Politics*. Kuala Lumpur: Oxford University Press.

——. 1998. *Thailand's Boom and Bust*. Bangkok: Silkworm Books.

——. 2004. *Thaksin: The Business of Politics in Thailand*. Bangkok: Silkworm Books.

Peck, Jamie. 2013. "Explaining (with) Neoliberalism." *Territory, Politics, Governance* 1, no. 2: 132–157.

Peck, Jamie, and Nick Theodore. 2012. "Follow the Policy: A Distended Case Approach." *Environment and Planning* A 44: 1–30.

Peck, Jamie, and Adam Tickell. 2002. "Neoliberalizing Space." *Antipode* 34, no. 3: 380–404.

Peck, Jamie, and Jun Zhang. 2013. "A Variety of Capitalism . . . With Chinese Characteristics?" *Journal of Economic Geography* 13, no. 3: 357–396.

Peterson, George. 2009. *Unlocking Land Values to Finance Urban Infrastructure.* Washington, DC: World Bank.

——. 2013. *Unlocking Land Values for Urban Infrastructure Finance: International Experience—Considerations for Indian Policy.* SSRN Scholarly Paper. Rochester, NY: Social Science Research Network.

Peterson, George, and Olga Kaganova. 2010. "Integrating Land Financing into Subnational Fiscal Management." World Bank Policy Research Working Paper 5409. Washington, DC: World Bank.

Phillips, David, Anthony Gar-On Yeh, and Kwi-Gon Kim. 1987. *New Towns in East and South-east Asia: Planning and Development.* Hong Kong: Oxford University Press.

Prakash, Gyan. 1999. *Another Reason: Science and the Imagination of Modern India.* Princeton, NJ: Princeton University Press.

Prakash, Vikram. 2002. *Chandigarh's Le Corbusier: The Struggle for Modernity in Postcolonial India.* Seattle: University of Washington Press.

Prinya, M. 1998. "More Debts and Deadlocks." *Bangkok Post 1997 Year End Review*, 46–47.

P. T. Bumi Serpong Damai. 1985. "BSD New City: Pre-Study Report." Pacific Consultants International Group, August.

Rachman, Noer Fauzi. 2011. "The Resurgence of Land Reform Policy and Agrarian Movements in Indonesia." PhD dissertation, University of California at Berkeley.

Ramanathan, Usha. 2006. "Illegality and the Urban Poor." *Economic And Political Weekly*, July 22, 3193–3197.

——. 2015. "The Questions We Should Be Asking Frequently about the Land Acquisition Act, and Answers from an Expert." http://in.news.yahoo.com/the-questions-we-should-be-asking-frequently-about-the-land-acquisition-act-060820434.html. Accessed July 17.

Reerink, Gustaaf. 2011. *Tenure Security for Indonesia's Urban Poor: A Sociolegal Study of Land, Decentralization, and the Rule of Law in Bandung.* Leiden: Leiden University Press.

Ren, Xuefei, and Liza Weinstein. 2013. "Urban Governance, Megaprojects, and Scalar Transformations in China and India." In *Locating Right to the City in the Global South*, edited by Tony Samara, Shenjing He, and Guo Chen, 107–126. New York: Routledge.

Renaud, Bertrand. 1995. "The 1985–1994 Global Real Estate Cycle: Its Causes and Consequences." The World Bank Financial Sector Development Department Policy Research Working Paper No. 1452. Washington, DC: World Bank.

Reserve Bank of India. 2008–2009. *Handbook of Statistics on the Indian Economy.* New Delhi: Reserve Bank of India.

Rithmire, Meg. 2013. "The 'Chongqing Model' and the Future of China." Harvard Business School Case No. 9-713-028.

Riverbank Holdings Pvt. Ltd. N.d. "Calcutta Riverside . . . Continuing Rich Traditions of Vibrant Calcutta." Unpublished PowerPoint presentation.

——. 2005. "Batanagar Master Plan, Kolkata, India." Prepared by HOK Planning Group, July.

Robison, Richard. 1986. *Indonesia: The Rise of Capital*. Singapore: Equinox.

——. 1988. "Authoritarian States, Capital-Owning Classes, and the Politics of Newly Industrializing Countries: The Case of Indonesia." *World Politics* 41, no. 1: 52–74.

——. 1990. *Power and Economy in Suharto's Indonesia*. Manila: Journal of Contemporary Asia Publishers.

Robison, Richard, and Vedi Hadiz. 2004. *Reorganising Power in Indonesia: The Politics of Oligarchy in an Age of Markets*. London: Routledge.

Robinson, Jennifer. 2006. *Ordinary Cities: Between Modernity and Development*. Oxon: Routledge.

——. 2011. "Cities in a World of Cities: The Comparative Gesture." *International Journal of Urban and Regional Research* 35, no. 1: 1–23.

——. 2016. "Comparative Urbanism: New Geographies and Cultures of Theorizing the Urban." *International Journal of Urban and Regional Research* 40, no. 1: 187–199.

Rolnik, Raquel. 2013. "Late Neoliberalism: The Financialization of Homeownership and Housing Rights." *International Journal of Urban and Regional Research* 37, no. 3: 1058–1066.

Rouanet, Hortense, and Ludovic Halbert. 2015. "Leveraging Finance Capital: Urban Change and Self-Empowerment of Real Estate Developers in India." *Urban Studies*. Online first. doi: 10.1177/0042098015585917.

Roy, Ananya. 2003. *City Requiem, Calcutta: Gender and the Politics of Poverty*. Minneapolis: University of Minnesota Press.

——. 2005. "Urban Informality: Toward an Epistemology of Planning." *Journal of the American Planning Association* 71, no. 2: 147–158.

——. 2009. "Why India Cannot Plan its Cities: Informality, Insurgence, and the Idiom of Urbanization." *Planning Theory* 8, no. 1: 76–87.

——. 2011. "Urbanisms, Worlding Practices and the Theory of Planning." *Planning Theory* 8, no. 1: 6–15.

Roy, Rajat. 2009. "Vedic Village Scam May Unearth Many Skeletons," *Business Standard*, August 31.

Sami, Neha. 2013. "From Farming to Development: Urban Coalitions in Pune, India." *International Journal of Urban and Regional Research* 37, no. 1: 151–164.

Sanderson, Henry, and Michael Forsythe. 2013. *China's Superbanks: Debt, Oil and Influence—How China Development Bank Is Rewriting the Rules of Finance*. New York: Bloomberg Press.

Santoso, Jo. 2009. *The Fifth Layer of Jakarta*. Jakarta: Centropolis.

Sassen, Saskia. 2013. "Land Grabs Today: Feeding the Disassembling of National Territory." *Globalizations* 10, no. 1: 25–46.

Sato, Yuri. 1993. "The Salim Group in Indonesia: The Development and Behavior of the Largest Conglomerate in Southeast Asia." *The Developing Economies* 31, no. 4: 408–441.

Schindler, Seth. 2014. "Producing and Contesting the Formal/Informal Divide: Regulating Street Hawking in Delhi, India." *Urban Studies*. Online first. doi: 10.1177/0042098013510566.

Schuman, Michael. 2013. "The Real Reason to Worry About China." Time Magazine Internet Edition, April 28. http://business.time.com/2013/04/28/the-real-reason-to-worry-about-china/. Accessed September 9, 2013.

Schwarz, Adam. 2004. *A Nation in Waiting: Indonesia's Search for Stability*. Singapore: Talisman Publishing.

Searle, Llerena. 2014. "Conflict and Commensuration: Contested Market Making in India's Private Real Estate Development Sector." *International Journal of Urban and Regional Research* 38, no. 1: 60–78.

Sengupta, Urmi. 2006. "Liberalization and the Privatization of Public Rental Housing in Kolkata." *Cities* 23, no. 4: 269–278.

——. 2013. "Inclusive Development? A State-Led Land Development Model in New Town, Kolkata." *Environment and Planning C: Government and Policy* 31, no. 2: 357–376.

Shatkin, Gavin. 2008. "The City and the Bottom Line: Urban Megaprojects and the Privatization of Planning in Southeast Asia." *Environment and Planning A* 40, no. 2: 383–401.

——. 2013. "Comparative Perspectives on Urban Contestations: India and China." In *Contesting the Indian City: Global Visions and the Politics of the Local*, edited by Gavin Shatkin, 293–311. Oxford: Wiley-Blackwell.

——. 2014. "Reconsidering the Meaning of the Singapore Model: State Capitalism and Urban Planning." *International Journal of Urban and Regional Research* 38, no. 1: 116–137.

Shatkin, Gavin, and Sanjeev Vidyarthi. 2013. "Introduction: Contesting the Indian City." In *Contesting the Indian City: Global Visions and the Politics of the Local*, edited by Gavin Shatkin, 1–38. Oxford: Wiley-Blackwell.

Shen, Jie, and Fulong Wu. 2012. "The Development of Master-Planned Communities in Chinese Suburbs: A Case Study of Shanghai's Thames Town." *Urban Geography* 33, no. 2: 183–203.

Sheng, Yap Kioe, and Sakchai Kirinpanu. 2000. "Once Only the Sky Was the Limit: Bangkok's Housing Boom and the Financial Crisis in Thailand." *Housing Studies* 15, no. 1: 11–27.

Shin, Hyun Bang. 2013. "The Right to the City and Critical Reflections on China's Property Rights Activism." *Antipode* 45, no. 5: 1167–1189.

Sidel, John. 1998. "Macet Total: Logics of Circulation and Accumulation in the Demise of Indonesia's New Order." *Indonesia* 66: 159–195.

Siemiatycki, Matt. 2013. "Riding the Wave: Explaining Cycles in Urban Mega-project Development." *Journal of Economic Policy Reform* 16, no. 2: 160–178.

Silver, Chris. 2007. *Planning the Megacity: Jakarta in the Twentieth Century*. London: Routledge.

Simone, Abdoumaliq, and Vyjayanthi Rao. 2012. "Securing the Majority: Living Through Uncertainty in Jakarta." *International Journal of Urban and Regional Research* 36, no. 2: 315–335.

Singh, M. 2008. The Future of Integrated Townships. *Economic Times* (New Delhi), January 25.

Sivaramakrishnan, K. C. 2011. "Urban Development and Metro Governance." *Economic and Political Weekly* 46, no. 31: 49–55.

Smith, Neil. 1996. *The New Urban Frontier: Gentrification and the Revanchist City.* New York: Routledge.

Stone, Clarence. 1989. *Regime Politics: Governing Atlanta, 1946–1988.* Lawrence: University Press of Kansas.

——. 1993. "Urban Regimes and the Capacity to Govern: A Political Economy Approach." *Journal of Urban Affairs* 15, no. 1: 1–28.

Struyk, Raymond, Michael Hoffman, and Harold Katsura. 1990. *The Market for Shelter in Indonesian Cities.* Washington, DC: Urban Institute.

Suehiro, Akira. 1989. *Capital Accumulation in Thailand, 1855–1985.* Bangkok: Silkworm Books.

Swyngedouw, Eric, Frank Moulaert, and Arantxa Rodriguez. 2002. "Neoliberal Urbanization in Europe: Large-Scale Urban Development Projects and the New Urban Policy." *Antipode* 34, no. 3: 542–577.

Szelenyi, Ivan. 2011. "Third Ways." *Modern China* 37, no. 6: 672–683.

Tan, Yingzi. 2015. "Shapingba Builds West China's Silicon Valley." *China Daily*, September 7.

TEC/DCA (Thai Engineering Co./Design Concept Co). 2005. "Final Report: Feasibility Study and Preliminary Design of Makkasan Workshop Area Development Project." State Railways of Thailand, May 27.

Thorburn, Craig. 2004. "The Plot Thickens: Land Administration and Policy in Post-New Order Indonesia." *Asia Pacific Viewpoint* 45, no. 1: 33–49.

Tian, Li. 2015. "Land Use Dynamics Driven by Rural Industrialization and Land Finance in the Peri-urban Areas of China: The Examples of Jiangyin and Shunde." *Land Use Policy* 45: 117–127.

Tiwari, Santosh. 2012. "Kelkar Sets Ball Rolling on Govt Land Monetization." *Rediff Business*, October 1. http://www.rediff.com/money/report/kelkar-sets-ball-rolling-on-govt-land-monetisation/20121001.htm. Accessed July 30, 2013.

Tong, Yanqi, and Shaohua Lei. 2010. "Large Scale Mass Incidents and Government Responses in China." *International Journal of China Studies* 1, no. 2: 487–508.

UNCTAD (United Nations Conference of Trade and Investment). 2013. "Inward and Outward Foreign Direct Investment Stock, Annual, 1980–2012." http://unctadstat.unctad.org/TableViewer/tableView.aspx. Accessed October 25, 2013.

United Nations. 2014. *World Urbanization Prospects, The 2014 Revision, File 3: Urban Population at Mid-Year by Major Area, Region and Country, 1950–2050 (thousands).* New York: United Nations Population Division. http://esa.un.org/unpd/wup/CD-ROM/. Accessed June 18, 2015.

United Nations Population Division. 2012. "World Urbanization Prospects: The 2012 Revision Population Database." http://esa.un.org/unup/index.asp. Accessed October 31, 2013.

Vidyarthi, Sanjeev. 2015. *One Idea, Many Plans: An American City Design Concept in Independent India.* New York: Routledge.

Wang, H., R. Tao, L. Wang, and F. Su. 2010. "Farmland Preservation and Land Development Rights Trading in Zhejiang, China." *Habitat International* 34, no. 4: 454–463.

Wang, De, Li Zhang, Zhao Zhang, and Simon Zhao. 2011. "Urban Infrastructure Financing in Reform-Era China." *Urban Studies* 48, no. 14: 2975–2998.

Webster, Douglas. 2000. "Financing City-Building: The Bangkok Case." Shorenstein APARC Working Paper Series. aparc.stanford.edu/publications/financing_citybuilding_the_bangkok_case.

Webster, Chris, Fulong Wu, and Yanjing Zhao. 2006. "China's Modern Gated Cities." In *Private Cities: Global and Local Perspectives*, edited by George Glasze, Chris Webster, and Klaus Franz, 151–166. London: Routledge.

Weinstein, Liza. 2008. "Mumbai's Development Mafias: Globalization, Organized Crime, and Land Development." *International Journal of Urban and Regional Research* 32, no. 1: 22–39.

——. 2009. "Redeveloping Dharavi: Toward a Political Economy of Slums and Slum Redevelopment in Globalizing Mumbai." PhD dissertation, University of Chicago.

——. 2014. *The Durable Slum: Dharavi and the Right to Stay Put in Globalizing Mumbai*. Minneapolis: University of Minnesota Press.

Weinstein, Liza, Neha Sami, and Gavin Shatkin. 2013. "Framing Contestations: Institutions and Actors in Contemporary Urban India." In *Contesting the Indian City: Global Visions and Politics of the Local*, edited by Gavin Shatkin, 39–64. New York: Wiley-Blackwell.

Whiting, Susan. 2011. "Values in Land: Fiscal Pressures, Land Disputes and Justice Claims in Rural and Peri-urban China." *Urban Studies* 48, no. 3: 569–587.

Wichit, C. 2004. "Making the Most of State Assets." *Bangkok Post* Mid-Year Economic Review.

Winarso, Haryo. 2000. "Residential Land Developers Behavior in Jabotabek, Indonesia." PhD dissertation, University College London.

Winarso, Haryo, and Tommy Firman. 2002. "Residential Land Development in *Jabotabek*, Indonesia: Triggering Economic Crisis?" *Habitat International* 26: 487–506.

Winarti, Agnes. 2007. "Concrete Walls Shut Residents Out." *Jakarta Post*, City News Section, October 11.

——. 2009. "Superblocks Pose Risks, Study Says." *Jakarta Post*, City Section, February 12.

Winters, Jeffrey. 1996. *Power in Motion: Capital Mobility and the Indonesian State*. Ithaca, NY: Cornell University Press.

——. 2011. *Oligarchy*. Cambridge: Cambridge University Press.

Wong, Kai Wen, and Tim Bunnell. 2006. " 'New Economy' Discourse and Spaces in Singapore: A Case Study of One-North." *Environment and Planning A* 38, no. 1: 69–83.

World Bank. 2010a. "Investigation Report: Cambodia Land Management and Administration Project." Inspection Panel Report No. 58016-KH.

——. 2010b. *The Urban Development Investment Corporations (UDICs) in Chongqing, China*. http://openknowledge.worldbank.org/handle/10986/2888. Accessed May 9, 2013.

Wu, Fulong. 2001. "China's Recent Urban Development in the Process of Land and Housing Marketisation and Economic Globalization." *Habitat International* 25, no. 3: 273–289.

———. 2002. "China's Changing Urban Governance in Transition Towards a More Market-Oriented Economy." *Urban Studies* 39, no. 7: 1071–1093.

———. 2015. *Planning for Growth: Urban and Regional Planning in China.* London: Routledge.

Wu, Fulong, and Klaire Webber. 2004. "The Rise of 'Foreign Gated Communities' in Beijing: Between Economic Globalization and Local Institutions." *Cities* 21, no. 3: 203–213.

Wu, Fulong, Fangzhu Zhang, and Chris Webster. 2013. "Informality and the Development and Demolition of Urban Villages in the Chinese Peri-urban Area." *Urban Studies* 50, no. 10: 1919–1934.

Xiang, Jian, and Jiang Wu. 2013. "A Public Service-Oriented Government Building Path in Chinese City: An Example from Public Rental Housing of Chongqing." *Canadian Social Science* 9, no. 4: 7–14.

Xu, Jiang, and James Wang. 2012. "Reassembling the State in Urban China." *Asia-Pacific Viewpoint* 53, no. 1: 7–20.

Xue, Charles, Ying Wang, and Luther Tsai. 2013. "Building New Towns in China: A Case Study of Zhengdong New District." *Cities* 30: 223–232.

Ye, Yumin, and Richard LeGates. 2013. *Coordinating Urban and Rural Development in China: Learning from Chengdu.* Cheltenham: Edward Elgar.

Yeoh, Brenda. 2005. "The Global Cultural City? Spatial Imagineering and Politics in the (Multi)cultural Marketplaces of South-east Asia." *Urban Studies* 42, no. 5/6: 945–958.

INDEX

Page numbers followed by letter *f* refer to figures.

access to urban space: efforts to retain, Calcutta Riverside project and, 169–70, 173; urban real estate megaprojects and conflicts over, 17, 25, 60. *See also* exclusion and segregation

accumulation by dispossession, 9, 137–38

affordable housing: in Chongqing, 180, 201–2, 203*f*, 204, 205, 209, 234; in Jakarta, 67, 113, 134–35; in Kolkata, 172–73, 235; urban real estate megaprojects and, 23

Africa: massive acquisition of rural land in, 97; neoliberalization processes and, 218

Agung Podomoro (developer), 135

Akosoro, Lana W., 114, 115, 120

Alterman, Rachelle, 91, 92

Ambuja Realty, 164, 165, 166

Angel, Shlomo, 28

Appadurai, Arjun, 145

architectural renderings, of urban real estate megaprojects, xi–xii, 4*f*; dual purpose of, 36; vs. reality, 5–6, 6*f*, 15, 30–31

Argo Manunggal Group, 121

Asian cities: diversity of, xiv–xv, 41–44; privatization of public space in, 45, 62–63, 235–36; rapid expansion of, xii; real estate turn in urban politics and remaking of, 236–37. *See also* new town projects; urban real estate megaprojects; *specific cities*

Asian financial crisis, 52; causes of, hypotheses regarding, 52–53; urban real estate megaprojects after, 58–59

Australia, property rights in, 91

authoritarian political systems: land monetization strategies in, 94, 96–98, 220–24; shifts in global economy and, 98

autonomy of state actors, and land monetization strategies, 88–93, 95*f*

Ayala Land Incorporated, 50

Baker, Chris, 39, 50, 54

Bakrieland (developer), 135

Balakrishnan, Pramod, 171

Bambang Trihatmodjo, 102, 121

Banerjee, Mamata, 159, 160

Bangalore Agenda Task Force (BATF), 16, 156

Bangkok (Thailand): Din Daeng Redevelopment Project in, 40, 51, 58, 78; Japanese foreign direct investment in, 33, 49; land values in, dramatic increase in, 50; Muang Thong Thani development near, 30, 43*f*, 44, 50, 214; property bubble of mid-1990s, 30; Rama III New Financial District in, 51; urban expansion in, 28

Bangkok Land Incorporated, 50

Bank Central Asia (Indonesia), 121

banking sector: in China, 68–69, 182–83, 197; in Indonesia, reforms of, 51, 66, 120; and urban land development in Asia, xiv, 51

Basic Agrarian Law of 1960 (BAL), Indonesia, 111

Bata Corporation, 168–69

Baviskar, Amita, 92, 143, 231

Beijing (China): Chongqing compared to, 196; Orange County development outside of, 191

Bello, Walden, 48

Benjamin, Solomon, xvii, 33, 89, 90, 99, 137, 142, 148, 231

Bhagwat, Aniket, 171

Bhagwat, Prabhakar, 171

Bhan, Gautam, 21, 22, 61, 92, 150, 155

Bhubaneshwar (India), 144, 146

Bimantara Group, 121

Bjorkman, Lisa, 74, 227

Blei, Alejandro, 28

Boeung Kak project (Phnom Penh, Cambodia), 1–2, 3*f*, 222; Great Garuda project (Jakarta) compared to, 213; rent seeking by state actors in, 1, 15, 24; stalling of, 2, 16, 222; state-corporate nexus in, 16

Bonifacio Global City (Metro Manila, Philippines), 4*f*, 30

Bo Xilai, 32, 70, 71, 177, 179, 196, 197–98, 201, 220

Bremmer, Ian, 99, 178

Brenner, Neil, 9, 24, 37, 78, 84, 217

BSD City. *See* Bumi Serpong Damai

Budianta, Melani, 107

Bukit Jonggol Asri proposal (Jakarta, Indonesia), 102–3, 105, 110*f*, 114, 120, 121

Bumi Serpong Damai (BSD City; Jakarta, Indonesia), 50, 66–67, 116, 122–32, 230; current state of, 123; developers involved with, 123–24; exclusion and segregation in, 130, 132; international consultants for, 126, 128; *kampungs* next to, 127–28, 127*f*, 132; land acquisition for, 126–27; location of, 126; location permit for, lobbying for, 125–26; phase one of, 129–30, 129*f*; phase two of, 130–31, 131*f*

Calcutta Riverside (Kolkata, India), 167–74, 169*f*; advertising for, 76*f*; ambiguity of "success" of, 168, 174; architects and planners for, 171; displacement resulting from, 174; efforts to address environmental degradation and social exclusion in, 170–73, 235; elements of, 172; land claims in, 168, 169; location of, 161*f*; negotiated nature of, 168, 172–73; planning process for, 30, 170–72 *calo tanah* (land brokers), in Indonesia, 114, 115

Cambodia: corporate dominance in land development of, 83; dispossession and displacement in, 2, 9, 97, 222; empowerment of local state actors in, 25; informal patterns of land occupation in, 2; land reclamation in, 1, 3*f*, 15, 97, 136, 213, 222; New Order Indonesia compared to, 136; opposition to forcible land acquisition in, 2, 16, 222; political economy of land grab in, 96, 97, 220–21; real estate turn in urban politics of, 55, 56

Canlubang Sugar Estate (Jakarta, Indonesia), 50

Caofeidian Eco-City (China), 224

capital accumulation: centrality of urban land to agendas of, xii, 13; by dispossession, 9, 137–38; land commodification and, 10, 11, 136, 177–78

CapitaLand (developer), 87

case studies, 7–8; and comparative practice of urbanism, 32–33; selection of, 31–32

CEO politicians, 35, 39, 74, 185

Chakravorty, Sanjoy, 155, 165

Chandigarh (India), 144, 146

Chang'an Automobile Company, 198, 205

Chatterjee, Partha, 89, 141–43, 145, 148

Chenggong project (Kunming, China), 5

chengzhongcun (villages in the city), 188, 191, 192

China, 67–72; banking system in, 68–69, 182–83, 197; *chengzhongcun* (villages in the city) in, 188, 191, 192; collective land ownership in, 187–88, 225; competition among state actors in, 25, 62, 178, 186, 224; conflicts over land in, 186–88, 228; "consolidated villages" in, 190, 192; contradictions in model of urban development in, 31–32, 71,

180, 215–16, 223–24; coordinated rural-urban development in, 79, 192–93; dispossession and displacement in, 20, 69, 86, 179, 181, 188, 192, 193; dualistic land rights regimes in, 187, 225, 226; eco-city projects in, 210–11, 224; ecological impacts of urbanization in, 69, 189; engineering of urban transition in, 186–87, 230–31; expansion of urban built-up areas in, 179; failed projects/ghost towns in, 5, 214; farmland conversion in, concerns regarding, 189–90; gated communities in, historical roots of, 45, 63, 190–91; gradual degradation of property claims in, 227; *hukou* (household registration) system in, 177, 183, 199–201, 203, 204–5; India compared to, 73, 174; land-centered accumulation project of, 24, 177–78, 181, 183, 210; Land Law of 1986 in, 183–84; land leasehold system in, 68, 181, 183–84; land-management authority in, 73, 90; local governments' search for new revenue streams in, 181, 184–85; local state actors in, empowerment of, 25, 180, 185, 223; model of urban development in, 67–72, 177; municipalities as key agents of territorial expansion in, 186–87; "nail households" in, 61; new town developments in, 5, 69, 179–80, 190–92, 206–7; protests against dispossession in, 86, 179, 187, 188, 193, 224; real estate turn in urban politics of, xiv, 56, 58; social inequality and spatial fragmentation in, 180, 190, 192, 208–9, 234; state capitalist urban planning in, 98, 99, 178, 180–86, 204, 209–10, 222, 223; state-corporate nexus in, 16; state land ownership in, 68, 83, 86, 91, 181; state-owned enterprises in, 16, 25, 94, 182; state rescaling in,

China *(cont.)*
24–25, 79, 180, 185, 223; tax sharing system in, 181, 184; university towns in, 207–8; urban development investment corporations (UDICs) in, 70–71, 185–86, 197, 201–2, 206; Urban Real Estate Management Law of 1994, 184; urban real estate megaprojects in, 5, 26, 190; Western models in new towns of, 191. *See also specific cities*
China Development Bank, 70, 182, 197
Chinese Communist Party (CCP): contradictions in state rescaling and, 79; control over banking system, 68, 182–83; control over local governments, 68, 181–83; control over politics and economy, 180–81; land markets used to legitimate power of, 86, 98; land monetization as strategy of growth used by, 68, 181; threats to legitimacy of, 178–79, 189–90, 192
Chongqing (China), 194–206; achievements of, 202–4, 206; affordable housing projects in, 180, 201–2, 203*f*, 204, 205, 209, 234; autonomy of land managers and development in, 90; cultural campaign in, 194–96; designation as province-level city, 196; economic growth of, 70, 198–99, 205; *hukou* (household registration) reform in, 177, 183, 199–201, 203, 204–5; infrastructure investment program in, 177, 194, 198, 207, 222; Jiangbeizui central business district in, model of, 70*f*; as laboratory for new models of urban development, 69–72, 197; land certificate exchange system in, 199, 203; land monetization and expansion of, 99, 219–20; map of, 195*f*; population of, 69, 196; relocation of rural residents in, 193; risks inherent in expansion of, 200–201, 204–5; selection for case study, 31–32, 180;

size of, 69; social segregation within new towns of, 234; social welfare programs in, 177, 180, 199, 201, 202–4; state appropriation of rent gaps in, 219; University Town in, 206, 207–8; urban development investment corporations (UDICs) and, 70–71, 197, 201–2, 206; Western New Town developments in, 206–9
Chuang, Julia, 188, 193, 200, 205
Ciputra Group, 50, 64, 66, 121, 123–24, 126
Civco, Daniel, 28
climate change: adaptation to, in urban planning, 59, 134, 212–13, 221; flooding caused by, 134, 212
collective land ownership, in China, 187–88, 225
Communist Party of India-Marxist (CPI-M): distribution of land to poor communities, 72; election wall painting in Kolkata, 163*f*; land acquisition push and election loss of, 21, 72, 140–41, 160–67, 216
consumer class, and urban real estate megaprojects in Asia, 19, 20
convergence in urban development, theories of, 41–44; critique of, 45
corporate actors: global economic processes and, 13; growing influence in development of urban space, 8, 16; shared interests with state actors, 8, 15–16, 24, 36, 45, 47–48, 118, 121, 122, 133. *See also* developers
corporations, states as, 35–36, 38–39
corruption: in China, 25, 68, 71, 179, 187, 216; in India, 73, 143, 144; in Indonesia, 98, 102, 103, 112, 132; local state actors and, 25, 68, 71, 73; real estate turn in politics and, 54; state capitalist model and, 99, 216, 223; in Thailand, 39, 54. *See also* rent seeking
courts: as agents in shaping urban development agendas, 91–93; Indian, on illegal encroachments by the poor, 61, 92, 155, 227

Cowherd, Robert, 20, 64, 102, 107
customary land tenure. *See* informal
    patterns of land occupation

Dabriwala, Sumit, 165, 170
Dankuni Township project (Kolkata,
    India), 164, 165–66, 167, 225
Delhi (India): Bhagidari program in,
    155–56; new town developments
    in, 153–54; "planned" vs.
    "unauthorized" colonies in, 22
democratic states, land monetization
    strategies used in, 224–25
developers: affordable housing
    initiatives and opportunities for, 135;
    and bankers, collusive transactions
    of, 120; monopsony rights of, 114;
    partnership with state actors, 8;
    speculative land banking by, 114–15;
    strategy of maximizing property
    values, 132, 133; and urban real
    estate megaprojects, xiii–xiv, 3–4
developmentalism, Indonesian claims of,
    80, 120, 135, 215, 234
Dharavi Redevelopment Project
    (Mumbai, India), 157, 226
Dick, Howard, 5, 19–20, 60, 64, 107
Din Daeng Redevelopment Project
    (Bangkok, Thailand), 40, 51, 58, 78
dispossession and displacement: in
    Cambodia, 2, 9, 97, 222; capital
    accumulation by, 9, 137–38; in
    China, 20, 69, 86, 179, 181, 188,
    192, 193; in India, 21, 61, 92, 158,
    164–67, 174, 227, 231; in Indonesia,
    97, 108, 229–30; legal frameworks
    and, 92, 158; new generation of
    urban real estate megaprojects and,
    214; in Philippines, 20–21; political
    economy of land grab and, 96, 97;
    political repercussions of, 21, 37, 140,
    220; state actors' rationalization of,
    229, 232; in Thailand, 40; urban real
    estate megaprojects and, 4, 7, 20–21,
    37, 60, 229–32. *See also* protests
DLF (developer), 57, 58, 154, 164, 166

DLF City (Gurgaon, India), 6, 6*f*, 153, 154
Doshi, Balakrishnan, 171
Doxiadis and Associates, 126
dualistic land rights regimes, 21–22; in
    Cambodia, 2; in China, 187, 225, 226;
    and constraints on commodification
    of urban space, 28–29; in India, 22,
    89, 137, 142, 226, 227; in Indonesia,
    21–22, 67, 80, 87, 104–6, 107,
    109–12, 116, 135, 187, 222, 225,
    228; and rent gaps, state's exploitation
    of, 99–100, 225–29

Eastwood City development (Metro
    Manila, Philippines), 59
eco-city projects, in China, 210–11, 224
ecological destruction, urban real estate
    megaprojects and, 4, 7; in Cambodia,
    2, 3*f*; in China, 69, 189; in India,
    Calcutta Riverside project and efforts
    to ameliorate, 171, 172, 173
ecological sustainability ideal, new
    generation of urban real estate
    megaprojects and, 210–11, 214
Emaar MGF (developer), 154
enclave developments, in Asian cities, 3,
    5; in China, 190, 191, 202, 206, 209,
    222; developer preferences for, 133;
    in India, 6, 6*f*, 167, 174; in Indonesia,
    106, 107, 128, 131*f*, 132, 133; new
    generation of urban megaprojects and,
    211, 214. *See also* gated communities
Europe: gentrification in, rent
    gap concept and, 26–27; urban
    redevelopment projects in, 17, 18–19
exclusion and segregation: Chinese urban
    development and, 180, 190, 192,
    208–9, 234; emergent urban conflicts
    over, 25; historical roots in Asia,
    235–36; Indonesian urban development
    and, 12, 127–28, 127*f*, 130, 132,
    218, 233–34; lasting consequences of,
    236–37; urban real estate megaprojects
    and, 4, 60, 214, 232–36
export processing zones (EPZs), in
    India, 138

Farid, Hilmar, 107

farmers: benefits of urban development for, 138; dispossession in Cambodia, 2, 9; dispossession in India, 21, 72, 140, 155, 159–60, 167; dispossession in Indonesia, 108, 229–30; informal claims to land, 11–12; real estate development by, 82–83, 138, 140, 157; resistance to displacement, 72, 77, 159, 164–65

farmland, in China: collective ownership of, 187–88, 225; conversion of, concerns regarding, 179, 189–90

Ferguson, James, 218

Firman, Tommy, 5, 51, 55, 63, 64, 65, 67, 103, 120

Fischer, Dominique, 51, 66, 120

flooding: in Jakarta, 134, 212, 213, 221; in Phnom Penh, 2

foreign direct investment (FDI), in Asia: in India, 56–57, 57f, 153, 154; rise in, 48–49, 49f; and urban expansion, 27, 33, 46, 47, 49

FoxConn, 198, 201, 205, 207

fragmentation. *See* spatial fragmentation

Gandhi, Mahatma, 143

gated communities: in China, 45, 63, 190–91; historical antecedents in Asia, 45, 62–63, 235–36; in India, effort to ameliorate, 173; in Indonesia, 42f, 44; Western models for, 41. *See also* enclave developments

Ghertner, Asher, 92, 140, 142, 155–56

ghost towns, in China, 214

Glassman, Jim, 48, 58

global financial crisis of 2008–2009: Chinese program of fiscal stimulus after, 182; and Indian real estate market, 58

Great Garuda plan. *See* National Capital Integrated Coastal Development Plan

Guangdong (China), developmental model of, 176, 179

Guangzhou (China), urban expansion in, 28; constraints on, 199

Gu Kailai, 196

Gurgaon (India), DLF City in, 6, 6f, 153, 154

Hadiz, Vedi, 104, 117, 118, 119

Halbert, Ludovic, xiv, xviii, 225

Harvey, David, 17, 137, 236

Hasan, Mirza, 125, 126, 128, 130

Haussmann, Georges-Eugène, 17

Heikkila, Eric, 20, 64, 107

Hewlett Packard, 198, 205, 207

Hiland Group (developer), 165, 168; elite idealism of, 170, 173

Hogan, Trevor, 20, 45, 62–63, 64, 191, 235

HOK (architecture firm), 30, 171

Hong Kong, as model of urbanism, 44

housing rights: national constitutions on, 91. *See also* affordable housing

Hsing, You Tien, 20, 25, 61, 62, 68, 69, 86, 177, 186, 187, 188, 224

Huang, Philip, 177, 199, 201, 204

Huang Qifan, 197, 198, 200, 204

Hudalah, Delik, 64, 113

hukou (household registration) system, in China, 183; Chongqing reform of, 177, 183, 199–201, 203, 204–5

Hun Sen, 222

inclusionary zoning, 23; in India, 234–35. *See also* affordable housing

India, 72–77; ambiguity of urban politics in, 139, 141–51; Bhaghidari scheme in, 227; China compared to, 73, 174; contestations over land in, 21, 62, 72, 140–41; diffused political power in, 25, 138; dispossession and displacement in, 21, 61, 92, 158, 164–67, 174, 227, 231; experimentation in models of urban development, 156–57; experiments in power in, 140, 141, 151; foreign direct investment in, 56–57, 57f, 153, 154; fragmented land ownership in, 138; inclusionary zoning regulation in, 234–35; Indonesia compared to,

139, 174; informal claims to land in, 22, 73, 89, 137, 142, 155–56, 226, 227; Jawaharlal Nehru National Urban Renewal Mission (JNNURM) in, 56, 74–75; Land Acquisition, Rehabilitation, and Resettlement Act of 2013, 75, 158, 226; Land Acquisition Act of 1894, 75, 76, 88, 155, 159, 226; land as tool of capital accumulation and state legitimation in, 149; land-management authority in, 73–75; land monetization in, 10, 141, 174–75, 224–25; liberalization agenda in, 150–51; municipal commissioners in, 144, 145; new town developments in, 5–6, 6*f*, 57–58, 144, 146, 153–54, 225; occupancy urbanism in, 89, 90, 99, 137, 148, 150; opposition to urban development in, 72, 76–77; political embededness of illegalities in, 148–50; political society in, 142, 143; poor communities in, tendency toward criminalization and stigmatization of, 61, 92, 227, 231; postliberaiization-era urban planning in, 147, 152–59; preliberalization-era urban planning in, 146–50, 151; public interest litigations (PILs) in, 92–93, 155, 227; real estate turn in urban politics of, 56–58; "smart city" initiative in, 158–59; Special Economic Zone Act in, 154; state control of land markets in, 88; statist agenda of development planning in, 144–45, 171; urban governance reform in, contradictions in, 79–80; Urban Land Ceiling and Regulation Act in, 147, 156; urban population of, growth of, 145; urban real estate megaprojects in, 26, 72, 77; vote bank politics in, 89–90, 137. *See also specific cities*

India Infrastructure Report (Mohan report), 152–53

Indonesia, 63–67; affordable housing projects in, 67, 113, 134–35; Asian financial crisis and, 52; autonomy of land managers and urban development in, 90; banking sector reforms in, 51, 66, 120; Basic Agrarian Law of 1960 (BAL), 111; *calo tanah* (land brokers) in, 114, 115; as capital exporter, 55; degradation of property claims in, 227; developmentalism veneer in, 80, 120, 135, 215, 234; dispossession and displacement in, 97, 108, 229–30; dualistic land rights regime in, 21–22, 67, 80, 87, 104–6, 107, 109–12, 116, 135, 187, 222, 225, 228; engineering of urban transition in, 230; exclusion and segregation in urban development of, 12, 127–28, 127*f*, 130, 132, 218, 233–34; family-based conglomerates with ties to Suharto in, 55, 65, 66, 102; foreign direct investment in, 49*f*; fusion of state and corporate interests in, 118, 121, 122, 133; India compared to, 139, 174; informal patterns of land occupation in, 21–22, 65, 80, 87, 104–6, 109–12; international architecture and planning firms and, 44, 64, 126, 128; *kampung* communities in, 12, 104–5, 105*f*, 109, 127–28, 127*f*, 132, 213, 218, 228; land management reforms in, 64–65; land-permitting process and land transfer in, xiv, 50, 55, 65–67, 97, 103, 105, 108, 113–14, 120, 219, 226; land-registration system in, 111–16; location permit *(ijin lokasi)* in, 112, 113, 114–15; major real estate players in, 66, 120–21, 123–24; New Order, corruption in, 102, 103; New Order, political economy of land grab in, 96, 97, 103–4, 116–22, 220; New Order, unraveling of, 119–20; New Order oligarchy in, 117–18; oil industry and economic fortunes of, 118, 119; postauthoritarian, 80, 228; real estate shift in urban politics of,

Indonesia *(cont.)*
    xiv, 53, 55; social function of land in,
    111; speculative land banking in, 67,
    114–15; state as intermediary in real
    estate market in, 112–13, 135; urban
    real estate megaprojects in, 4–5, 26.
    See also Jakarta
informality: in India, 148–50; as mode
    of governing, 22, 61, 148, 162,
    226–27
informal patterns of land occupation:
    in Cambodia, 2; in cities of Global
    South, 11–12; in India, 22, 73, 89,
    137, 142, 155–56, 226, 227; in
    Indonesia, 21–22, 65, 80, 87, 104–6,
    109–12. *See also* dualistic land rights
    regimes
infrastructure development: in
    Chongqing, 177, 194, 198, 207, 222;
    land grants for, 56; land monetization
    translated into, 222
international architecture and planning
    firms, designs by: in India, 30, 171;
    in Indonesia, 44, 64, 126, 128; in
    Thailand, 44
International Monetary Fund (IMF),
    Asian financial crisis and, 52, 53

Jakarta (Indonesia), 63–67; Bukit
    Jonggol Asri proposal for, 102–3,
    105, 114, 120, 121; Bumi Serpong
    Damai (BSD City) in, 50, 66–67,
    116, 122–32, 230; Canlubang Sugar
    Estate in, 50; flooding in, 134, 212,
    213, 221; Japanese foreign direct
    investment in, 33, 49; *kampung*
    communities in, marginalization
    of, 12, 104–5, 105*f*, 109, 213,
    218; Kebayoran Baru in, 108; land
    monetization in, 135; land values in,
    dramatic increase in, 50, 120; Lippo
    Cikarang project in, 50, 121; Lippo
    Karawaci project in, 42*f*, 50, 131–32;
    map of, 110*f*; National Capital
    Integrated Coastal Development Plan
    (Great Garuda plan) for, 59, 134,
    212–13, 221; population of, 63, 108;
    Pulo Mas in, 108; real estate boom
    in, 65; runaway urbanism in, 107,
    133, 213; selection for case study,
    31; Senayan Sports Complex in, 108;
    superblock developments in, 133–34;
    traffic congestion in, 133; unregistered
    lands in, 87, 104, 105, 106, 109–12;
    Western models of architecture and
    design in, 106–7, 128, 130
Jakarta Metropolitan Region (JMR),
    108; dispossession of periurban
    farmers in, 229–30; enclavization
    in, 132; expansion of, 64, 65; former Dutch plantations in, 115;
    fragmentation of, 67, 106, 221; new
    town developments in, 4–5, 30, 42*f*,
    44, 50, 64, 102, 103–4, 108–9, 115,
    233–34; political arrangements and
    spatial development of, 121–22;
    population of, 63, 108; "sleeping
    land" in, 67, 115
Japan: foreign direct investment in
    Southeast Asia, 33, 47, 48, 49;
    Tsukuba Science City in, 65
Jawaharlal Nehru National Urban
    Renewal Mission (JNNURM), 56,
    74–75, 156
John Portman and Associates, 126

kampung communities (Indonesia),
    104–5, 105*f*, 109, 213; increased
    political sway of, 228; marginalization
    of, 12, 127–28, 127*f*, 132, 218
Kapadia, Kiran, 171
Keppel (developer), 87, 164
King, Ning, 121
Kolkata (India): abortive new town
    projects on periurban fringe of, 72;
    Bidhannagar (Salt Lake City) in, 146;
    CPI-M election wall painting in, 163*f*;
    Dankuni Township project in, 164,
    165–66, 167, 225; dispossession
    accompanying urban development

in, 164–65; Housing Infrastructure Development Corporation (HIDC) in, 76; inclusionary zoning regulation in, 234–35; informality as mechanism of governance in, 162; land acquisition and transfer to developers in, 219, 220; Left Front's land monetization strategy in, 160–62; map of, 161*f*; political shifts in, forcible land acquisition and, 21, 72, 140–41, 160–67, 216, 220; population of, 72; postliberalization urban planning in, 163–64; Rajarhat new town development in, 162, 163; resistance to urban megaprojects in, 216; selection for case study, 31; Singur development plans in, 72, 77, 159–60, 162, 164, 167; "unmapping" of, 150; Vedic Village near, 166. *See also* Calcutta Riverside

Kolkata West International City, 30, 164, 167

Kusno, Abidin, xviii, 8, 20, 22, 64, 67, 87, 107, 135, 229–30

Land Acquisition, Rehabilitation, and Resettlement Act of 2013 (India), 75, 158, 226

Land Acquisition Act of 1894 (India), 75, 76, 88, 155, 159, 226

land brokers *(calo tanah)*, in Indonesia, 114, 115

land commodification, 14; appreciation of land values and push toward, 14, 46; in China, 177–78, 181, 183, 210; dualistic land rights regimes and constraints on, 28–29; government policies encouraging, 47; in Myanmar, 136; as rent seeking, 10–11; state interest in, 17; as strategy of accumulation, 10, 11, 13, 136; as technology of governing, 10, 11. *See also* land monetization

land grab, political economy of, 33, 95*f*, 96–98, 220–24; in Cambodia, 96, 97,

220–21; in Suharto-era Indonesia, 96, 97, 103–4, 116–22, 220

Land Law of 1986 (China), 183–84

land leasing: in China, 68, 181, 183–84; in Singapore, 87

land monetization: and disruptive pressures, xv; speculative interest in, 19, 36; state actors and, xiii, 10, 14; state strategies for, 29, 33, 36, 84, 95–101, 95*f*, 222, 224–25; state strategies for, variables shaping, 14–15, 85–95; state transformation through, in India, 174–75; as tactic of rent seeking, 10–11, 96, 136, 221; use of term, 14

land ownership. *See* collective land ownership; dualistic land rights regimes; state land ownership

land permitting, and land transfer in Indonesia, xiv, 50, 55, 65–67, 97, 103, 105, 108, 113–14, 120, 219, 226

land reclamation: in Jakarta, 212–13, 221; in Phnom Penh, 1, 3*f*, 15, 97, 136, 213, 222

land values, increases in: in Bangkok, 50; foreign direct investment and, 50; government policy responses to, 13, 45, 219–25; in India, 150–51; in Jakarta, 50, 120; in Metro Manila, 50; and push for land commodification, 14, 46; and state rescaling, 25

Lao Meng Khin, 1, 16

law: and dispossession and displacement, 92, 158; and politics of land development, 90–93, 100

Leaf, Michael, xviii, 22, 109, 114, 115, 124, 227

Leisch, Harald, 132

Levien, Michael, 138, 153, 154, 164

Liem Sioe Liong, 117. *See also* Salim, Sudono

Lin, George Chu-Sheng, 188, 189

Lippo Cikarang project (Jakarta, Indonesia), 50, 121

Lippo Group (Lippo Land
    Development), 50, 121, 131
Lippo Karawaci project (Jakarta,
    Indonesia), 42*f*, 50, 131–32
Logan, John, 209
London (UK), Docklands in, 18

Magar, Satish, 83, 157
Magarpatta City (Maharashtra, India),
    82–83, 101, 138, 140, 157
Makkasan Redevelopment Project
    (Thailand), 59
Malaysia: as capital exporter, 55;
    Singapore's growth and, 223
Manila (Philippines). *See* Metro Manila
Marcos, Ferdinand, 53
McKinsey (consulting firm), on urban
    regions as economic drivers, 38,
    46–47
Mehta, Mukesh, 157
Metro Manila (Philippines): Ayala South
    development in, 50; Bonifacio Global
    City in, 4*f*, 30; dispossession and
    displacement in, 20–21; Eastwood
    City development in, 59; Japanese
    foreign direct investment in, 33, 49;
    land values in, dramatic increase in,
    50; urban expansion in, 28
Modernland (developer), 135
Modi, Narendra, 141, 158, 160, 231
Mohan, Rakesh, 152
Molla, Gaffar, 167
Molotch, Harvey, 209
monopsony rights, 114
Muang Thong Thani development
    (Bangkok, Thailand), 30, 43*f*, 44,
    50, 214
Mukherjee, Dulal, 171
Mumbai (India): Dharavi
    Redevelopment Project in, 157, 226;
    Shivajinagar resettlement area in,
    74, 227; vote bank politics and land
    development in, 90
Myanmar: dominance of state actors in,
    94; land commodification in, 136

National Capital Integrated Coastal
    Development Plan (Great Garuda
    plan), Jakarta, 59, 134, 212–13, 221
Navi Mumbai, 146
Nehru, Jawaharlal, 73, 143
neighborhood unit concept, 146–47
neoliberalism, as technology of
    governing, 10, 221
neoliberalization of urban policy,
    8; broad implications of, 218; in
    China, 210, 218; in cities of Global
    South, 11–12; debate on, 8–9,
    11–12; distinct forms of, local
    political economies and, 217, 219; as
    externally imposed force, questioning
    of, 12–13, 214–15, 216–17;
    government agency in, 9–10, 12–13;
    in India, 139; in Indonesia, 135–36,
    218; in Western cities, 11
Neotia, Harish, 165
New Delhi (India): population
    displacement in run-up to
    Commonwealth Games, 21. *See also*
    Delhi
new town projects: in China, 5, 69,
    179–80, 190–92, 206–7; in India,
    5–6, 6*f*, 57–58, 144, 146, 153–54,
    225; in Indonesia, 30, 42*f*, 44, 50, 64,
    102, 103–4, 108–9, 115, 233–34;
    plans for, 5; social segregation within,
    234; studies of, 19–20; use of term,
    18; veneer of developmentalism in,
    135, 215, 234
New York City: Battery Park City in,
    18; Tammany Hall investments in, 17
Nilekani, Nandan, 156

occupancy urbanism, 33, 89, 90, 95*f*,
    99–100, 137, 148; in India, 89, 90,
    99, 137, 148, 150
Ong, Aihwa, xviii, 8, 9–10, 84, 188,
    190, 210, 221
opposition, to urban real estate
    megaprojects: effectiveness of, xiv,
    40; in India, 72, 76–77, 228; legal

frameworks and, 92; vs. state rhetoric of globalization-driven development, 140. *See also* protests

Orange County (Beijing, China), 191

Pamuntjak, M., 65

parastatal land-development agencies, 16, 100; in India, 163–64

Parent, Jason, 28

Paris (France), Haussmann's reconstruction of, 17

Parnell, Susan, 11, 217, 218

Pasuk Phongpaichit, 35, 39, 50, 54

Patel, Bimal, 171

Peck, Jamie, 9, 84, 182, 217, 219

People's Action Party (Singapore), 87, 98, 223

Perry, Clarence, 146–47

Peterson, George, 23, 28, 88, 138

Philippines: Asian financial crisis and, 52; banking sector reforms in, 51; corporate capture of state in, 118; dispossession and displacement in, 20–21; foreign direct investment in, 49*f*; occupancy urbanism in, 99, 100; real estate turn in urban policy of, 50–51, 53; state's land monetization strategy in, 224; urban real estate megaprojects in, 26, 51, 58, 59. *See also* Metro Manila

Phnom Penh (Cambodia), 222; Boeung Kak project in, 1–2, 3*f*, 15, 16, 222; land reclamation in, 1, 3*f*, 15, 97, 136, 213, 222

Plaza Accord of 1985, 33, 48

political conflicts, forcible land acquisition and, 21, 37, 140, 220

political society, in India, 142, 148; critique of concept of, 143

poor communities, in India: public interest litigations (PILs) against, 92–93, 155, 227; tendency toward criminalization and stigmatization of, 61, 92, 227, 231; threats to, 141, 231; and vote bank politics, 89, 90

population growth, in Asia: and urban expansion, 46; and urban real estate megaprojects, 19, 27

property rights: global economic change and new contestations in, 13; legal ambiguity in India, 73; national constitutions on, 90–91; splintered regimes of, 21–22; urban real estate megaproejcts and debates over, 17. *See also* dualistic land rights regimes

protests, against dispossession and displacement: in Cambodia, 2, 16, 222; in China, 86, 179, 187, 188, 193, 224; in Thailand, 40

PT Tunggal Reksakencana, 50

public interest litigations (PILs), in India, 92–93, 155, 227

public-private partnerships, in land development: in India, 153, 163–64; and state-corporate nexus, 16; in Thailand, 39

Pune (India): Lavasa resort near, 153; Magarpatta City development in, 82–83, 101, 138, 140, 157

Rachman, Noer Fauzi, 112

Rajarhat new town development (Kolkata, India), 162, 163

Rama III New Financial District (Bangkok, Thailand), 51

real estate boom, in Asia, 50–52; early stages of, 27; financial crisis following, 52; impact on urban politics, 53; origins of, 46–49

Real Estate Indonesia (REI), 66, 124

real estate turn in urban politics, xiii, xiv, 14–15, 37–38, 53–59, 215; actor-centered perspective on, 13; after Asian financial crisis, 58–59; in Cambodia, 55, 56; central elements of, 55; in China, 56, 58; contradictions inherent in, 59, 60–62; different outcomes of, 77; in India, 56–58; in Indonesia, 53, 55; origins of, 33, 46–47; in Philippines,

real estate turn in urban politics *(cont.)*
50–51, 53; and remaking of Asian
cities, 236–37; synchronicity with
changes in property sector, 47–48; in
Thailand, 53–55; in Vietnam, 55–56
Reerink, Gustaaf, 112
Ren, Xuefei, 143
rent gaps: buildup in early stages of
real estate boom, 27; dualistic land
rights regimes and, 99–100, 225–29;
emergent, government exploitation of,
118, 219, 225–29; government role in
creation of, 47; and urban real estate
megaprojects, spatial and temporal
patterns of, 26–29, 123
rent seeking: increasing land values
and, 13; Indonesian land-permitting
process and, 114; land monetization
as tactic of, 10–11, 96, 136, 221;
urban real estate megaprojects
and, 24
Riady, Mochtar, 50, 121
Rimmer, Peter, 5, 19–20, 60, 64, 107
Robinson, Jennifer, 11, 12, 32, 45,
217, 218
Robison, Richard, 66, 104, 117,
118, 119
Rouanet, Hortense, xiv, 225
Roy, Ananya, xviii, 12, 22, 61, 105–6,
142, 148, 149, 162, 163, 165,
226–27
Roy, Rajat, 167

Sahara Group (developer), 154
Salim, Anthony, 124
Salim, Sudono (Liem Sioe Liong), 66,
117, 120, 123
Salim Group, 66, 120–21
Sami, Neha, xvii, 82, 138, 144,
145, 157
Santoso, Jo, 130
Sassen, Saskia, 97, 98
Sentul City (developer), 103
Shanghai (China): Chongqing
compared to, 196; constraints on
urban development in, 199; housing

investment in, 184; land leasing
in, 183; as model of urbanism, 20,
155; new town projects in, 190;
Pudong development district in,
197; Songjiang City near, 42*f*, 44,
191; Thames Town outside of, 191;
Xintiandi district in, 43*f*, 44, 190
Shatkin, Gavin, 21, 25, 29, 58, 87, 99,
144, 145, 223
Shen, Jie, 191
Shivajinagar resettlement area (Mumbai,
India), 74, 227
Shukaku Incorporated, 1
Sidel, John, 80, 90, 104
Silver, Chris, xviii, 66, 102, 108,
124, 129
Sinarmas Group, 121, 123, 124,
126–27, 130
Singapore: as capital exporter,
55; land markets as tool for
regime legitimation in, 223; land
monetization and expansion of,
99; as model of urbanism, 20, 44,
155; public housing new towns
in, 87; public investments through
land monetization in, 24; social
engineering and political control in,
10; state capitalist urban planning in,
98, 99, 222–23; state land ownership
in, 87; state-owned enterprises in, 94
Singur development (Kolkata, India),
72, 77, 159–60, 162, 164, 167
Sino-Singapore Tianjin Eco-City
(China), 224
Smith, Adam, 204
Smith, Neil, 26–27
social impact assessment requirements,
in India, 158
Songjiang City (Shanghai, China), 42*f*,
44, 191
Southern California model, replication
in Asian cities, 44, 64, 102, 128,
130, 191
South Korea, as capital exporter, 55
spatial fragmentation: Chinese real
estate megaprojects and, 180,

190, 192, 208–9, 234; in Jakarta Metropolitan Region (JMR), 67, 106, 221

Special Economic Zone Act (India), 154

speculative land banking, 67, 114–15

state(s): addiction to land development, 210, 224; as corporations, 35–36, 38–39; diversity of roles in land markets, 94; legitimation of, urban real estate megaprojects and, 86, 98–99, 149, 223

state actors: in authoritarian settings, 94; autonomy of, and land monetization strategies, 88–93, 95*f*; conflict among different levels of, 25, 61–62, 178, 186, 224; decentralization of powers and responsibilities, trend toward, 24–25, 180, 185, 223; and dispossession, rationalization of, 229, 232; exploitation of urban land as means to power, xiii; global economic processes and, 13; land commodification and rent seeking by, 10–11; as market actors, 35–36; and neoliberalization of urban policy, 9–10, 12–13; shared interests with corporate actors, 8, 15–16, 24, 36, 45, 47–48, 118, 121, 122, 133; strategies for land monetization, 29, 33, 36, 84, 95–101, 95*f*, 222, 224–25; and urban real estate megaprojects, xiii, xiv, 8, 14, 15, 18, 31, 98

state capitalism (term), 178

state capitalist model of urban planning, 33, 95*f*, 98–99, 222; in China, 98, 99, 178, 180–86, 204, 209–10, 222, 223; contradictions inherent in, 223–24; government legitimation and empowerment though, 222–23; in Singapore, 98, 99, 222–23

state land ownership: in China, 68, 83, 86, 91; as constraint on capitalization of land rents, 28; in Singapore, 87; and strategies of land monetization, 85–88, 93, 95*f*

state-owned enterprises (SOEs): in China, 16, 25, 94, 182; and state-corporate nexus, 16

state rescaling: in China, 24–25, 180, 185, 223; contradictions inherent in, 78–79; emergent urban conflicts over, 25, 61–62; trend toward, 24–25, 37–38

Stone, Clarence, 93

Sudwikatmono, 66, 124

Suharto, 66; on evictions, 102; fall of, 98; family-based conglomerates with ties to, 55, 65, 66, 102; family-stage of rule of, 119–20; land management reforms during regime of, 64–65; land monetization under, 135; oligarchic power structure under, 117–18, 120; political economy of land grab under, 96, 97, 103–4, 116–22; urban development industry under, 109; veneer of state developmentalism under, 80, 120

superblock developments, in Jakarta, 133–34

SWA group, 64

Szelenyi, Ivan, 204, 206

Tata Corporation, 77, 159, 160

Thailand: banking sector reforms in, 51; as capital exporter, 55; corporate capture of state in, 118; financial crisis/real estate bust in, 52; foreign direct investment in, 49*f*; Makkasan Redevelopment Project in, 59; real estate shift in urban politics of, 53–55; Thaksin government in, 35, 39, 54–55; urban real estate megaprojects in, 26, 39–40, 51. *See also* Bangkok

Thaksin Shinawatra, 35, 38, 39, 54–55

Thames Town (Shanghai, China), 191

Theodore, Nick, 9, 84, 217, 219

Tokyo (Japan), Tsukuba Science City in, 65

Trihatmodjo, Bambang, 102, 121

Tweed, Willia

UDICs. *See* urban development
investment corporations
Unitech (developer), 154, 164
United States: gentrification in, rent
gap concept and, 26–27; Southern
California model in, replication in
Asian cities, 44, 64, 102, 128, 130,
191; urban redevelopment projects
in, 18–19; urban regime theory in
context of, 93
university towns, in China, 207–8
urban development investment
corporations (UDICs), in China,
70–71, 185–86, 197, 201–2, 206
urban land: centrality to agendas of
capital accumulation, xii, 13; political
struggle associated with, 36
Urban Land Ceiling and Regulation Act
(India), 147, 156
urban megaprojects (term), 18
Urban Real Estate Management Law of
1994 (China), 184
urban real estate megaprojects, in Asia,
3–4; after Asian financial crisis,
58–59; benefits vs. costs of, 7, 23;
"best case" scenario for, 174; case
studies of, 7–8, 31–32; critical issues
associated with, 4, 7, 20–21, 37, 60,
213–16, 229–36; developers and,
xiii–xiv, 3–4; diversity of form in,
41–44, 42*f*–43*f*; earliest examples
of, 26, 33; ecological sustainability
ideal in new generation of, 210–11,
214; as experiments in governance,
8; factors propelling, 19, 27; failed,
5, 16, 30, 72; field visits to, 30, 32;
foreign investment and, 27, 33, 49;
and legitimation of state power, 86,
98–99, 149, 223; models for, 20; new
generation of, 213–14; predatory
vs. developmental, 84; questions
regarding, 7; recent studies of, 19–20;
redistribution of financial benefits

of, 23–24; reforms preceding, 33;
and rent seeking, 24; spatial and
temporal patterns of, rent gap theory
of, 26–29; state actors and, xiii, xiv,
8, 14, 15, 18, 31, 98; state objectives in,
36; state vs. corporate objectives in,
16–17; typology of state strategies
in, 95–101, 95*f*; U.S. and European
projects compared to, 18–19; use
of term, 18; wealth generation and
economic opportunities in, 7, 23.
See also architectural renderings;
specific countries, cities, and projects
urban regime theory, 93; departures
from, 94

Vidyarthi, Sanjeev, 25, 87, 145, 147
Vietnam, real estate turn in urban
politics of, 55–56
vote bank politics, 89–90, 137

Wang Shaoguang, 204
Wang Yang, 176
Weinstein, Liza, xviii, 73, 74, 90, 142,
143, 144, 145, 152, 157
Western models, and urban development
in Asia, 20, 41, 44, 64, 102, 106–7,
128, 130, 191
Widjaya, Eka Tiptja, 121, 124
Winarso, Haryo, 5, 51, 55, 65,
113, 115, 118–19, 120, 121,
126, 130
Winters, Jeffrey, 104, 117, 118, 119
World Bank: on Boeung Kak project,
2; "The East Asian Miracle" report,
48; on urban regions as economic
drivers, 38
Wu, Fulong, 41, 44, 45, 68, 181, 184,
185, 189, 190, 191, 192, 193, 201,
206–7

Xintiandi development (Shanghai,
China), 43*f*, 44

CPSIA information can be obtained
at www.ICGtesting.com
Printed in the USA
LVOW10s2313230917
549849LV00001B/116/P